A GUIDE TO FIELD

BIRDS

OF NORTH AMERICA

by CHANDLER S. ROBBINS, BERTEL BRUUN,

and HERBERT S. ZIM

Illustrated by ARTHUR SINGER

 GOLDEN PRESS • NEW YORK
Western Publishing Company, Inc.
Racine, Wisconsin

PREFACE

This book was truly a cooperative venture involving a team of authors, artist, editors, and professionals in book design and production. Our team was aided by many individuals and institutions which provided both technical and practical assistance in our day-by-day efforts. We gratefully acknowledge help from, and extend our sincere thanks to the following: for assistance in preparing the range maps, David and Margaret Bridge; for converting the map data into final maps, Ahza Cohen, Christine Swirnoff, and Margaret Mayer; for measurement data, C. Douglas Hackman, Mel Garland, Gladys H. Cole, and Willet T. Van Velzen; for access to field notes, Erik Hansen; for assistance with skins and literature, Finn Salomonsen. For tape recordings, Peter Paul Kellogg and the Laboratory of Ornithology, Cornell University, Marguerite and David Howard, and Sveriges Radio, for help in producing Sonagrams, Howard E. Winn, Robert W. Ficken, W. J. L. Sladen, and Richard Penney. Seventeen Sonagrams were reproduced from the Peterson Field Guide Series record albums, *A Field Guide to Bird Songs* and *A Field Guide to Western Bird Songs*, through the kind permission of Houghton Mifflin Company and the Laboratory of Ornithology, Cornell University. Others who helped in reading the text, in checking art, and in reviewing families include John W. Aldrich, the late Robert Porter Allen, Dean Amadon, Oliver L. Austin, Jr., James Baird, John Bull, Kai Curry-Lindahl, Don R. Eckelberry, Eugene Eisenmann, Eugene Kridler, Roxie Laybourne, Charles O'Brien, Robert L. Pyle, Eleanor C. Robbins, Samuel D. Robbins, Jr., William B. Robertson, Peter Scott, Francis G. Scheider, Lester Short, Alexander Sprunt IV, George B. Stevenson, and Leslie M. Tuck.

The U.S. National Museum and the American Museum of Natural History provided most of the bird skins which the artist used in conjunction with his field notes and photographs. The University of Maryland and Johns Hopkins University made available the use of their audiospectrographs. The U. S. Bureau of Sport Fisheries and Wildlife provided access to their bird distribution maps from which our range maps were made.

C.S.R.
B.B.
H.S.Z.

TABLE OF CONTENTS

4

INTRODUCTION

About 1,780 species of birds representing 97 families live and breed on the continent of North America. When Central America and Mexico are dropped out, the number of breeding birds (permanent residents and migrants) falls to about 645 species. Another 50 or so migratory species are regular or casual visitors. All of these represent 75 families. Perhaps 100 more species occur accidentally. This last group is not an integral part of the North American bird population.

The 645 or so breeding species in North America north of Mexico total less than 8 per cent of the world's 8,600 or so birds, but North America makes up almost 17 per cent of the world's land. This relative discrepancy may only reflect the fact that North America, north of Mexico, has no true tropical component in its climate.

The number of species gives only part of the picture of avian life. The other factor is bird population, something much more difficult to establish. Populations have been estimated in limited areas but not often for a continent. At its peak, at the end of summer, the bird population of North America (north of Mexico) has been estimated at some 20 billion, and the world population of birds at about 100 billion. These rough estimates suggest that North America with about 17 per cent of the world's land and perhaps 20 per cent of its birds may be at least an average place to watch and study them. An average bird population of about three birds per acre is a reasonably good one.

Any interested person can find birds to observe and study, even in our urban centers. No one has seen all of the North American avian species, but a recent survey disclosed that a score of serious bird students, both amateur and professional, have each seen over 600 species north of the Mexican border. Many more watchers have "life lists" of 500 or more species, and it is common for an amateur to see and identify 300 species or more. Building up a large life list is not in itself a major goal, yet without accurate identification based on wide experience, all other observations may be suspect.

Birding amply satisfies our curiosity about all animal life. The joys of discovery and the aesthetic appeal of avian species provide rewarding experiences for the observer. But in addition, the study of birds is one of the few fields of biological science where the contributions of amateurs continue to be important. Beginners who keep species lists while birding make a start. Those who add notes on numbers seen, weather, terrain, and details of bird behavior soon discover that the data in their field notes conjure up provocative questions and hypotheses. These, in turn, require further, more detailed, or more extensive observations, which may eventually yield new facts —the very core of a scientific contribution.

Map based on Life Areas of N.A., by John W. Aldrich, *Journal of Wildlife Management*, Oct. 1963.

SCOPE This guide covers a continental land mass of over 9 million square miles. Geographically and climatically, North America ranges through a rich variety of subtropical, temperature, and arctic environments. Mapped above are the major natural vegetative regions, which depend on latitude, altitude, rainfall, and other factors. The distribution of birds tends to fit into these natural areas and even more closely into the specific habitats that they include. Bear these natural regions in mind when using the range maps.

Arctic-Alpine	Pacific Rain Forest	Mesquite-Grassland
Open Boreal	East Deciduous Forest	Pinyon-Juniper
Closed Boreal	Grasslands	Chaparral-Oak Woodland
No. Hardwood-Conifer	Oak-Savannah	Southern Evergreen
Aspen Parkland	Northern Desert Scrub	Mexican Pine and Pine-Oak
Montane Woodland	Southern Desert Scrub	Tropical Areas (combined)

Robin

Wilson's Petrel

Bridled Tern

BREEDING BIRDS comprise those which nest regularly north of Mexico. Some are rare and local. Most can be found at the proper time and place. About 645 species.

REGULAR VISITORS breed in other areas but are seen here as migrants, mostly along the coast or on offshore waters. Some may be abundant at times. About 30 species.

CASUAL VISITORS are migrants that stray here occasionally in small numbers. Most apt to be seen in fall with flocks of regular migrants or during severe coastal storms. About 25 species.

BIRDS IN THIS BOOK

This book covers the three groups of birds outlined above and so includes all species of wild birds likely to be found north of Mexico. For all birds included there are at least five North American records in the present century. This criterion is important, for the last category, Casual Visitors, includes Old World birds that wander here occasionally and unpredictably. Other tropical and Old World species have been found here fewer than 5 times since 1900. These birds of accidental occurrence are not included in this guide. Not included also are species now extinct, introduced birds released experimentally or on a small scale, and escaped birds that are not established and spreading.

Included as breeding birds are introduced species that are spreading and breeding regularly. Three gamebird species, the Chukar, Gray Partridge and Ring-necked Pheasant, are so established. Recent additions to the songbird list are the Blue-gray Tanager and the Red-whiskered Bulbul, both breeding in south Florida. If present patterns become established, such birds as the Elegant Tern, Hook-billed Kite, Scarlet Ibis, and others may be added to the list of regular breeders.

Hybrids between closely related species sometimes occur in the wild. Four of the most spectacular and best known hybrids are included. Observers should also watch for albinism, which occurs occasionally in most species of wild birds. Pure white or pale brown forms are rare. More frequently the normal plumage is modified by white feathers on the wings or tail or in patches on the body. Melanism is a condition that produces effects opposite of albinism. Dark colored birds occasionally appear, especially among the hawks. This condition is less common than albinism.

NAMES OF BIRDS Common species of birds may have many local or regional names. For example, the Bobwhite is called partridge in many parts of the South, as is the Ruffed Grouse throughout much of the North. Only the common names adopted by the American Ornithologists' Union (Check-List of North American Birds, 5th edition) are used in this guide. These names will avoid confusion. For your convenience, some widely used alternate names, especially those formerly used by the A.O.U., are listed in the index. The scientific names used (including accent marks to aid in pronunciation) are also those of the A.O.U. Check-List. Changes in the classification of birds occur as we learn more about them. Interpretation of the new knowledge varies and so the number of species, families, and orders may also vary according to different authorities.

Each species of bird is assigned a Latin or scientific name, which is accepted and understood by scientists throughout the world. The scientific name consists of two parts—the genus, followed by the species name, as in *Párus carolinénsis* (Carolina Chickadee). These Latin names are often descriptive and indicate avian relationships better than common names. Closely related species belong to the same genus, closely related genera to the same family, and closely related families to the same order. All birds belong to the Class Aves. The largest order of birds (Passeriformes) encompasses a great many families and genera. Its members show much variation in appearance and habits, though all have common characteristics that put them in one order. Our several species of buntings, for example, all belong to the Order Passeriformes (perching birds) and to the family Fringillidae (finches and sparrows). But while the Indigo Bunting *(Passerina cyánea)* is closely related to the Lazuli Bunting *(Passerina amoéna)*, it is very different in appearance and habits from the Lark Bunting *(Calamospiza melanócorys)* and the Snow Bunting *(Plectróphenax nivális)*.

Some species are further subdivided into subspecies (races or geographic forms). Scientific names of subspecies have three parts, as *Párus carolinénsis impiger*, the Florida form of the Carolina Chickadee. Most subspecies are not recognizable in the field. They are not treated separately in this book, except for a few conspicuous examples.

Of the 27 orders of living birds, 20 are represented in North America north of Mexico, some by only a single species (as the trogons and parrots). The largest order, Passeriformes, includes 27 families with over 300 species in North America. About 170 families of birds are currently recognized. The 75 families that occur in North America are treated in this book. The text often includes a brief introduction that summarizes the field characters common to orders and families or other groups of birds.

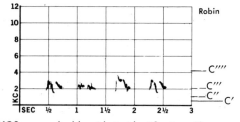

BIRD SONGS are valuable aids in identification. Many experts can identify the majority of songbirds by the song. Words cannot describe bird songs adequately, nor can songs be shown accurately on a musical staff. By methods developed by Dr. Peter Paul Kellogg of the Laboratory of Ornithology, Cornell University, bird songs can be recorded in the field and then reproduced either audibly or visually. Audible reproductions (by tapes or phonograph records) are ideal for learning bird songs at home, and the new visual reproductions of bird songs can be used in the field. Called audiospectrograms or Sonagrams, these visual reproductions are electronically made by a sound spectrograph. The bird song diagrams in this book are photographs of Sonagrams. Most of the recordings were made in the field by the senior author.

Sonagrams have been used in many scientific publications. This is the first time they have appeared in a field guide. They are essentially an electronic refinement of the method introduced by Aretas A. Saunders in 1935. The typical Sonagram in this guide shows 2½ seconds of song. The graph has grid lines at ½-second intervals. Pitch, usually up to six kilocycles per second, is marked in the left margin at two kilocycle intervals. For pitch comparison, middle C of the piano and the four octaves above middle C are indicated in the right margin of the enlarged Sonagram above. Middle C has a frequency of 262 cycles per second. The frequency doubles with each succeeding octave: C′ is 523, C″ is 1046, C‴ is 2093 and C⁗ (top note on piano) is 4186 cycles per second. Sonagrams show more detail than the ear can detect at normal speed; the best way to learn to use Sonagrams is to compare them with recordings played at half speed.

A knowledge of music helps in interpreting Sonagrams but is by no means necessary. Even a person who is tone deaf can detect the differences in pattern, timing, and quality of a song. Before attempting to interpret Sonagrams of unfamiliar birds, study those of some familiar sounds and of birds that you know well.

Three toots on an automobile horn are easily read. The "wolf whistle" shows how a whistle appears as a single narrow line which

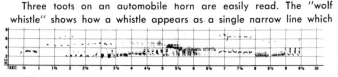

Brewer's Sparrow

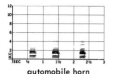

automobile horn

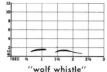

"wolf whistle"

ticking clock

rises and falls as the pitch changes. Compare it with the Eastern Meadowlark. A mechanical sound such as the ticking of a clock has no recognizable pitch, but each tick appears in the Sonagram as a vertical line, indicating that it has a wide frequency range. Compare the clock ticks with the Short-billed Marsh Wren.

Songs that are very high in pitch (6-12 kilocycles) are shown on an extra high Sonagram. Older people may not hear these notes. Some birds, such as thrashers, have very long songs, of which only a typical portion is shown. For some others with typical songs that exceed 2½ seconds (House Wren, Purple Finch), a shorter complete song has been used. Study these very common songs. The Bobwhite's consists of a faint introductory whistle, a short loud whistle, and a longer upward-slurred note that is not as pure as the preceding whistle. The Black-capped Chickadee's "phoebe" song is a series of whistles which you can easily imitate. The first note is a full tone higher than the second.

Many bird songs have overtones or harmonics that give a richness of quality to each note. These show on the Sonagram as generally fainter duplicate notes at octaves above the main or fundamental pitch. High-pitched harmonics are "drowned out" by the louder lower notes to which our ears are more sensitive.

Birds, like people, have individual and geographical differences in their voices, yet any typical song is distinctive enough to be recognized by an experienced observer.

With a little practice you will learn to visualize from Sonagrams the approximate pitch of an unfamiliar bird song (in relation to a species you know); the quality (clear, harsh, buzzy, mechanical); the phrasing (separate notes, repetitions, trills, continuous song, or phrases); the tempo (even, accelerating, or slowing); the length of individual notes and of the entire song; and changes in loudness.

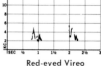

Red-eyed Vireo

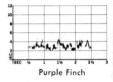

Purple Finch

Eastern Meadowlark

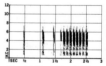

Short-billed Marsh Wren

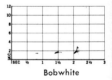

Bobwhite

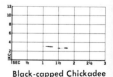

Black-capped Chickadee

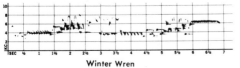

Winter Wren

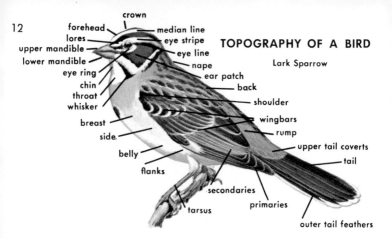

TOPOGRAPHY OF A BIRD

Lark Sparrow

crown, forehead, median line, lores, eye stripe, upper mandible, eye line, lower mandible, nape, eye ring, ear patch, chin, back, throat, whisker, shoulder, breast, wingbars, side, rump, belly, upper tail coverts, flanks, tail, secondaries, primaries, tarsus, outer tail feathers

DESCRIBING BIRDS is hardly necessary if you identify a species at sight with the help of a friend or a guidebook. However, the use of the correct descriptive terms becomes important with birds that you cannot immediately identify. Then you will want to make detailed notes on appearance and behavior. The accuracy of such notes will be augmented by the use of the terms illustrated above and below. Your description and notes submitted to an expert or used in checking other references may solve your identification problem.

The use of correct terminology will also aid you in making comparisons and in checking variations in color and pattern of local birds. Knowing the terminology helps focus your attention on specific parts of a bird as you observe it. Sometimes such details as an incomplete eye-ring or the color of the undertail covers will clinch an identification.

PARTS OF WING

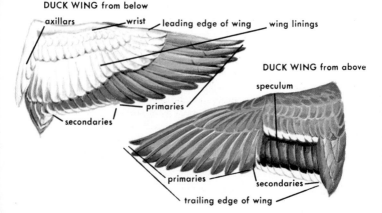

DUCK WING from below

axillars, wrist, leading edge of wing, wing linings, primaries, secondaries

DUCK WING from above

speculum, primaries, secondaries, trailing edge of wing

BIRD WATCHING AND BIRD STUDY

Persons who live in suburbs or rural locations can enjoy bird watching right at home. Planting shrubs and evergreens for shelter and providing food and water will attract some species in large numbers, and a much larger variety in small numbers. Many observers have identified 50 or more species in a suburban yard. A window feeder and a bird bath with dripping water will bring into view birds that might otherwise stay in the shubbery.

Birds are best seen by going afield to parks, sanctuaries, open areas, and shores. On such trips a pair of prism binoculars (6 to 8 power, with central focus) is almost essential. For work with waterbirds, a spotting 'scope (12 to 30 power) is extremely helpful. Camera fans will want a 35mm camera with focal plane shutter, a telephoto lens, and tripod.

You will see more birds if you walk slowly and quietly, alone or in small groups. Do not wear brightly colored clothing. If you watch from your parked car remember that the car serves as a blind and birds will approach closer than if you are on foot. If you are quiet or partly concealed you can sometimes attract songbirds and get them close by "squeaking"—sucking air through your lips or noisily kissing the back of your hand. Some species will respond to crude imitations of their song, and any song or call that you can imitate well may cause other birds to burst into song.

Local bird clubs, Audubon groups, or ornithological societies are found in almost every state and Canadian province, especially in the larger cities. These clubs hold meetings, lectures, and field trips at which you will be welcome and through which you can broaden your interest and experience. Many groups publish newsletters or journals. Meetings occasionally feature motion pictures or slides of birds and other wildlife. Audubon screen tours also present outstanding wildlife films and lectures. For help in locating these and other nature societies consult the Conservation Directory of the National Wildlife Federation, your state conservation department, or the library or newspaper of your home town or in places where you travel.

National Parks, Monuments, and National Wildlife Refuges are often excellent places to observe birds. Rangers or naturalists are glad to answer questions. State and private sanctuaries, local parks, and zoos can also prove helpful and stimulating. Many larger cities or universities have museums with bird collections, and study here can greatly aid field recognition. A number of private camps and tours emphasize bird study. The National Audubon Society camps have outstanding programs in nature education.

HOW TO USE THIS BOOK

These four pages can aid you in using your field guide effectively to identify birds quickly and accurately in the field. Begin to use the book before you go birding. In spare moments at home or while traveling thumb through its pages. Note the silhouettes that appear with the introductions to families and other groups. These will give you a quick impression of the form of a "typical" bird in a particular group as compared to birds with similar silhouettes. Silhouettes of birds in the group illustrated are in black. Those of birds of similar shape, which may be confused with species illustrated, are in blue.

Scan the full-color illustrations at the far right. These are usually the male birds in breeding plumage. Do not study each picture for details. At first, glance quickly at the bird and its name and then move on. Do this scores of times. Open the book at random or work through an interesting family. The person who does this will become increasingly sure about recognizing members of a family or a genus, such as herons, quails, woodpeckers, chickadees, and others. He may not be able to enumerate all the quail or heron characteristics, but he will recognize the birds on sight. This preparation will be an important aid to identification.

Later scan the range maps, read the text, and review the illustrations, making note of details that separate one species from another. Each person will develop his own system for recalling facts, such as underlining words, drawing arrows pointing to species characteristics, or writing marginal notes and records.

Use the book in the field as much as possible. When birds are on the move, check the silhouettes to help place a bird within a recognized group. Gradually, experience will highlight species characteristics, and in time only the barest glimpse will enable you to identify some species. With others, and with females and immature birds, careful observations and comparisons will always be essential. Constant review by thumbing through the book will fix details in your mind and will refresh your memory of species seen.

No single technique can be the key to birding or to using a field guide. Each person's pattern of observation and learning is, in some ways, unique. As experience, skill, and interest increase, you will discover techniques and devices that are best and most satisfying for you. Become familiar with the features of this book listed on the next pages and with the ways that data are presented in the text, maps, and Sonagrams so that birds can be checked in the field with a minimum of effort.

1. In general, this guide follows a "natural" or evolutionary order, progressing from the least to the more advanced families of birds. However, minor departures have been made to set up comparisons; for example, the white herons are grouped together (p. 93), and all herons (pp. 92-98) have been placed next to the cranes.

2. Illustrations feature the adult male, usually in breeding plumage. Next, the female. Immatures (im.) are illustrated when noticeably different from adults. Juvenal (juv.) plumage is shown for some species. Birds not labeled are adults in which sexes are similar. Otherwise ♂ indicates the male, ♀ the female. Most birds typically seen in flight are illustrated in a flying position. If birds have very different summer and winter plumages, these are also shown. The color phases of a few species are given and comparison illustrations call attention to similar species on a different page.

3. The common and scientific names (and accent marks to aid pronunciation) are from the *A.O.U. Check-List of North American Birds,* 5th edition, 1957. The index also gives some widely used alternate common names, especially those from previous editions of the *A.O.U. Check-List.*

4. Both text and illustrations attempt to point out the behavior of birds as an identification aid. Watch for patterns of flight, walking, feeding, courtship, nest building, and care of young. Such observations will increase your ability to recognize some birds at a glance.

5. The text attempts to evaluate the abundance of most species of breeding birds and regular visitors within their principal geographic range. Remember that at the edge of a species' range its abundance decreases rapidly.

When modified by the word *local,* the terms below indicate relative abundance in a very restricted area.

An *abundant* bird is one very likely to be seen in large numbers every time by a person visiting its habitat at the proper season.

A *common* bird may be seen most of the time or in smaller numbers under the same circumstances.

An *uncommon* bird may be seen quite regularly in small numbers in the appropriate environment and season.

A *rare* bird occupies only a small percentage of its preferred habitat or occupies a very specific limited habitat. It is usually found only by an experienced observer.

6. The range maps use North America as a base except for birds of limited range. The winter range of a species is shown in blue (A); the summer or breeding range in red (B). Purple (C) shows where the bird occurs all year. Within its range a bird is found only in certain habitats, such as cattail marshes or pine woods.

Areas through which migrants pass as they move north in spring are shown with red hatching upward from left to right (D). The area of fall migration is shown by red hatching downward from left to right (E). Cross-hatching (F) shows where a species may be seen in both spring and fall but where it does not breed or winter.

The black isochronal lines show the average first arrival date where birds migrating to the north may be seen about the first of March (solid line—G); first of April (dotted line—H); first of May (dashed line—I) and first of June (dots and dashes—J). Finally, the dashed lines in blue and in red bound areas where some species occasionally extend their range in winter (K) or in summer (L).

The maps are based on data tabulated for many years by the U.S. Fish and Wildlife Service.

7. Some species are highly adaptable and are widely distributed within their range. Others are very restricted. Altitude, moisture, type of vegetation, availability of food, and other factors determine the environment in which birds live. The text lists some of the more important habitats for most species.

8. Besides verbal descriptions of songs and their normal frequency per minute, songs or calls of many species are pictured by Sonagrams (see pp. 10-11). This is a new scientific technique that gives a true "picture" of a song. Study the Sonagram while the bird is singing, or while you listen to a recording. You should soon be able to recall typical songs. Remember that a Sonagram pictures only a single characteristic song. Many birds have several songs, but these often have many basic similarities.

9. The measurements of total length are original figures based on

10"

11½"

SCRUB JAY

actual field measurements, from the tip of the bill to the tip of the tail, of thousands of live birds hand-held in natural positions. These live measurements are shorter than conventional ones (of dead birds, stretched "with reasonable force"). The single figure given for length (L) is a median or average figure for the adult male, rounded to the nearest ¼ inch in small birds and to the nearest ½ inch or 1 inch in larger birds. Individual birds may be 10 per cent longer or shorter. Thus a bird recorded as L 10" may be between 9 and 11 inches. If the sexes differ appreciably in size this is usually mentioned. On larger flying and soaring birds an average wingspan (W) measurement also is given.

10. In the text a number of terms have been abbreviated to save space and convey information quickly. Besides such common abbreviations as months, states, and countries, you will also find: feet: ′, inches: ″, length: L, wingspan: W, immature: im., juvenal: juv., number of songs per minute: x/min.

LOONS (*Order* Gaviiformes, *Family* Gaviidae) are specialized for swimming and diving. Powerful legs attached at the rear of the body give extra leverage to the large webbed feet. Loons come ashore only to breed and to nest. They are silent in winter. In flight the head is lower than the body. The wingbeats are fast, uninterrupted by gliding. When diving, the swimming bird hops up and forward to begin the plunge, but it can also submerge stealthily from a sitting position. Loons eat fish, crustaceans, and some water plants. Eggs, 2-3.

COMMON LOON
Gávia immer

The most common loon, breeding along lakes and rivers. Its yodel-like laugh is given frequently, near the nest and in flight, especially at night. Varies considerably in size. Note its dark, evenly-tapered bill and, in summer, its cross-banded back. In winter the head and neck are darker than the Red-throated Loon's. Common Loons migrate in small flocks; most go to the coast.

YELLOW-BILLED LOON
Gávia ádamsii

The largest loon, and the most northern; breeds on lakes in the tundra. The bill is straw-colored; the upper half is straight, the lower half curved up, in contrast to the dagger-like bill of the Common. The head is darker and the white spots on back are larger and fewer than the Common Loon's. Both species have similar calls.

ARCTIC LOON
Gávia árctica

Nearly circumpolar, but rare in eastern North America. Breeds on tundra lakes. The Arctic is smaller than the two preceding loons; its light gray crown and white stripes on the side of the throat are diagnostic. In winter the back is gray with pale feather edgings. The bill is thin and straight, more slender than Common Loon's. The Arctic is so like the small race of the Common Loon that identification in winter is risky outside its normal range. Call is an ascending whistle.

RED-THROATED LOON
Gávia stelláta

Common in its breeding range on both fresh and salt water, wintering mainly along the coast. Often migrates in flocks. It is nearly as long as the Arctic Loon but is much slimmer. The light-colored, upturned bill is a good field mark. In summer plumage the white stripes extend up the back of the head. In winter the back is gray with tiny white spots. Call, a rapid quacking.

cormorant   scaup   merganser   loon   grebe

YELLOW-BILLED LOON
L 25" W 60"

summer   winter

COMMON LOON
L 24" W 58"

winter

summer

ARCTIC LOON
L 18" W 47"

winter   summer

winter   summer

**RED-THROATED
LOON**
L 17" W 44"

Red-throated
raises wing
higher than
other loons.

Arctic Loon   Red-throated Loon

20

GREBES (*Order* Podicipediformes, *Family* Podicipedidae) are swimming and diving birds, smaller than loons, with flat lobes on their toes. The short legs are far back on the body; the tail is very short; wings are short. Their flight is weak and hurried; they taxi for several yards before becoming airborne. The head is held low in flight. Grebes dive and pursue small aquatic animals. Courtship displays are often elaborate, accompanied by wails and whistles. Nest in floating marsh vegetation; eggs, 2-9.

WESTERN GREBE   *Aechmóphorus occidentális*

Locally abundant, breeding in colonies in lake vegetation. Winters along the Pacific Coast and in some inland areas, often in large flocks. A large black and white grebe with a long straight neck. The bill is much longer and more needle-like than in other grebes.

RED-NECKED GREBE   *Pódiceps grisegéna*

A long-necked grebe. Uncommon; in ponds and lakes during the summer. It winters mainly in salt water on both coasts. In all plumages, light throat contrasts with dark neck. Stockier appearance and heavy bill distinguish it from Western, Horned, and Eared Grebes.

HORNED GREBE   *Pódiceps auritus*

This commonest grebe (except in Southwest) has a thin straight bill. Nests on lakes and ponds; winters in salt water, often in flocks. In winter it is told from Red-necked and Eared Grebes by white face and neck.

EARED GREBE   *Pódiceps cáspicus*

A small grebe with a thin upturned bill and high, rounded back. It breeds in colonies and is common on shallow lakes. In winter plumage head and neck (more slender than Horned Grebe's) are gray with white ear and throat patches. Most winter inland.

PIED-BILLED GREBE   *Podilýmbus pódiceps*

Pied-billed Grebe

Fairly common in shallow fresh water, rare in salt water. A small, solitary, stocky grebe with a high chicken-like bill. Rarely flies; escapes by diving. Call, a series of low slurred whistles.

LEAST GREBE   *Pódiceps dominicus*

A tiny grebe with a slender dark bill. Uncommon; in southern Rio Grande Valley; rare and local farther north.

Pied-billed Grebe

WESTERN GREBE
L 18″ W 40″

take off

courtship dance

RED-NECKED GREBE
L 13″ W 32″

summer

winter

Horned

head comparison

HORNED GREBE
L 9½″ W 24″

winter

summer

Eared

Eared

EARED GREBE
L 9″ W 23″

winter

summer

Pied-billed

winter

im.

summer

PIED-BILLED GREBE
L 9″

summer

LEAST GREBE
L 6½″

winter

summer

TUBENOSES (Order Procellariiformes) have external tubular nostrils. They are birds of the sea, coming ashore on remote islands and shores only to breed. They nest in colonies; feed on squid, fish, and other marine life, usually at or near the surface. All have hooked beaks. The sexes are similar. Silent away from the breeding grounds. Lengths given are for birds in flight.

FAMILIES OF TUBENOSES OCCURRING OFF OUR COASTS

Albatrosses (Diomedeidae) Large birds, including the longest winged species. Long, narrow wings, very heavy hooked beak.   p. 22

Fulmars, Shearwaters, and Large Petrels (Procellariidae) Large birds, though considerably smaller than the albatrosses. The bill is generally thinner, with a pronounced tooth at the end. pp. 22, 24, 26

Storm Petrels (Hydrobatidae) Small birds, scarcely larger than swallows. Bills are short and the legs fairly long.   p. 28

ALBATROSSES are primarily birds of the Southern Hemisphere, with only three species breeding north of the equator. They have tremendously long wingspreads (11′ in the Wandering Albatross). Though capable of powerful direct flight, they are gliders, soaring on stiffly held wings. The single egg is laid on the ground.

LAYSAN ALBATROSS   *Diomedéa immutábilis*

This white-bodied albatross nests on mid-Pacific islands; occurs far offshore, but regularly in summer close to the Aleutians. The black mantle covers upper wings and back. Seldom follows ships.

BLACK-FOOTED ALBATROSS   *Diomedéa nigripes*

Our only all-dark albatross. Occurs regularly as close as ten miles off the Pacific Coast. Often rests on the water; feeds on squid and fish at night. Told from the dark Pacific shearwaters by larger size and heavier bill.

FULMARS (*Family* Procellariidae) strongly resemble gulls in appearance and in scavenging habits, but typically are found much farther at sea. Nest on high sea cliffs; lay 1 egg.

FULMAR   *Fulmárus glaciális*

A large gull-like tubenose. In its light color phase it can be told from gulls by the stiff flight, the habit of flapping and gliding, the heavy head and neck, the shorter tail, and, at close range, by the tubular nostrils. Dark-phase birds are paler than Sooty Shearwaters (p. 26), have shorter wings and a broader tail. Fulmars follow ships, often over long distances.

ern

frigatebird

gull

storm petrel

shear-water

albatross

albatross

shearwater

storm petrel

LAYSAN ALBATROSS
L 28″ W 85″

**BLACK-FOOTED
ALBATROSS**
L 28″ W 80″

FULMAR
L 18″ W 42″

dark phase

light phase

● **SHEARWATERS** differ from fulmars in having longer, narrower wings, a narrower tail, and a longer, thinner bill. The flight pattern is similar, a few deep wingbeats and a long glide, usually close to the water. Their food is small fish and crustaceans. Nocturnal on breeding grounds. Lay a single egg.

PINK-FOOTED SHEARWATER   *Púffinus creátopus*

A large common Pacific tubenose; breeds in Chile. Often seen in flocks with Sooty and Manx Shearwaters. Larger than the Sooty, with slower wingbeats; much larger than the Manx, with less contrasting colors. Most common from May to Nov., but a few are seen all year round. Does not follow ships.

CORY'S SHEARWATER   *Púffinus diomedéa*

This largest Atlantic shearwater has plumage the same as the Pink-footed's, but bill is yellow, rather thick. Compare with Greater. Sometimes soars, the only Atlantic shearwater to do so. Does not follow ships.

GREATER SHEARWATER   *Púffinus grávis*

A large, fairly common, Atlantic shearwater, breeding Nov.-Apr. in the Tristan de Cunha Islands. Black cap and white on the tail are pronounced. In May and June it migrates north over the western Atlantic; in Oct. and Nov. it moves south over the eastern Atlantic. Larger and heavier than either Audubon's or Manx.

AUDUBON'S SHEARWATER   *Púffinus lherminiéri*

A very small, rather common Atlantic shearwater; breeds in the Bahamas. There is no white on the tail. Has longer tail and shorter wings than Manx's. Wingbeats are much faster than other shearwaters'.

NEW ZEALAND SHEARWATER   *Púffinus búlleri*

Rare but regular off Calif. (Monterey), where it is seen with other shearwaters in the fall. A slender shearwater with a dark cap. Note the W-shaped pattern above, light wing tips below. Flight is lighter than Manx's.

MANX SHEARWATER   *Púffinus púffinus*

Rare on the Atlantic but common on the Pacific Coast. It is much smaller than the Pink-footed and its back and wings are dark, where the New Zealand Shearwater has light areas. Wingbeat and flight are fast.

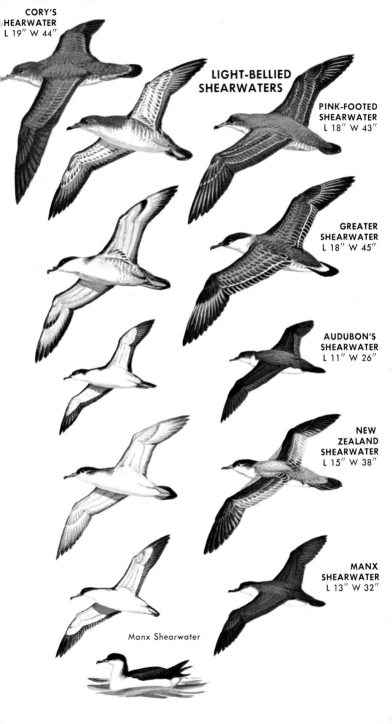

CORY'S HEARWATER
L 19" W 44"

LIGHT-BELLIED SHEARWATERS

PINK-FOOTED SHEARWATER
L 18" W 43"

GREATER SHEARWATER
L 18" W 45"

AUDUBON'S SHEARWATER
L 11" W 26"

NEW ZEALAND SHEARWATER
L 15" W 38"

MANX SHEARWATER
L 13" W 32"

Manx Shearwater

SOOTY SHEARWATER — *Púffinus gríseus*

A large, dark, gray-brown bird of cool waters. Abundant in fall off West Coast, uncommon on the East. The only dark-bodied shearwater in west Atlantic, and the only one in the Pacific with contrasting wing linings. Bill is dark. Told from Pink-footed by dark body, smaller size, and faster wingbeats. It is larger than the Slender-billed, which is all dark below.

SLENDER-BILLED SHEARWATER — *Púffinus tenuiróstris*

A fairly large, slender shearwater breeding in southern Australia. Told from Pale-footed by smaller size, shorter tail, dark legs, and dark bill. Generally separable from Sooty by more crooked wings and dark wing linings, but a few of each species have the underwing pattern of the other, so single birds cannot always be told. Uncommon; flocks appear in late fall, later than the Sooty.

PALE-FOOTED SHEARWATER — *Púffinus carnéipes*

A very large species and a very rare and irregular visitor to the West Coast. Larger than the Sooty and the Slender-billed, with a large, dark-tipped, yellowish bill and flesh colored feet and legs. Similar in shape and habits to the Pink-footed, which is believed by some to be a light-colored subspecies of the Pale-footed. Most likely to be seen in July and August.

LARGE PETRELS, also called Gadfly Petrels, are in the same family as fulmars and shearwaters. In flight and behavior they can be regarded as intermediate between the shearwaters and the smaller storm petrels. Their very fast flight resembles that of shearwaters, but the angle of the wing is like the storm petrels'. These birds do not follow ships at sea; they eat fish and shrimp. Nest in burrows; 1 egg.

BLACK-CAPPED PETREL — *Pteródroma hasitáta*

A widespread tubenose, nowhere common, and a casual summer visitor to eastern North America during storms. Dark above and light below, it can be confused only with Manx and Audubon's Shearwaters, neither of which has a white rump and white hind neck.

SCALED PETREL — *Pteródroma inexpectáta*

A medium-sized petrel from New Zealand, a casual summer visitor to the Gulf of Alaska. Note the contrast between the throat and belly. The heavy black bar on the underside of the wing is unique; from above, the light upper surface contrasts with the dark leading edge.

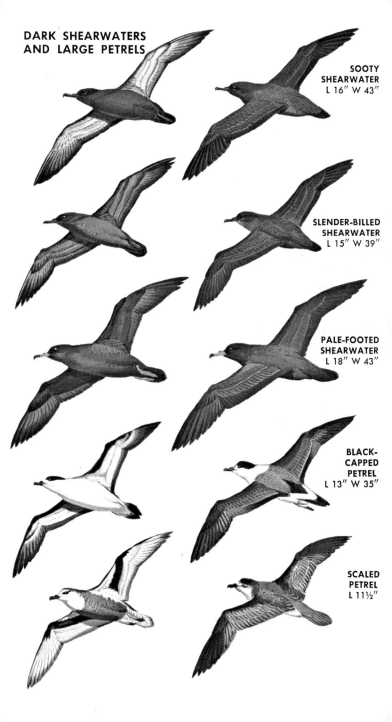

DARK SHEARWATERS
AND LARGE PETRELS

SOOTY
SHEARWATER
L 16″ W 43″

SLENDER-BILLED
SHEARWATER
L 15″ W 39″

PALE-FOOTED
SHEARWATER
L 18″ W 43″

BLACK-
CAPPED
PETREL
L 13″ W 35″

SCALED
PETREL
L 11½″

STORM PETRELS (*Family* Hydrobatidae) are small birds of open water, feeding on tiny fish, shrimp, and planktonic animals. They flutter and hop over the waves, pattering with webbed feet. The sturdy bill is hooked, and the tubular nostrils can be seen at close range. Found singly or in flocks. Lay a single egg.

BLACK PETREL   *Loomelánia melánia*
Rather common off the southern Calif. coast in winter months, but also seen locally in summer. This largest of the black petrels has dark underwings, long legs, and a forked tail. Flight is graceful, wingbeats rather slow. Follows ships, often in small flocks. Nests in burrows.

ASHY PETREL   *Oceanódroma homóchroa*
Common only locally, Apr.-Nov. Stocky build, medium size, pale wing coverts above and below. Flight is more fluttering than the larger Black Petrel's.

FORK-TAILED PETREL   *Oceanódroma furcáta*
Abundant in the northern Pacific, where it breeds. This lightest-colored storm petrel has a light head, underparts, wing patch, and light underwing with a dark leading edge. The tail is forked. Glides more than other petrels and has shallower wingbeat.

LEACH'S PETREL   *Oceanódroma leucórhoa*
Uncommon and local in summer. Medium-sized, dark, with a prominent white rump (except in southern California) and gray wing patch. Tail is forked; feet are dark. Leach's is smaller than the Black and has darker underwings than those of the Ashy. Flight is butterfly-like, quite different from that of Wilson's.

WILSON'S PETREL   *Oceanites oceánicus*
Very common off Atlantic Coast, June-Sept. Dark brown with white rump, light wing patch, long legs, and yellow feet. Tail is rounded. Dances over the surface with wings held high. Often follows ships in loose flocks.

HARCOURT'S PETREL   *Oceanódroma cástro*
Casual on both coasts during storms. Almost identical to Leach's. Told in hand by shape of white rump band, less deeply forked tail.

LEAST PETREL   *Halocypténa microsóma*
This smallest, rare, all-dark petrel ranges north on W. Coast to San Diego in summer. Note wedge-shaped tail, dark feet.

BLACK PETREL
L 8½″ W 18″

petrel at
burrow

ASHY PETREL
L 7″ W 16″

Ashy Petrel
from below

**FORK-TAILED
PETREL**
L 7½″ W 18″

Leach's Petrel

**LEACH'S
PETREL**
L 7½″ W 19″

Wilson's Petrels

**WILSON'S
PETREL**

L 6½″ W 16″

**HARCOURT'S
PETREL**
L 8½″ W 18″

**LEAST
PETREL**
L 5½″ W 13″

PELICANS AND THEIR ALLIES (Order Pelecaniformes) are large aquatic fish-eating birds with all 4 toes webbed. Most nest in large colonies and are silent outside the breeding grounds. There are six families: Tropicbirds (Phaëthontidae), Pelicans (Pelecanidae), Frigatebirds (Fregatidae), Gannets and Boobies (Sulidae), Cormorants (Phalacrocoracidae), and Anhinga (Anhingidae). Tropicbirds, Frigatebirds, Gannets, and Boobies lay one egg. Cormorants, Anhinga, and Pelicans lay 3-5.

RED-BILLED TROPICBIRD   *Phaëthon aethéreus*
A rare regular visitor to southern California coast in fall; highly pelagic and seldom seen close to shore. Adults usually have a long streamer tail, red bill. Immature's bill is yellow. Fishes by diving ternlike into the water. The flight is pigeon-like, with strong wingbeats.

WHITE-TAILED TROPICBIRD   *Phaëthon leptúrus*
A casual visitor off the Southeast coast after storms. Similar to the Red-billed but smaller, with a heavy black band on the wing in place of the black streaking, and a short eye line. Immature lacks the streamer tail.

BROWN PELICAN   *Pelecánus occidentális*
A locally common breeder on both coasts, rarely found on fresh water. Adult has a light head and a gray-brown body. Immature is uniformly dull brown above, lighter below. An excellent flier, with a powerful stroking flight alternating with short glides, which often carry the bird only inches above the water. Flies with head drawn back to the shoulder; rarely soars. Small flocks fly in long lines. Dives into the water from heights of 30' for small fish. Semi-tame birds often beg for food on fishing piers.

WHITE PELICAN   *Pelecánus erythrorhýnchos*
Locally common in breeding colonies of several hundred pairs on the West Coast and also on lakes. Black area of wing includes all the primaries and half of the secondaries. Flat, rounded plate on the bill is seen in breeding season only. Flight is an alternation of flapping and gliding. Migrates in long lines in V-formation and often soars at great heights. Fishes by wading in shallows, often in flocks, scooping up fish with its large bill. Does not dive. Some non-breeding birds spend the summer at their wintering grounds.

loon   gull   tropicbird   pelican   frigatebird   gannet   cormorant

RED-BILLED TROPICBIRD
L 34″ W 44″

Red-billed

WHITE-TAILED TROPICBIRD
L 26″ W 37″

White-tailed

BROWN PELICAN
L 41″ W 90″

winter

im.

summer

diving

winter

WHITE PELICAN
L 50″ W 110″

im.

fishing formation

summer

32

MAGNIFICENT FRIGATEBIRD — *Fregáta magníficens*

Common during summer in Florida Keys; occasional on Southeast, Gulf, and West coasts during storms. Note prominent crook in narrow wing, and long slender tail. Pouch of the male is inflated during courtship. Robs gulls and terns in flight; also takes small fish and marine refuse from surface, but does not land on the water. A very efficient glider, it soars to great heights without moving a wing.

GANNET — *Mórus bassánus*

Common in summer near breeding islands; winters on the ocean; often visible from shore, especially during east winds. Note its double-ended silhouette. Dark wing tips on white body identify the adult. Nests in large colonies. Feeds by diving from 50′ or more into the water and swimming underwater for short distances. In migration, flies just above the water, often in lines. Wingbeats are rather stiff, alternately flaps and glides.

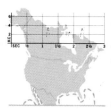

BLUE-FACED BOOBY — *Súla dactylátra*

A regular visitor in summer to Dry Tortugas, Fla.; very rare on mainland. All the flight feathers and the face are black; the skin near the bill is slaty. Immature is dark above with a pale band around the neck. A tropical gannet, it is larger than the other two boobies but smaller than the Gannet, which it resembles in habits.

BROWN BOOBY — *Súla leucogáster*

A regular visitor to the Gulf Coast, quite rare in Calif. It is the only booby that has its entire upper parts dark. Immature is uniformly dark above and lacks the sharp white and brown contrast below. A tropical gannet breeding along all warm oceans, it resembles the Gannet in habits and behavior.

BLUE-FOOTED BOOBY — *Súla neboúxii*

A casual visitor to Salton Sea, Calif., and the lower Colo. River. From above, the white patch on the upper back and (in adult) the large white rump are the best marks. The underwings are dark. Both immature and adult have blue feet, very bright in the adult. The bluish bill of the adult also is diagnostic. This tropical bird breeds in the Gulf of Calif. and along the west coast of Mex. and S.A. Behavior, gannet-like.

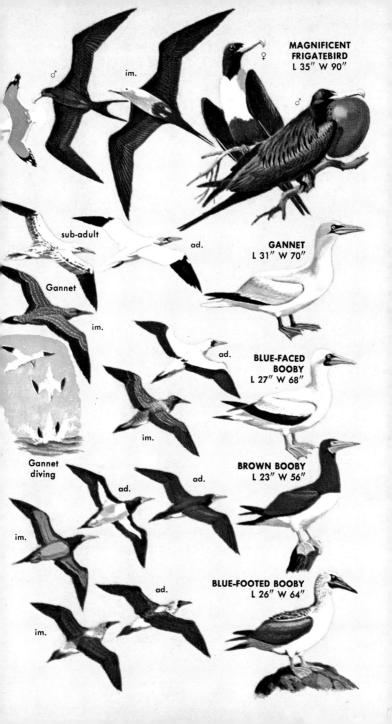

MAGNIFICENT FRIGATEBIRD
L 35" W 90"

♂

im.

♀

♂

sub-adult

ad.

GANNET
L 31" W 70"

Gannet

im.

Gannet diving

ad.

im.

BLUE-FACED BOOBY
L 27" W 68"

im.

ad.

ad.

BROWN BOOBY
L 23" W 56"

im.

ad.

im.

ad.

BLUE-FOOTED BOOBY
L 26" W 64"

● **CORMORANTS AND ANHINGA** are fish eaters that dive from the surface and swim underwater. They often perch with wings half open to dry. Migrate in V-formation; usually are silent.

GREAT CORMORANT
Phalacrócorax cárbo

Our largest cormorant and the only one with a white throat patch. The bill is yellower and heavier than Double-crested's. In breeding season adult has a white flank patch; immature has belly whiter than neck.

BRANDT'S CORMORANT
Phalacrócorax penicillátus

A common, short-tailed, crestless Pacific cormorant. The throat is dark (blue in breeding season) with dull yellow margin behind. The immature is dark below, as is the smaller immature Pelagic, but has a large pale Y on its breast.

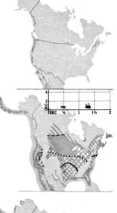

DOUBLE-CRESTED CORMORANT
Phalacrócorax auritus

The most common cormorant. Found on inland lakes and rivers, but mainly seen along the coast. The throat pouch is orange; the crests seldom are visible. Like other cormorants, it slants its bill upward while swimming. Immature birds are white on the breast, dark on the belly.

PELAGIC CORMORANT
Phalacrócorax pelágicus

A small cormorant of the Pacific Coast, with a thin bill and a slender neck. The throat pouch and face are dull red. It has a double crest and a white flank patch in spring. Immature is all dark.

OLIVACEOUS CORMORANT
Phalacrócorax oliváceus

A small, rather common, unwary bird with slender bill and green eyes; just reaches the Louisiana coast.

Olivaceous Cormorant

RED-FACED CORMORANT
Phalacrócorax úrile

Resident in the Aleutians. It resembles the Pelagic but has more and brighter red on the face and a blue pouch. Immature is told from Pelagic by the longer bill.

ANHINGA
Anhinga anhinga

Common in fresh-water swamps, ponds, and lakes, where it spears fish. Often swims with only head and neck exposed. Long straight bill, long tail, and white wing and back plumes differentiate it from cormorants. Usually seen singly, but may soar very high in flocks.

GREAT CORMORANT L 30" W 60"

im.

Great Cormorant

BRANDT'S CORMORANT L 29" W 50"
head only

Double-crested

DOUBLE-CRESTED CORMORANT L 27" W 50"

im.

PELAGIC CORMORANT L 22" W 40"

im.

Pelagic

RED-FACED CORMORANT L 28" W 48"

head only

OLIVACEOUS CORMORANT L 22" W 40"

im.

♀

♀

♂

partially submerged

ANHINGA L 28" W 47"

drying wings

● **WATERFOWL** (*Order* Anseriformes, *Family* Anatidae) in North America are divided into seven subfamilies: one each for swans and geese, and five for ducks. Waterfowl are aquatic, with webs between the three front toes. They have long necks and narrow pointed wings, and most have short legs. They differ from loons and grebes in having flattened bills with tooth-like edges that serve as strainers. Their flattened bodies are well insulated with down feathers. Young hatch down-covered and can walk and swim a few hours after hatching.

Whistling Swan

Canada Goose

Mallard

SWANS, the largest of the waterfowl, are characterized by long necks—longer than their bodies. American species, all white, are graceful in the air and on water. They patter along the surface when taking flight. The young are brownish. Swans dip for aquatic plants in shallow water. Eggs, 3-10. p. 38

GEESE are intermediate between swans and ducks in size and other characteristics, but form a distinctive group. Sexes are alike. Geese are heavier and longernecked than ducks. They molt once a year, as do swans. Legs of most are placed farther forward than in ducks and swans. This is an adaptation for grazing. Eggs, 3-8. p. 40

SURFACE-FEEDING DUCKS are the first of the five duck subfamilies. Ducks are smaller than swans and geese and have flatter bills and shorter legs. Surface-feeding ducks are birds of ponds, lakes, and slow rivers, where they feed on water plants. They fly strongly and take off with a sudden upward leap. In flight their secondary wing feathers show a bright patch—the speculum. Nest on the ground (except Wood Duck); eggs, 5-12. p. 44

TREE DUCKS form a connecting link between ducks and the larger waterfowl. They are long-legged, long-necked ducks. They fly somewhat like geese. Tree ducks live along lakes and ponds and feed on water plants by tipping. They also graze like geese and occasionally damage crops. Lay 10-15 eggs.   p. 50

BAY DUCKS and sea ducks fall into a single subfamily (all have a lobed hind toe). Expert divers, their legs are set far back. Bay ducks breed along northern lakes, and most winter in huge rafts in tidal estuaries or along ice-free coasts. Feed mainly on aquatic plants. Most nest on the ground; lay 4-14 eggs.   p. 52

SEA DUCKS and bay ducks have flat bills. In taking off, they patter along the surface. Sea ducks dive deeper than bay ducks and feed more on mollusks. Sea ducks breed more along the coast than on inland lakes. In winter they are more strictly coastal than the bay ducks. Nest on the ground; eggs, 4-8.   p. 54

STIFFTAILS are little, chunky, southern ducks living in lakes and fresh-water bays. Their rather long stiff tails give them their name. Eggs, 5-11.   p. 60

MERGANSERS have long slender bills modified for seizing fish. Mergansers take off slowly, as sea ducks do. Nest in hollow trees (except Red-breasted). Eggs, 6-18.   p. 60

Black-bellied Tree Duck

Ring-necked Duck

Common Eider

Ruddy Duck

Red-breasted Merganser

SWANS (*Subfamily* Cygninae) are heavy, white, long-necked birds of lake and river shores. They dip head and neck into the water to feed on bottom vegetation. They also browse on shore grasses. There is no black on the wing tips. Sexes are similar. Immatures are grayish-brown above, white below. Swans have a deep, ponderous flight, with neck extended. Fly in V-formation or in lines.

MUTE SWAN
Cýgnus ólor

An Old World species introduced into eastern North America and commonly seen in parks. It breeds in the wild locally on Long Island and on the N.J. coast and is slowly extending its range south. No other swan breeds in eastern U.S. When swimming, it holds neck in a graceful S-curve, with the bill pointed downward; the secondary wing feathers are often raised. The adult has an orange bill with a black knob. The dull rose bill of the immature is black at the base. The voice, a low grunt, is seldom heard. Wingbeats of flying birds produce a singing note.

WHISTLING SWAN
Ólor columbiánus

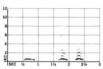

Our most common swan; breeds in the Far North and winters in large flocks in shallow fresh or brackish water. It migrates by day and by night, flying in long V's. When swimming, it is told from the Mute Swan by its silhouette. The neck is held straight, the bill level; secondaries are not raised. The adult's black bill often, though not always, shows a bright yellow spot; this spot is always lacking in the Trumpeter Swan. The immature is light gray-brown; single birds can be mistaken for immature Mute Swans, but the bill of the immature Whistling is pink, dusky only at the tip. The call, a muffled, musical whistle, can be mistaken for the honking call of the Canada Goose.

TRUMPETER SWAN
Ólor buccinátor

This largest swan, recently close to extinction, is now increasing in Yellowstone Park, Wyo., in Red Rocks Lake, Mont., and in parts of the Canadian Rockies. Very rare outside its breeding range, but sometimes is found along the West Coast in winter. Narrow flesh-colored stripe at base of mandible is hard to see but diagnostic. Immatures have black base and tip to their pink bill; their feet are dull yellow. Call is a loud, low-pitched, trumpeting: a low note followed by about 3 on a higher pitch.

SWANS

pelican Mallard eider goose swan

threat
posture

MUTE SWAN
L 40″

im.

WHISTLING SWAN
L 36″ W 85″

im.

TRUMPETER SWAN
L 45″ W 95″

im.

GEESE (*Subfamily* Anserinae) are large plump birds with a long neck, short legs, and a broad round-tipped bill. They feed on grains, grass sprouts, and some marine vegetation and fly with deep, powerful wingbeats. Geese usually migrate in noisy flocks, in V-formation or in long undulating lines. Sexes look alike.

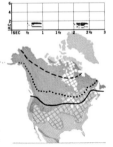

CANADA GOOSE
Bránta canadénsis

The most common and best-known goose, identified by the black head and neck and broad white cheek. It breeds on lake shores and coastal marshes. Gather in large flocks after the breeding season and graze in open fields within commuting distance of water. They migrate by day and by night. There are at least ten recognized subspecies, which differ greatly in size and slightly in color. The characteristic honking is well known; the smaller races have a cackling call.

BRANT
Bránta bérnicla

A small, locally common, dark goose with a short neck and lacking the white cheek of the Canada. The white neck mark is lacking in the immature. Flight is rapid, usually low over the water, often in flocks strung out in a long line. Breeds in the Arctic; winters in coastal bays. Its food is aquatic plants, mainly eel grass, taken by tipping. Once nearly extinct, it is now regaining its former numbers. The voice is a soft *rronk*.

BLACK BRANT
Bránta nígricans

Common locally. A small, dark, western goose, very similar in plumage, habits, and voice to the Brant, but with black on the breast and belly. The immature has more black below and lacks the white neck marking.

BARNACLE GOOSE
Bránta leucópsis

An Old World species, occurring casually along the East Coast in fall, generally in flocks with other geese. Recognized by entire white face. Immature is like adult. It nests in Greenland, winters in Europe.

EMPEROR GOOSE
Philácte canágica

A small gray goose, breeding along marshy shores in Alaska and wintering along the Alaskan coast. A few stragglers get as far south as coastal northern Calif. Note the adult's orange legs and the dark undertail coverts, a trait found in both adult and immature.

GEESE

CANADA GOOSE
L 16-25" W 50-68"

small race

large race

BRANT
L 17" W 48"

im.

BLACK BRANT
L 17" W 48"

im.

Black Brant

EMPEROR GOOSE
L 18" W 53"

BARNACLE GOOSE
L 19" W 56"

im.

WHITE-FRONTED GOOSE   *Ánser álbifrons*

A common gray goose on its principal wintering grounds, but rare east of the Mississippi. It breeds on the arctic tundra. In winter usually seen in large flocks. This is our only goose with irregular black markings on the light gray underparts, and the only one south of Alaska with orange or yellow legs. The white face of the adult contrasting with the brown head and neck is a good close-up field mark. Immature is best told from immature Blue Goose by the yellow bill, the yellow legs, and the call, a high, squealing *wah wah wah wah*.

BLUE GOOSE   *Chén caeruléscens*

Abundant in its principal Middle West range; uncommon east of Mississippi River. The adult has the head, neck, and legs of the Snow Goose and the dark body of the White-fronted Goose. The immature is almost identical to the immature White-fronted, but has a gray-brown bill and legs; it is darker than the immature Snow Goose. The Blue Goose is similar in habits to the Snow, often occurs in mixed flocks with it, and occasionally hybridizes with it. The hybrid has a dark back, but is much lighter on the underparts. Call of short, muffled notes suggests Whistling Swan's.

SNOW GOOSE   *Chén hyperbórea*

The larger of our two white geese. Locally abundant in large flocks. The adult is pure white with black wing tips. Both the adult and the pale gray immature are very similar to the rare Ross' Goose, from which they may be told by the larger size and heavier bill. The immature Snow Goose resembles and often occurs with the immature Blue, but is much paler and grayer. Call similar.

ROSS' GOOSE   *Chén róssii*

The smallest and rarest of the North American geese. It breeds in the Arctic, winters almost exclusively in the Central Valley of Calif. It is very similar to the Snow Goose, with which it occurs, but it averages smaller. The bill is comparatively shorter than the Snow Goose's and lacks its dark streak. At very close range, the bill of the adult shows warty protuberances at its base. The immature is a lighter gray than the immature Snow Goose, and the legs are pinker. The only call of Ross' Goose is a weak, grunting noise.

WHITE-FRONTED GOOSE
L 20" W 60"

im.

BLUE GOOSE
L 19" W 58"

im.

Snow Goose

im.

SNOW GOOSE
L 19" W 59"

im.

ROSS' GOOSE
L 16" W 51"

🔵 **SURFACE-FEEDING DUCKS** (*Subfamily* Anatinae) are the common ducks that dabble and tip in the shallows of fresh- and salt-water marshes. Surface-feeders are agile fliers that take off nearly vertically. Most do not dive. Male and female have different plumages. Most have a bright distinctive rectangle of color (the speculum) on the hind edge of each wing. In early summer the males assume a drab eclipse plumage; a second molt restores the usual colorful plumage by early fall. Though chiefly vegetarians, they eat some mollusks, insects, and small fish.

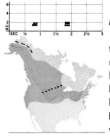

MALLARD   *Ánas platyrhýnchos*

This wide-ranging bird is the most abundant duck in the Miss. Valley; it is common in ponds and fresh-water marshes through most of its range. Male is recognized by its green head, white neck band, and rusty breast. Female is a mottled brown. Both have a blue speculum, broadly bordered in front and back with white. Mexican Duck has the same speculum. Mallards are often found with Black Ducks and Pintails. Voice, a loud quack.

MEXICAN DUCK   *Ánas diazi*

Rare and local resident in upper Rio Grande Valley of N. Mex. Similar to female Mallard, but shier; prefers same habitat. Recognized in flight by its darker tail and, at close range, by the unmarked bill of male and the dark ridge on the upper mandible of the female.

BLACK DUCK   *Ánas rúbripes*

The most abundant surface-feeding duck in the East, found in shallow coastal waters and in ponds. Note in all plumages the white wing linings that contrast with the dark body, and the violet-blue speculum with only a trace of a white border. The pale head shows more contrast to the dark body than in the female Mallard. Bill of male is not mottled. Voice same as Mallard's.

MOTTLED DUCK   *Ánas fulvigula*

Common resident in fresh and brackish marshes. Intermediate in plumage between the Black Duck and female Mallard, it has a distinct white border behind the speculum, but not in front. Also told from Mallard by darker tail, pale head, and yellower bill. In winter, Mallards and Black and Mottled Ducks use the same marshes. In Jan. Mottled Ducks are paired; Blacks and Mallards generally are not. Voice is like Mallard's.

SURFACE-FEEDING DUCKS

Mallard
take off

landing

feeding

MALLARD
L 16" W 36"

♂

♀

♂

♀

♀

♂

♀

Mexican

MEXICAN DUCK
L 15"

♂

♀

BLACK DUCK
L 16" W 36"

♂

♀

MOTTLED DUCK
L 15"

♂

♀

46

PINTAIL
Ánas acúta

The most widely distributed North American duck. Abundant in West, common in the East. Found on lakes, ponds, and bays, where it is seen in huge flocks except in the breeding season. Pintails are slim and very agile, with slender pointed wings. Note the male's sharp tail plumes, white underparts, and dark head. The female has a longer neck and a longer, more pointed tail than other mottled ducks. The speculum is metallic brown with a white rear border. Call is a short whistle. The Bahama Duck (*Ánas bahaménsis,* L 13"), a straggler in the Southeast, resembles the female Pintail but has white on the tail, white cheeks, and a mottled red bill.

GADWALL
Ánas strépera

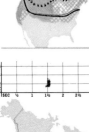

Uncommon. Seen most often with Pintail and widgeon, it rarely congregates in large flocks. Unlike other surface-feeding ducks, the Gadwall dives regularly. Note the male's plain head, dark bill, gray body, and dark tail coverts. The Black Duck is browner, with a yellow bill. The female is lighter brown than the Black Duck, and usually shows white in the wing when swimming. The speculum of both sexes is white with some brown and black; the feet are yellow. Call, very low and reedy.

AMERICAN WIDGEON
Maréca americána

A common duck, feeding largely on aquatic vegetation, occasionally coming ashore to eat shoots of grains and grasses. Recognized by large white patch on the forewing, most distinct in male. Except in the breeding season, widgeons congregate in large flocks. Unlike most ducks, they fly in tight flocks and not in long open V's. The male also shows a white crown and flanks and dark tail coverts. The female at rest is told from female Gadwall by pale head and bluish bill. Call is of 2 or 3 soft whistles, the last note lower.

EUROPEAN WIDGEON
Maréca penélope

This Old World duck is a regular fall visitor to the northern coasts of North America, though never in large numbers. Usually seen with the similar American Widgeon. Male European has rusty head and gray sides; American is opposite. Female is duller on the side and browner on the head than female American. In flight note darker axillars. Call is a high, descending whistle.

PINTAIL
L 18½" W 35"

♂
♀
♂
♀
♀

GADWALL
L 14½" W 35"

♂
♀
♂
♀

AMERICAN WIDGEON
L 14" W 34"

♀
♂
♂
♀

EUROPEAN WIDGEON
L 13½" W 32"

♀
♂
♂
♂

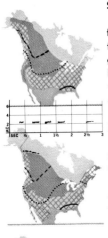

SHOVELER — *Spátula clypeáta*

Abundant in the central and western part of its range; found mainly in ponds and flooded marshes, where it feeds in shallow water. From below, the male alternates green, white, red, white, and black. Identify both sexes by the flat head, long spatulate bill, and large blue wing patch. On the water it rides low in front, bill held downward. Quack like a Mallard; also a low clucking.

BLUE-WINGED TEAL — *Ánas díscors*

A small, rather common, shy duck found on ponds, marshes, and protected bays, often with other surface-feeders. Like all teals, it flies rapidly in small, tight flocks. Both sexes have a pale blue area on the forward edge of the wing, and a green speculum. The male has the white crescent on the face and the white flank patch. Male peeps; female has a soft quack.

CINNAMON TEAL — *Anas cyanóptera*

This very small duck is common within its range and in the same habitat as the Blue-winged, which it resembles in behavior. The male is cinnamon red on head and underparts; otherwise its plumage is the same as that of the Blue-winged. The female is virtually identical to the female Blue-winged. Voice is similar to Blue-wing's.

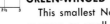

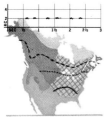

GREEN-WINGED TEAL — *Ánas carolinénsis*

This smallest North American surface-feeding duck is common on small ponds and lakes in summer. In winter it prefers fresh water to salt. Male is told by its dark head and the vertical white stripe on the side. Female resembles female Blue-winged, but has a smaller bill and lacks the large blue wing patches. It flies fast in small tight flocks. Call, a short whistle.

COMMON TEAL — *Ánas crécca*

A rare visitor from the Old World found with the Green-winged. Male Common Teal has a white horizontal line above the wing instead of the vertical stripe. Females alike. Call, like Green-winged's.

BAIKAL TEAL — *Ánas formósa*

This Asian breeder is a casual visitor to Alaska. Note the male's distinctive face pattern. The female is told from Green-winged by the distinct white patch at base of bill. Both male and female have a green speculum with a white border.

SHOVELER
L 14" W 31"

BLUE-WINGED TEAL
L 11" W 24"

CINNAMON TEAL
L 11" W 25"

GREEN-WINGED TEAL
L 10½" W 24"

COMMON TEAL
L 10½"

BAIKAL TEAL
L 11"

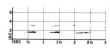

WOOD DUCK
Aix spónsa

This is a common duck of open woodland around lakes and along streams. The large head, the short neck, and the long square tail are good field marks. No other duck has the long slicked-back crest. The dull-colored female has a white eye ring. Males in eclipse plumage resemble the female, but have much white under the chin. Flight is rapid; Wood Ducks dodge agilely between the trees. They feed on plant materials, from duckweed to acorns (which are crushed in the gizzard), and some insects. Nesting is in natural tree cavities, but Wood Ducks also use nest boxes. The call is a distinctive rising whistle.

TREE DUCKS *(Subfamily* Dendrocygninae) are not all arboreal; whistling ducks would be a more appropriate name. The sexes look alike. Tree ducks are very shy. When alarmed, they raise their heads and look around, as geese do. Flight is strong, the wingbeats rather slow. In flight the feet project beyond the tail, head and feet droop down below the body line. In landing, tree ducks extend their head and feet downward until the bill nearly touches the ground. Tree ducks are particularly fond of corn, but other seeds are eaten, as are acorns. Feeding is at night. Tree ducks do not dive. Call, a shrill whistle.

FULVOUS TREE DUCK
Dendrocygna bícolor

Rather common in marshlands within its range, also in rice fields and sometimes ponds. In all plumages has a deep tawny yellow head and underparts, with a dark back and wings. The bill is dark, almost black; the feet have a dull bluish tone. Use the white rump and white side markings as secondary field marks. The white streakings on the neck are not always visible. The bird is not often seen because of its nocturnal feeding habits. It rarely perches in trees and never nests in them.

BLACK-BELLIED TREE DUCK
Dendrocygna autumnális

Rather common within its breeding range but only a straggler outside. It is found in much the same habitat as the Fulvous, though to a larger degree in wooded country. The best field marks are the black underparts and the large white areas on the wings. The bill is red, yellow, and blue, and the feet are pink. Female is duller. It frequently perches in trees and sometimes nests in holes in the trunk or in forks in the branches.

WOOD DUCK
L 13½" W 28"

eclipse plumage

♂

♀   ♂

♀   ♂

♀

TREE DUCKS

**FULVOUS
TREE DUCK**
L 13" W 36"

im.   ♂

♂

**BLACK-BELLIED
TREE DUCK**
L 13" W 37"

● **BAY DUCKS** (*Subfamily* Aythyinae) commonly winter in protected coastal bays and river mouths. These ducks dive from the surface and swim under water. They are heavy birds that run along the surface as they take off. They eat more animal food than surface-feeding ducks. Calls of most are short low croaks.

REDHEAD
Aýthya americána

This common duck summers on ponds and lakes and winters in tidewater. It often mixes with other bay ducks, forming flocks of hundreds of birds. The male has a large round head, a light bill, dark breast, and white underparts. The female's rounded head, plain bluish bill, and lack of conspicuous eye ring and white face patch distinguish it from the Ring-necked and scaups.

CANVASBACK
Aýthya valisinéria

This locally abundant duck winters more in saltier waters than does the Redhead. It mixes less with other bay ducks, though it is often found near them. Both male and female resemble the Redhead, but are noticeably lighter backed and larger, and have a distinctly flattened head profile. The bill and head profile and the male's white back are the best field marks.

RING-NECKED DUCK
Aýthya colláris

Common in woodland ponds. In winter more confined to fresh water than other bay ducks. The vertical white stripe on the side and the solid black back are the best field marks of the male. The female can be told by its distinct narrow white eye ring, ringed bill, and broad gray wing stripe. The Tufted Duck (*Aýthya fulígula*, L 12″), casual on northern coasts, lacks vertical stripe on side, has white wing stripes; female lacks facial markings.

GREATER SCAUP
Aýthya marila

Locally common, but not as abundant as Lesser Scaup; usually in salt water. Long white wing stripe and rounded head help distinguish both sexes from Lesser Scaup (head color of males not reliable). Female scaups are told from other divers by the white face. Call, *scaup*.

LESSER SCAUP
Aýthya affinis

Abundant, especially inland. White wing stripe is shorter than in Greater Scaup. At very close range the smaller "nail" at the tip of the bill is diagnostic.

BAY DUCKS

REDHEAD
L 14½″ W 33″

CANVASBACK
L 15″ W 34″

TUFTED DUCK
♂ head
L 12″

RING-NECKED DUCK
L 12″ W 28″

GREATER SCAUP
L 13″ W 31″

Greater Scaup

Lesser Scaup

LESSER SCAUP
L 12″ W 29″

COMMON GOLDENEYE *Bucéphala clángula*

Common in lakes and rivers in forested country, where it nests in cavities or even nest boxes. Winters along the coast and on lakes and rivers. Note the round dark head, the puffy crest, the wing patch, and the loud musical whistling of the wings. The male has a round white facial spot; the female a white collar. Usually goldeneyes are seen in pairs or small flocks. Their flight is very fast. When feeding, they prefer deeper water than other bay ducks. Call suggests Common Nighthawk's.

BARROW'S GOLDENEYE *Bucéphala islándica*

Rather common in West; winters on coasts and rivers. Male is told from Common Goldeneye by white facial crescent, purple head, and blacker sides. The crest tends to be more flattened and pointed to the rear. Female has less white on wing than Common and darker head; and in spring and early summer the short bill is entirely yellow, not black with a yellow tip. Eats crustaceans.

BUFFLEHEAD *Bucéphala albéola*

Summers on wooded lakes and rivers; common in winter in tidewater, generally in loose flocks. Unlike other diving ducks, it takes off without running along the water surface. The male is distinguished by the large white patch on its puffy greenish head. Small white cheek patch of the female also is diagnostic. In flight it is told from goldeneyes by whiter head (male), the small wing patch (female), and the lack of wing whistle.

SEA DUCKS (*Subfamily* Aythyinae) are heavy, rather large, short-necked diving ducks usually seen along coasts, rarely inland. In winter they often occur in large flocks, frequently of mixed species. Most live on mollusks.

HARLEQUIN DUCK *Histriónicus histriónicus*

Uncommon and shy. Summers on swift rivers and along arctic shores. Winters in the heavy surf along rocky coasts. The male is recognized by its dark and light pattern (appears dark at a distance), small size, and long tail. Female is smaller and darker than goldeneyes, lacks the white wing patch in flight, and has distinct head spots. Seldom found with other ducks, though occasionally with scoters. Harlequin often swims with its long tail tilted upward or slowly raises and lowers it.

COMMON GOLDENEYE L 13" W 31"

♀ winter

BARROW'S GOLDENEYE L 13" W 31"

♀ winter

♀ Common ♂

♀ Barrow's ♂

BUFFLEHEAD L 10" W 24"

♀ ♂

♀ ♂

Bufflehead

courtship display

SEA DUCKS

HARLEQUIN DUCK L 12" W 26"

♂ ♂

♀

♂ ♂

COMMON EIDER
Somatéria mollíssima

Abundant, but winters so locally in huge rafts (off Chatham, Mass., and in Alaska) that it is rare at other coastal locations. At close range the female and immature male can be told from other eiders by the sloping profile and by the long slender frontal shield, which extends much farther up the forehead than in the other eiders (twice as far above nostril as in King Eider). Male in first winter is intermediate between female and first spring plumage shown. Flight is heavy and laborious, with the head held low. Flocks fly in lines a few feet over the surface. Feed on mollusks and crustaceans. Call is a low, slurred moan.

KING EIDER
Somatéria spectábilis

Rare in U.S. but common in the Far North. The King Eider behaves very much like the Common Eider, with which it often occurs. The black back, white foreparts, and heavily shielded bill are good field marks for the male. The large white wing patches are unlike those of any other sea duck. The female is told from scoters (p. 58) by its uniform head coloration and stocky build, from Common Eider by the bill profile and richer brown plumage. Not so strictly confined to salt water. Immatures migrate farther south than adults.

SPECTACLED EIDER
Lampronétta físcheri

Rare in North America, though common on the coast of Siberia. A few winter in the Aleutian Islands. A heavy duck, with a very clumsy appearance. The faded green head and large white eye patch of the male are diagnostic, as is the black breast. The female can be told at close range from the larger Common Eider by the faint spectacle and the low feather line on the upper mandible.

STELLER'S EIDER
Polysticta stélleri

This small Asiatic eider is uncommon where it occurs along the Alaskan coast. Its shape is like Mallard's, but the bill is stubbier and the tail longer. The black collar of the male continues down the back as a dark line. The female is a uniform dark brown except for a blue speculum bordered with white. Both sexes have a tiny rounded crest. Their wings whistle in flight like goldeneyes'. Unlike other eiders, male helps rear the young.

EIDERS

♀

♂

♂ First Spring

♂

♀

♂

COMMON EIDER
L 17″ W 41″

♂

♂ First Spring

♂

♀

♂

KING EIDER
L 16″ W 37″

♂

♂

♀

♂

SPECTACLED EIDER
L 15″ W 36″

♀ ♂

♂

♂

STELLER'S EIDER
L 12″ W 29″

♂

♂

♀ ♂

Steller's
♀

Common

King

Common Eider

58

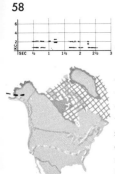

OLDSQUAW
Clángula hyemális

Abundant within its range. Summers on tundra lakes. Winters in loose flocks in deep lakes, along coasts, and often far out to sea. This is the only diving duck that is dark in front and white behind at the water line. The distinctive needle-like tail plumes of the male are shared only by the Pintail (p. 46), which has no white on the face or black on the breast. In flight the Oldsquaw, quite short and stocky, is the only white-headed duck with all-dark wings. It's flight is fast and it migrates chiefly at night. A very vocal duck, it is often noticed by its yodel-like whistle before it is seen.

COMMON SCOTER
Oidémia nigra

Despite its name, the least common of the scoters in most areas, but locally abundant on its breeding grounds in Alaska and along the coast in winter. The male is the only all-black duck in North America. (White-winged Scoters may appear all black at a distance.) Note the plump, short-necked scoter body and the prominent yellow protuberance on its black bill. Bills of other male scoters are orange. The dark cap and gray face of the female may not be seen in poor light. The female may have some yellow around the nostril. Legs and feet are black (orange or pink in other scoters).

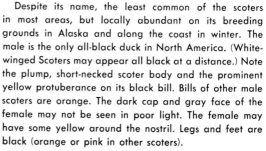

WHITE-WINGED SCOTER
Melanítta deglándi

Often abundant. Found in mixed flocks with other scoters. This largest scoter is the one most likely to be found inland. The male has a dark protuberance on the bill, which is otherwise orange. In both sexes the best field mark is the contrast between dark body and white wing patch (not always visible when swimming). Rides on the water in tight flocks; flies in loose flocks over short distances, in long lines when migrating. Female scoters are browner than the blackish males.

SURF SCOTER
Melanítta perspicilláta

In many places the most common scoter. The male has a long, thick-based, multicolored bill and prominent white markings on nape and forehead. The female is told from the Common Scoter by the two white cheek spots and from the White-winged by lack of wing patches. The Surf Scoter is more agile than other scoters. It seldom flies in line formation.

OLDSQUAW
L 15" W 30"

summer

♂

♀

♀

♂

♀

♂

winter

COMMON SCOTER
L 14" W 33"

♀

♀

♂

♀

♂

♀

WHITE-WINGED SCOTER
L 16" W 38"

im.
♀

♂

ad.
♀

♂

♂

SURF SCOTER
L 14" W 33"

im.
♀

♂

♂

ad.
♀

♂

scoters at sea

● **STIFF-TAILED DUCKS** (*Subfamily* Oxyurinae) are small and stubby, with a short thick neck. In swimming the tail is often held up at a jaunty angle. They dive and sometimes sink slowly, as grebes do.

RUDDY DUCK
Oxyúra jamaicénsis

Common in summer on lakes and ponds with floating vegetation, in winter on estuaries, lakes, and rivers. The wings are short and rounded; the flight is fast and uneven, with rapid wingbeats. Both sexes are identified by the white cheeks under the dark cap and by the long uptilted tail.

MASKED DUCK
Oxyúra domínica

A casual visitor to the southeastern U.S. from West Indies and Mexico. Largely in fresh water; nests in trees. Note male's black face and large white wing patch. Recognize female by dark face lines, white wing patches.

● **MERGANSERS** (*Subfamily* Merginae) are fish-eating diving ducks with a long thin bill serrated on the sides. Flight is rapid, with the body held very straight and horizontal. All three North American species have a white wing patch, and all except the male Common show a crest.

COMMON MERGANSER
Mérgus mergánser

A large, common, fresh-water species, seldom found in salt water. Longer and slimmer than goldeneyes, and the male is whiter behind. The male's green head, which seldom appears crested, often looks black. The female has more of a crest; the distinct white throat and sharp contrast between neck and breast distinguish it from the female Red-breasted. Call, low, short quacks.

RED-BREASTED MERGANSER
Mérgus serrátor

Common, especially along seacoasts in winter. Both sexes have the shaggy crest. The male is told by the reddish-brown chest patch. Females, which have more crest than female Common, lack contrast between head and throat. Call, low, short quacks.

HOODED MERGANSER
Lophódytes cucullátus

Uncommon; in wooded lakes and streams. The male's black-bordered white cockade and its dark sides set it off from the smaller Bufflehead (p. 54). Female is told by its bushy crest, dark face and body and merganser bill. Call is very low and toneless.

RUDDY DUCK
L 11" W 23"

winter ♂

♂

♀

summer

courtship display

MASKED DUCK
L 10" W 20"

♀

♂

♂

♀

COMMON MERGANSER
L 18" W 37"

♂

♀

♂

RED-BREASTED MERGANSER
L 16" W 33"

♂

♀

♂

HOODED MERGANSER
L 13" W 26"

crest lowered

♂

♀

♂

♂

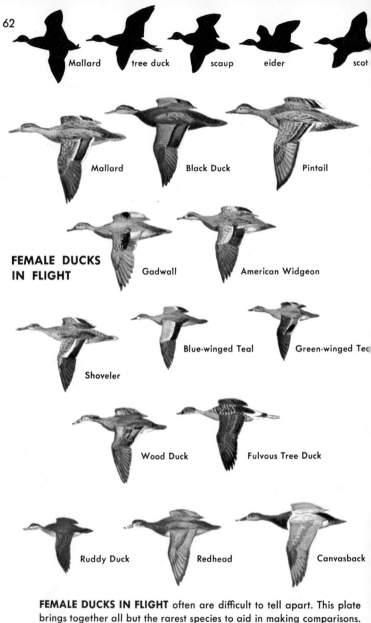

Mallard   tree duck   scaup   eider   scot

Mallard   Black Duck   Pintail

FEMALE DUCKS IN FLIGHT

Gadwall   American Widgeon

Shoveler   Blue-winged Teal   Green-winged Tea

Wood Duck   Fulvous Tree Duck

Ruddy Duck   Redhead   Canvasback

FEMALE DUCKS IN FLIGHT often are difficult to tell apart. This plate brings together all but the rarest species to aid in making comparisons. Summer and winter plumages of females are identical (except Old-

Mallard   tree duck   scaup   eider   scoter

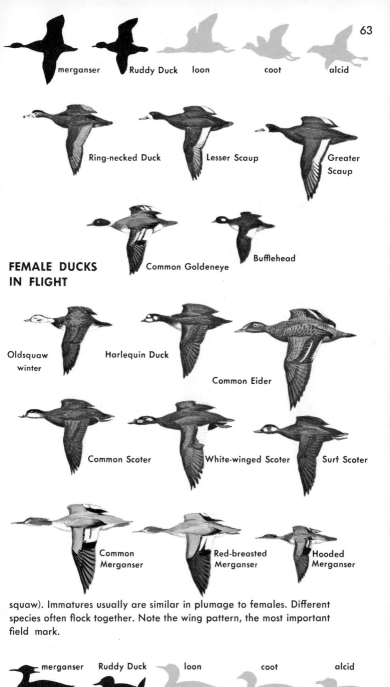

merganser Ruddy Duck loon coot alcid

Ring-necked Duck Lesser Scaup Greater Scaup

Common Goldeneye Bufflehead

FEMALE DUCKS IN FLIGHT

Oldsquaw winter Harlequin Duck Common Eider

Common Scoter White-winged Scoter Surf Scoter

Common Merganser Red-breasted Merganser Hooded Merganser

squaw). Immatures usually are similar in plumage to females. Different species often flock together. Note the wing pattern, the most important field mark.

merganser Ruddy Duck loon coot alcid

● **VULTURES, HAWKS, AND FALCONS** (Order Falconiformes) are diurnal flesh eaters. Most take live prey; some are scavengers. All have a heavy, sharp, hooked bill, and toes with strong, curved talons. Sexes are usually alike, but females are generally larger than males. There is much individual variation in color. Immatures differ from adults, and several species have light and dark forms.

FAMILIES OF VULTURES, HAWKS, AND FALCONS

TURKEY VULTURE   *Cathártes áura*

A common carrion eater, scavenging in fields and along roadsides. Immature has a black head. Soars in wide circles, holding wings in broad V and tilting quickly from side to side. Feeding vultures are soon joined by others flying in from beyond the range of human vision.

BLACK VULTURE   *Córagyps atrátus*

Common, but less so than the Turkey Vulture. Recognized at a great distance by its short-tailed, longer-necked silhouette, horizontal wing position, and relatively weak, heavy flight, an alternation of laborious, deep flapping and short glides. White patches near wing tips are distinctive. This carrion eater often invades settlements to feed on garbage and small animals.

CALIFORNIA CONDOR   *Gýmnogyps californiánus*

Almost extinct; limited to small area in mountains of southern Calif. Note striking underwing pattern, heavy beak. Soars on long wide wings held in a straight line.

vulture   buteo   gull   kite   falcon   accipiter   pigeon

VULTURES

TURKEY VULTURE
L 25″ W 72″

flight profile

im.

BLACK VULTURE
L 22″ W 54″

flight profile

CALIFORNIA CONDOR
L 45″ W 120″

im.

flight profile

KITES include two subfamilies of hawk-like birds. All are graceful on the wing, capable of swift flight and effortless soaring; hover while hunting. When prey is spotted, they do not dive (stoop), as do other hawks, but slip downward, feet first, to seize their prey before swooping (kiting) upward. Kite populations in North America have declined dangerously.

WHITE-TAILED KITE
Elánus leucúrus

Rare; in open country, grasslands, and marshes. The adult is easily recognized by the white tail and black wing patch. The immature can be told by the long white tail and pointed wings; its plumage changes to adult's during the first winter. In flight wings are held with tips pointed downward, gull fashion. Feeds largely on rodents and insects. Does not migrate.

MISSISSIPPI KITE
Ictínia misisippiénsis

Uncommon; in brushlands and open woods near water. Adult recognized by plain gray underparts and pale head; immature from other hawks by its graceful, almost swallow-like flight and notched black tail (barred below). Often seen in flocks when feeding or migrating. Feeds in flight on insects caught in the air and on the ground; also known to take mice, toads, and small snakes.

SWALLOW-TAILED KITE
Elanoídes forficátus

Fairly common in swamps, marshes, river banks, and open forests. This most graceful of all North American hawks is told in all plumages by the striking black and white pattern and swallow tail. Immature plumage is like adult's, but speckled. Somewhat gregarious in its habits. In hunting the bird may drift along slowly just a few feet above treetops or low over the ground, outstretched wings and tail in constant motion as it balances on the air currents. Often feeds in flight.

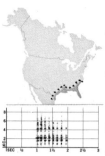

EVERGLADE KITE
Rostrhámus sociábilis

A South American species. In North America a very rare but tame resident at Lake Okeechobee and Loxahatchee Refuge, Fla. Tail of male is distinctive. Easily told from Marsh Hawk (p. 68) by broad wings, dark body and by white on tail, not rump. Flight is floppy, not kite-like. Feeds solely on a fresh-water snail (*Pomacea*), which it removes from the shell with its long hooked beak. Nests, usually in loose colonies, are a few feet above water.

KITES

WHITE-TAILED KITE
L 14½″ W 40″

im.

im.

im.

im.

MISSISSIPPI KITE
L 12½″ W 36″

SWALLOW-TAILED KITE
L 21″ W 50″

♂

♂

EVERGLADE KITE
L 15″ W 44″

♀

ACCIPITERS feed mainly on birds and small mammals. These long-tailed hunters with short rounded wings fly rapidly with short wing-beats interrupted by glides. Females are larger than males, so species overlap in size. Sexes are similar in plumage.

GOSHAWK *Accipiter gentilis*
An uncommon to rare, secretive hawk of northern forests, large enough to prey on grouse and squirrels. Recognized by its size (larger than crow), its gray or blue-gray underparts, and in all plumages the broad white eye stripe. Note also the white fluffy undertail coverts. Tail is comparatively longer than in Cooper's. Call, a long series of short high notes.

COOPER'S HAWK *Accipiter coóperii*
Uncommon; in open woodlands and wood margins. Best told from Sharp-shinned by rounded tail; also has slower wingbeat. As in other accipiters, the immature shows rich brown streaking. A very fast and powerful hawk. Call, a series of 15-20 cackling notes.

SHARP-SHINNED HAWK *Accipiter striátus*
Fairly common over most of North America in open woodlands and wood margins. The tail is narrower and more square-cut than that of Cooper's, which it greatly outnumbers during migration. This smallest accipiter preys on small birds up to the size of pigeons. Like other accipiters, it migrates during all daylight hours; flies just above the treetops in early morning, often soars high at midday. Call like that of Cooper's, but with quality of Sparrow Hawk's.

HARRIERS are slim with long rounded wings and long tails. In hunting they glide swiftly a few feet above the ground, holding their wings above the horizontal. Sexes differ greatly in color.

MARSH HAWK *Circus cyáneus*
A slim common hawk of grasslands and marshes; feeds largely on rodents. The white rump is prominent. Shares hunting grounds with Rough-legged, which is much heavier and shorter tailed. In gliding, the wings, long and narrow, but not as pointed as a falcon's, are held above the horizontal. Flies a few feet above the ground, tilting from side to side. Migrating birds fly high, often soar. Distress call, about 10 sharp notes.

ACCIPITERS

GOSHAWK
L 19″ W 42″

♂

im. ♀

♂

♀

♂

im. ♀

COOPER'S HAWK
L 15½″ W 28″

♀

♀

im. ♀

SHARP-SHINNED HAWK
L 10½″ W 21″

♀ ♂

♀

hovering

♂

MARSH HAWK
L 16½″ W 42″

BUTEOS, the largest subfamily of the Accipitridae, are the soaring hawks, which circle overhead and drop upon their prey in a steep dive. Broad rounded wings, a robust body, and a broad fanned tail distinguish them. Usually lone hunters, but two species migrate in flocks. In migration they tend to follow ridges and shorelines.

ROUGH-LEGGED HAWK   *Búteo lagópus*

An uncommon open-country bird living almost entirely on rodents. The broad dark band on the white tail, black at the bend of the wing, and the black belly are the best field marks. Tail and wings are longer than in other buteos except the Ferruginous. There are two color phases and much individual variation. Often seen hovering. Call, a thin whistle usually slurred downward.

FERRUGINOUS HAWK   *Búteo regális*

Locally common on the Great. Plains; feeds entirely on rodents. Note V of dark legs against belly of light phase (this contrast is lacking in the immature.) The head is usually light in contrast to the darker rusty back. The tail is always very light and unbanded, the primaries light and black tipped. Two color phases; the dark one rare. Does not hover. Call similar to Rough-legged's.

RED-TAILED HAWK   *Búteo jamaicénsis*

A well-known and common buteo; nests in woodlands, feeds in open country. The uniformly colored tail of the adult—reddish above, light pink beneath—and the dark belly band are the best field marks. The tail of the immature is finely streaked. Body is heavier than other buteos', plumage extremely variable. Often perches on poles or treetops, rarely hovers. A less common race resembles Harlan's Hawk (p. 72), but lacks the dark terminal band on the tail. Call is a high, faint scream.

RED-SHOULDERED HAWK   *Búteo lineátus*

One of the most common hawks of eastern North America, breeding in moist woodlands, often close to cultivated fields. Note the reddish shoulder patches, uniformly colored underparts, translucent "windows" at the base of the primaries, and narrow white bands on the dark tail. Wings and tail are comparatively longer than those of Red-tailed or Broad-winged Hawks. Red-shoulders often hunt from a perch for rodents, insects, and small birds. Call often imitated by Blue Jay.

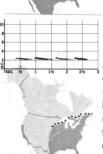

BUTEOS

hovering

dark phase

light phase

ROUGH-LEGGED HAWK
L 19″ W 52″

light phase

dark phase

FERRUGINOUS HAWK
L 20″ W 54″

light phase

dark phase

RED-TAILED HAWK
L 18″ W 48″

im.

im.

RED-SHOULDERED HAWK
L 16″ W 40″

SWAINSON'S HAWK · *Búteo swaínsoni*

A dark-breasted western hawk; especially common on the plains. The head, back, primaries, and chest are dark, contrasting in the light adult phase with the light belly. Note the heavy terminal band on the long finely barred tail. The rare dark phase appears all black except for the face and the banded tail. Glides with wings slightly uptilted; migrates in flocks. Feeds largely on gophers and rats; also eats grasshoppers. Usually perches near the ground. Call is like Rough-legged Hawk's.

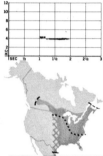

BROAD-WINGED HAWK · *Búteo platýpterus*

A woodland species, common and rather tame. Adult is easily recognized by the broadly barred tail. Immature, with characteristic buteo shape, has white underwing surface contrasting with black tips on primaries. It lacks the belly band of the much larger Red-tail (p. 70). Shape in flight is like Red-tail's. The Broad-wing hunts from a perch, flashing into action upon the appearance of a large insect, mouse, or small reptile. It characteristically migrates in large flocks. Call is a thin whistle suggesting Eastern Wood Pewee's.

HARLAN'S HAWK · *Búteo hárlani*

An uncommon buteo of the plains and one of the most difficult hawks to identify. In all plumages this bird strongly resembles the Red-tailed Hawk (p. 70), but the tail is mottled dark on white, with a definite terminal band—never barred. The primaries, always black-tipped, are finely barred, unlike Rough-legged and Ferruginous Hawks. Two color phases interbreed, and the offspring show a mingling of characteristics. Preys on rabbits and chipmunks. Call like Red-tail's.

HARRIS' HAWK · *Parabúteo unicínctus*

A very dark buteo of the Southwest; common in mesquite brushland, less so in desert areas. Harris' Hawk is slimmer than most buteos and has a longer tail. Tail of adult is black with white on tip and base. Chestnut on shoulder and thigh is very distinctive. Immature resembles Red-shouldered, but tail has more white at tip and base, more like the immature Marsh Hawk's. The more robust buteo shape and manner of flight should prevent confusion with the Marsh Hawk. Preys on mice, gophers, lizards, and small birds. Call is loud and rasping.

BUTEOS

light phase

SWAINSON'S HAWK
L 18" W 49"

light phase

dark phase

Swainson's Hawk im.

im.

BROAD-WINGED HAWK
L 13" W 33"

HARLAN'S HAWK
L 19" W 50"

dark phase

dark phase

light phase

dark phase

HARRIS' HAWK
L 18" W 43"

im.

BLACK HAWK
Buteogállus anthracínus

This black buteo is rare in U.S. In flight the dangling yellow legs, the two white bands on the tail, and the white base of the outer primaries identify the adult. Immatures are best identified by their buffy underwings and wide-winged silhouette. The wings and tail are wide, even for a buteo. Flight is alternate flapping and gliding. From woodlands near water it hunts land crabs, toads, and crayfish, its commonest foods.

ZONE-TAILED HAWK
Búteo albonotátus

A black buteo of wooded canyons and rivers. Both adults and immatures seem to mimic Turkey Vulture in plumage and in habit of soaring, with wings frequently tilted in a V. The white tail bands of the adult are often partly concealed when the bird is hunting. The wings are longer and slimmer than most buteos'. Flight is slow and sluggish. Eats small mammals, reptiles, and birds.

WHITE-TAILED HAWK
Búteo albicaudátus

A rather common hawk of the border, south to Argentina, in grasslands and the edge of the desert. The adult is told by light gray appearance and a very prominent black terminal band on the white tail. The immature is dark, almost eagle-like in color, with an unmarked grayish tail. The wings are held in a V when soaring, and the tail is short. Feeds on small animals.

SHORT-TAILED HAWK
Búteo brachyúrus

A small resident buteo of swamps and coastal areas, rare and local in the U.S. In both color phases the head and back are dark and the tail is black with three white bands. The short tail gives it a chunky appearance. Buffy-breasted immature resembles immature Broad-winged Hawk. Note pure white or jet black wing linings of adult. Feeds on lizards, snakes, and rodents.

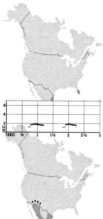

GRAY HAWK
Búteo nítidus

A small gray buteo found mostly south of the Mexican border. Rare and local in U.S. in woods along streams. Flight is rapid and direct. The all-gray adult can be told from the White-tailed by the three wide black bands on the tail. Whitish rump is characteristic of both adult and immature. Lizards are its preferred food. Has a variety of loud, high, slurred calls.

SOUTHERN BUTEOS

im.

BLACK HAWK L 20″ W 48″

im.

ZONE-TAILED HAWK L 19″ W 47″

im.

WHITE-TAILED HAWK L 21″ W 48″

dark phase

light phase

SHORT-TAILED HAWK L 14″ W 35″

im.

GRAY HAWK L 15″ W 35″

im.

GOLDEN EAGLE
Aquila chrysáëtos

A rare bird of remote mountains, tundra, grasslands, and deserts. Both adults and immatures have the rich dark brown body plumage. The golden neck feathers are seen only at close range. The broad white tail band and white wing patches of the immature are good field marks. Note its buteo flight with very long rounded wings. Legs are feathered to the toes. Feeds mostly on rodents. Call, rapid sharp chips.

BALD EAGLE
Haliaéetus leucocéphalus

Rare and local along shores. Adult plumage, white head and tail on brown body, is unmistakable. Immatures are brown, mottled irregularly with white until their fourth year. Bill is much heavier than Golden Eagle's, and legs are feathered halfway down the tarsus. Flies with deep strokes, soars on flattened wings. Note large head, short tail. Chief food is fish. Call similar to Golden Eagle's, but softer.

OSPREYS (fish hawks) are worldwide in distribution near fresh or salt water. Fish, the only prey, are taken at or just below the surface. The birds hover, often 50′ to 150′ high, then suddenly plunge, sometimes going completely under the water.

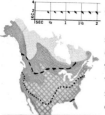

OSPREY
Pandion haliáetus

Uncommon; along seacoasts, lakes, and rivers. Conspicuous crook in long wings and black "wrist" mark confirm identification of adults and young at great distances. Plumage is dark above, white below. Except when migrating at a height, they flap more than they sail. Wingbeats are slow and deep. Wings are held in an arched position. Call, a series of loud, clear whistles.

CARACARAS AND FALCONS, though dissimilar in looks and behavior, are closely related. Caracaras are tropical American, with one species ranging into the U.S. They feed on carrion.

CARACARA
Caracára chériway

This uncommon and local long-legged scavenger of the prairies and open scrublands spends much time on the ground. In flight the large head and beak, long neck, long tail, white throat, and black-banded white tail set it apart from the vultures, with which it often associates. Call, a low rattle.

L 32″ W 78″

GOLDEN EAGLE

im.

ad.

flight profile

BALD EAGLE
L 32″ W 80″

im.

flight profile

OSPREY
L 22″ W 54″

flight profile

Bald Eagle
im.

Osprey

CARACARA
L 21″
W 48″

Black Vulture
for comparison

Osprey fishing

Turkey Vulture
for comparison

Caracara

im.

FALCONS are streamlined hawks with long pointed wings, large heads, and tails that narrow at the tip. They are rapid on the wing, with a direct, choppy, powerful flight, though they sometimes soar with the tail spread open.

GYRFALCON
Fálco rustícolus

An arctic bird, rarely wandering south of Canada. White phase is mostly in Greenland, black in western Canada, and the more common gray phase in between. Preys on birds and rodents. Has a slow wingbeat and fast flight. Note the large size and pale facial markings.

PRAIRIE FALCON
Fálco mexicánus

A light brown falcon of the plains, occasionally found in wooded areas. Black axillars (base of underside of wings) are diagnostic. Plumage is much paler than Peregrine Falcon's. Flight is strong, rapid, and usually low. Call, a series of short loud notes.

PEREGRINE FALCON
Fálco peregrínus

A rare local falcon of coasts, mountains, and woods. Best field marks are facial pattern, dark cap, and large size. Flight is fast; only Prairie Falcon is swifter. Rarely soars. It preys almost entirely on birds. Call, a long series of slurred notes.

PIGEON HAWK
Fálco columbárius

This uncommon small dark falcon of open areas is told by the absence of a black facial pattern and by prominently barred tail and pointed wings. Flight is direct with steady wingbeats, often low over the ground; seldom soars. It often captures shorebirds, pigeons, mice, and insects. Call is a series of sharp *biks*.

SPARROW HAWK
Fálco sparvérius

Sparrow Hawk

The smallest and most common falcon in open and semi-open country. The only small falcon with two "whiskers" on each side of face and the only one with a rusty back. Hunts from poles or trees; frequently hovers. Eats insects primarily. Call, a sharp *killy killy killy*.

APLOMADO FALCON
Fálco femorális

Rare; along the Mexican border. Tail is proportionately longer and wider than those of most falcons. Note the distinctive white line below the black cap.

Pigeon Hawk

FALCONS

gray phase

GYRFALCON
L 20″ W 48″

white phase

black phase
im.

im.

Peregrine Falcon

PRAIRIE FALCON
L 16″ W 40″

Prairie Falcon

PEREGRINE FALCON
L 15″ W 40″

♀

♂

PIGEON HAWK
L 12″ W 23″

♀

♂

♂

♀

♂

SPARROW HAWK
L 8½″ W 21″

♂

Sparrow Hawk hovering

ad.

im.

APLOMADO FALCON
L 14″ W 35″

HAWKS IN FLIGHT are best studied at concentration spots during migration. In some places more than 1,000 buteos and accipiters can be seen in one day. Hawks tend to move along shores rather than cross large bodies of water. Concentrations may be seen along lake and ocean shores and along mountain ridges, where updrafts will aid their flight. Some good places to observe hawk migrations are:

Hawk Mt., Kempton, Pa., all hawks	spring and fall
Great Lakes, south shores, all hawks	Mar. and Apr.
Great Lakes, north shores, all hawks	Sept. and Oct.
Cape May, N.J., accipiters, falcons, Ospreys	Sept. and Oct.

LONG-TAILED HAWKS

Goshawk p. 68

Gyrfalcon p. 78

Cooper's Hawk p. 68

Peregrine Falcon p. 78

Sharp-shinned Hawk p. 68

Prairie Falcon p. 78

Pigeon Hawk p. 78

Marsh Hawk p. 68

Sparrow Hawk p. 78

Mississippi Kite p. 66

DARK BUTEOS

LIGHT BUTEOS

Rough-legged Hawk
p. 70

dark phase

Rough-legged
Hawk p. 70

light phase

Ferruginous Hawk
p. 70

dark phase

Ferruginous
Hawk p. 70

light phase

Red-tailed Hawk
p. 70

dark phase

Red-tailed
Hawk p. 70

light phase

Harlan's Hawk
p. 72

Red-
shouldered
Hawk p. 70

light phase

Swainson's Hawk
p. 72

dark phase

Swainson's
Hawk p. 72

Broad-winged
Hawk p. 72

● **GALLINACEOUS BIRDS** (Order Galliformes) are heavy-bodied, chicken-like land birds. All have a short heavy bill with the upper mandible strongly decurved. The wings are short and rounded. Tails vary from short to very long. Legs are rather long. Their flight is not fast, but they can burst into full flight with rapid wingbeats from a sitting position. When flushed, seldom fly more than a few hundred feet. All are capable runners that forage on the ground for seeds and insects. Males of most species are more colorful than the females. Males of many species have elaborate courtship displays that include strutting, raising or spreading of specialized feathers on the head, neck, and tail, and the inflating of air sacs in the neck. Beating of the air with their wings or the release of air from the air sacs produces characteristic courtship sounds. They are mainly non-migratory.

FAMILIES OF GALLINACEOUS BIRDS

Chachalacas and others (Cracidae) Large, long-legged, long-tailed, chicken-like woodland birds. Eggs, 3-4.   p. 82

Turkeys (Meleagrididae) Very large long-legged birds with a long broad tail. Head and neck bare. Eggs, 10-12.   p. 82

Grouse (Tetraonidae) Medium-sized birds with moderate to long tail. Nostrils and feet covered with feathers. Courtship displays often elaborate. Ground dwellers. Eggs, 7-12.   p. 84

Quails, Partridges, and Pheasants (Phasianidae) Small to large birds of fields or open country. Quails, the smallest, are natives of the New and Old Worlds. Eggs, 6-16. Partridges, from Europe, are larger. Eggs, 8-16. Pheasants, from Asia, are largest.   p. 88

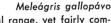

TURKEY   *Meleágris gallopávo*

Gone from most of its original range, yet fairly common locally in open woodland or forest clearings. Similar to the familiar barnyard turkey, but slimmer and with rusty, not white, tip to the tail. Turkeys roost in trees at night. They are weak fliers and prefer to avoid danger by running. Their food is acorns, fruit, and seeds. The male, or gobbler, calls (gobbles) in the early morning to summon the hens of his harem.

CHACHALACA   *Órtalis vétula*

Locally abundant in woodlands and thickets, preferring clearing in heavy growth. This large, long-tailed, arboreal species is quite unlike any other U.S. bird. Note the plain olive back and iridescent green tail. The patch of dull pinkish skin on the side of the throat becomes red on the male in spring. Outer edge of tail is tipped with white. Sexes similar. Call is a loud repetition of its name.

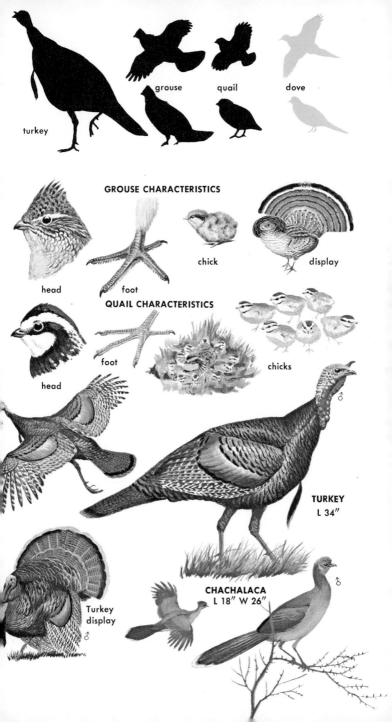

turkey

grouse

quail

dove

GROUSE CHARACTERISTICS

head

foot

chick

display

QUAIL CHARACTERISTICS

head

foot

chicks

TURKEY
L 34"

Turkey
display ♂

CHACHALACA
L 18" W 26"

BLUE GROUSE
Dendrágapus obscúrus

Common in deciduous woodlands in summer, in mountain thickets of fir in winter. The male is told by its plain gray plumage and the orange or yellow patch of skin above the eye. The female is a dark mottled brown; has a black tail with a pale gray terminal band. Birds in the northern Rockies lack the tail band. The male produces deep booming sounds from his inflated neck sacs. These are purple on interior birds and orange on coastal birds.

SPRUCE GROUSE
Canachites canadénsis

A fairly common, very tame grouse of coniferous forests. The male is gray above, black below, with white spots on the sides. Bare skin above the eye is red. In the eastern race, the tail has a chestnut band. Western race has white spots on upper tail coverts. The mottled female is rustier than Blue Grouse, darker than Ruffed Grouse, with brown terminal band on blackish tail. Generally silent; hooting is extremely low pitched.

RUFFED GROUSE
Bonása umbéllus

Usually fairly common, but the population is variable. A summer resident of clearings in open woods; winters in conifers. Two color phases occur, gray and red, differing mainly in the tones of the finely barred tail with its black terminal band. The male attracts females by a display pattern and by "drumming" the air with rapidly beating wings.

SHARP-TAILED GROUSE
Pedioecétes phasianéllus

Locally common in prairies and brushland. Underparts are light. The narrow pointed tail is white-edged, distinguishing it in flight from female pheasant (p. 90) and prairie chicken (p. 86). The mottled body feathers produce an overall buffy appearance. During courting display male gives deep pigeon-like coos.

SAGE GROUSE
Centrocércus urophasiánus

Common in sagebrush country, summering in the foothills and wintering on the plains. Both sexes are recognized by their large size, black bellies, and long, pointed tails. Note also the white breast of the male and the black throat divided by a white band. Its principal food is sagebrush. During display male utters short, deep, bubbling notes.

display

♂

Northern Rocky Mt. races

♂ Blue Grouse

♂ Spruce Grouse

♀

♂ display

Sharp-tail display
♂

display
♂

Sage Grouse

♂

BLUE GROUSE
L 17″

♀ ♂

SPRUCE GROUSE
L 13″

♀ ♂

gray phase

red phase

♂ ♂

RUFFED GROUSE
L 14″

SHARP-TAILED GROUSE
L 15″

SAGE GROUSE
L 22″

♀

GREATER PRAIRIE CHICKEN   *Tympanúchus cúpido*

Uncommon and very local; in virgin grasslands and prairies. May be told from other prairie birds by the short, rounded, blackish tail that contrasts with the brown body plumage. The males have long tufts of feathers on the sides of the neck and orange air sacs that are inflated during courtship. The tail of the female is barred. The Sharp-tailed Grouse (p. 84), which may occur in the same habitat, shows a pointed brown tail bordered with white. During display the male makes a weird, deep, hollow sound.

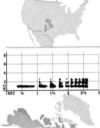

LESSER PRAIRIE CHICKEN   *Tympanúchus pallidicinctus*

Even less common than the Greater, and found more in arid regions. It is smaller and paler, with reddish air sacs. Both species have courtship, or booming, grounds where the males gather to display before the females. Courtship sound is higher in pitch than in the Greater Prairie Chicken.

WILLOW PTARMIGAN   *Lagópus lagópus*

Common in the Arctic; winters in deep thickets or on windswept tundra not covered by snow. The summer male is more reddish than other ptarmigans. The female is similar in plumage to the smaller Rock Ptarmigan, but has a proportionately larger bill. Winter birds are all white, except for black tail. The principal food is willow leaves. Winters in small flocks.

ROCK PTARMIGAN   *Lagópus mútus*

Common in mountain areas, usually above the tree line. In summer the male is lighter and more yellow than the larger Willow Ptarmigan, but females are virtually identical except for size and bill. In winter both sexes are white, faintly tinged with pink; tail is black in both sexes, and the male has a black line through the eye. Found in pairs in the summer, in flocks in winter. Call, very low pitched and grating.

WHITE-TAILED PTARMIGAN   *Lagópus leucúrus*

Locally common above timberline. This is the only ptarmigan with no black on the tail. Unwary in the wild, it runs from danger in preference to flying. Its staple food is Dwarf Willow, although it also eats the needles of Alpine Fir. Call is hen-like.

Sharp-tailed
for comparison

Greater
Prairie
Chicken

display

♂

**GREATER PRAIRIE
CHICKEN
L 14″**

display

♂

**LESSER PRAIRIE
CHICKEN
L 13″**

**WILLOW
PTARMIGAN
L 13″**

molting

summer

♀

♂

winter

**ROCK
PTARMIGAN
L 11″**

molting

summer

♀

♂

♂

winter

**WHITE-TAILED
PTARMIGAN
L 10″**

molting

♀

♂

winter

summer

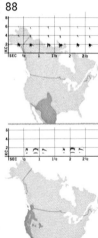

SCALED QUAIL
Callipépla squamáta

Usually common, but population fluctuates from year to year. A bird of dry semi-desert country. Sexes are alike, gray-backed, scaled underneath, with a prominent cottony white crest that gives the birds a very pale appearance. Normally gregarious, usually found in flocks (of up to 100 birds). Seldom flies, preferring to run. Has a sharp, two-syllable call.

CALIFORNIA QUAIL
Lophórtyx califórnicus

Common in mixed woodlands and increasing in large city parks. Note the male's black face outlined in white, its bluish chest, and white marking on the gray flanks. Both sexes have scaling on the belly. The similar Gambel's Quail has a plain belly (with black spot in the male). Usually seen in flocks, feeding on the ground. Call of 3 slurred notes, the middle one highest and loudest.

GAMBEL'S QUAIL
Lophórtyx gámbelii

This is a common quail of drier habitats than the California, which it resembles. Ranges barely meet. Note the chestnut flanks, broadly streaked with white in both sexes. The black belly patch can also be used to separate the male from the California. The teardrop topknot, common to both species, distinguishes them from all other quail. Call is similar to California Quail's.

MOUNTAIN QUAIL
Oreórtyx píctus

This largest of North American quails is common in mountain regions in mixed woodlands and chaparral. The thin head plume is distinctive; the vertical white streaks on the flanks and the chestnut throat also are good field marks. Sexes are similar, but the female is duller than the male. These quail are hard to flush. Call, a loud crowing note or a soft *whook*.

HARLEQUIN QUAIL
Cyrtónyx montezúmae

Rather common, but local on open woodland slopes under oaks or pines. The male is easily identified by the face pattern and the heavily spotted flanks. The dull brown female has enough traces of the male's face pattern to identify it. When approached, Harlequins often squat and hide rather than fly. Call is a gentle whistle, louder and more varied at dusk.

WESTERN QUAILS

SCALED QUAIL
L 8"

CALIFORNIA QUAIL
L 8"

♀ ♂

GAMBEL'S QUAIL
L 8½"

♂ ♀

MOUNTAIN QUAIL
L 9"

♀ ♂

HARLEQUIN QUAIL
L 7"

protective
crouching

90

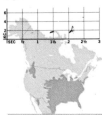

BOBWHITE
Colínus virginiánus

Abundant in brush, abandoned fields, and open pine-lands, but avoids deep forests. A chunky reddish-brown quail with a gray tail. The male is identified by the white throat and eye line; in the female these areas are buffy. In winter found in flocks (coveys) of up to 30 birds. When disturbed, all burst into flight at once. Call is a whistled *bob-bob-white*, 4-6/min.

● **INTRODUCED GALLINACEOUS BIRDS** of many species have been released in the U.S. and Canada, but most have not become established. The three species below have succeeded in adapting to their new environment sufficiently to become common in several areas.

CHUKAR
Aléctoris graéca

Locally common, this large European partridge prefers open, rocky, barren lands. Sexes are similar, with a light olive-brown back, creamy underparts with chestnut striping on the flanks, and a cream-colored face with a prominent black border. In flight (strong and direct) the reddish legs are visible. Feeds on grass shoots, seeds, grain, and insects. The male calls *chu-kar*.

RING-NECKED PHEASANT
Phasiánus cólchicus

Common in open woods and on farmland in brush, hedgerows and cornfields. Much larger than other gallinaceous birds except the Turkey. Both sexes have the long pointed tail and short rounded wings. The male is much more colorful. Plumage variable, depending on origin of released stock. Female is told from the smaller Sharp-tailed Grouse (p. 84) by the much longer tail, large bill and bare legs. Flight is strong, but only for short distances. Pheasants roost in trees. Feeds mostly on waste grains, seeds, and berries. The loud, 2-syllable call is followed by a muffled rapid beating of wings.

GRAY PARTRIDGE
Pérdix pérdix

Locally abundant on agricultural lands, especially those under irrigation. In flight the rusty tail is a good field mark. Larger than the Bobwhite, this partridge is much grayer, especially on the breast. The face and throat are orange-brown without a black border. Usually silent, but a fast repetition of a one-tone whistle is sometimes heard.

BOBWHITE
L 8"

CHUKAR
L 10"

**RING-NECKED
PHEASANT**
L 27"

**GRAY
PARTRIDGE**
L 10"

Pheasant

HERONS AND THEIR ALLIES (*Order* Ciconiiformes) are wading birds with long legs, neck, and bill. Most feed on aquatic animal life in shallow water. Some have long plumes, or aigrettes, in the breeding season. Wings are broad and rounded; tail is short. Eggs, 2-6.

FAMILIES OF HERONS AND THEIR ALLIES

Herons and Bitterns (Ardeidae) Bill straight. Flight slow, with head drawn back. Most nest in colonies. Calls, hoarse croaks.   p. 92

Wood Ibises (Ciconiidae) Bill heavy, decurved. Flight slow with neck outstretched. Head of adult bare.   p. 98

Ibises and Spoonbills (Threskiornithidae) Bill thin and decurved or flat and spoon-shaped. Fast wingbeats, neck outstretched.   p. 98

Flamingos (Phoenicopteridae) Legs and neck extremely long; bill stout, hooked. Flight ponderous, neck outstretched but drooping.   p. 98

GREAT WHITE HERON   *Árdea occidentális*
This largest North American heron is locally common in salt water along the coast of southern Fla. and the Fla. Keys. Bill is yellow, legs yellowish. Very closely related to Great Blue Heron. Does not flock.

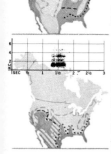

COMMON EGRET   *Casmeródius álbus*
Common along streams, ponds, rice fields, salt- and fresh-water marshes, and mudflats. The plumage is white, bill yellow, legs and feet glossy black. White phase of Reddish Egret (p. 94) has flesh-colored, black-tipped bill and bluish legs. Larger than any other white heron except the Great White. In flight, the Common Egret holds its neck in a more open S than do other white herons.

SNOWY EGRET   *Leucophóyx thúla*
Common, mostly in fresh- and salt-water marshes, but sometimes in ponds and rice fields. Plumage snow white, bill thin and black, with bare yellow skin at the base. Legs black, feet bright yellow in adult, duller in immature. Immature Little Blue Heron (p. 94) has bluish bill, greenish legs. Snowy is slimmer and more active than other white herons. Flight is less abrupt than Cattle Egret's.

CATTLE EGRET   *Bubúlcus ibis*
An Old World species recently naturalized in North America; common and spreading. Seen in flocks in pastures, feeding on insects. The yellow or orange bill and the neck are shorter and thicker than in other herons. Note buffy-orange crest, breast, and shoulders in breeding plumage. Adult's legs are yellowish to pinkish.

egret

ibis

Wood Ibis

spoonbill

flamingo

WHITE HERONS

GREAT WHITE HERON
L 38″ W 70″

Common Egret
open curve

Reddish Egret
for comparison

COMMON EGRET
L 32″ W 55″

Snowy Egret
tight curve

white
phase

im. Little Blue
Heron for
comparison

SNOWY EGRET
L 20″ W 38″

display

breeding

im.

CATTLE EGRET
L 17″ W 37″

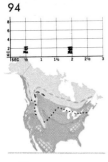

GREAT BLUE HERON   *Árdea heródias*

This largest of the dark herons is common on fresh water as well as salt. Head is largely white, underparts are dark. This pattern is reversed in the Louisiana Heron. When hunting, Great Blue walks slowly through shallows or stands with head hunched on shoulders. A rare hybrid between this species and the Great White occurs in Fla. Bay. Called Würdemann's Heron, it is like a Great Blue with a white head and neck. Alarm call of both is a series of about 4 hoarse squawks.

REDDISH EGRET   *Dichromanássa ruféscens*

An uncommon, dark heron of salt-water flats. Larger than the Louisiana. The head and neck are quite shaggy. The bill usually is dark at the tip and flesh-colored at the base, a trait also distinguishing the rare white phase (p. 93). Very active when feeding—running, hopping, and flapping as it pursues fish.

LOUISIANA HERON   *Hydranássa trícolor*

A common heron of salt-water shores. This dark heron with white underparts appears more slender-necked than other herons. An active feeder, though less so than the Reddish Egret. Often wades in deep water.

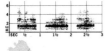

LITTLE BLUE HERON   *Flórida caerulea*

A common, small, dark heron of both fresh and salt water. Note the dark slaty-blue back and underparts, with a warm brown on the head and neck. The bill is bluish, with a black tip; the legs are bluish-green. The Reddish Egret is larger, much paler, and thicker necked. The more active Louisiana has white on the underparts and is not so stocky. The immature Little Blue is white with a dark-tipped bluish bill and greenish legs. Molting one-year birds (Calico Herons) are blotched blue and white.

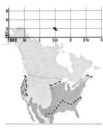

GREEN HERON   *Butorídes virescens*

Common, locally abundant, in both fresh and salt water. Found more than other herons in small ponds and along wooded streams. Looks more blue than green. Told by its small size, dark underparts, and bright orange or yellow legs. Flight is rapid, with deep wingbeats. Appears all dark at a distance. The crest is not always visible. Neck is comparatively shorter than that of other herons. Call, a sharp, descending *kew*.

BLUISH HERONS

Great Blue Heron
soon after take off

GREAT BLUE HERON
L 38" W 70"

REDDISH EGRET
L 25" W 46"

splay

white phase

Reddish Egret
canopy feeding

LITTLE BLUE HERON
L 22" W 41"

LOUISIANA HERON
L 22" W 38"

...siana Heron
feeding

im.

1 year

GREEN HERON
L 14" W 25"

im.

96

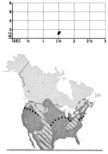

BLACK-CROWNED NIGHT HERON

Nycticorax nycticorax

Night herons are characterized by heavy bodies, short thick necks, and, in this species, short legs. A common heron of fresh-water swamps and tidal marshes. The adult is dark-backed and entirely white below. The Louisiana Heron (p. 94) has a white belly, but is a long slender bird. The heavily streaked immature can be confused only with the Yellow-crowned Night Heron and American Bittern. Flies in loose flocks. Often inactive by day, roosting in trees. Fishes more at night. Call, a single *kwawk,* is most frequently heard at night.

YELLOW-CROWNED NIGHT HERON

Nyctanássa violácea

Much less common than the Black-crowned. Hunts at night, but frequently is seen feeding by day. Watch for the distinct black and white face on the otherwise gray adult. The immature is similar to the immature Black-crowned, but has a shorter, thicker bill, longer legs, and grayer plumage with smaller light spots on the back. In flight part of the tarsus extends beyond the tail. Call is slightly higher pitched than Black-crowned's.

AMERICAN BITTERN   *Botaúrus lentiginósus*

Rather common but very elusive in the tall vegetation of fresh-water marshes. Most active at dusk and at night. Sometimes hides by freezing in position with head pointed upward. The best field mark for a sitting bird is the black whisker mark, which no other heron or bittern has. In flight the blackish flight feathers are diagnostic. Seldom calls when flushed. Does not flock. On the breeding ground it makes a hollow croaking or "pumping" sound, *oonck-a-tsoonck.*

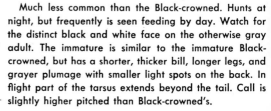

LEAST BITTERN   *Ixobrýchus exilis*

Common but very shy, usually remaining hidden in tall fresh-water grasses and sedges. This smallest heron is a weak flier. It will run or climb rather than take wing; seldom flies more than 100'. Both sexes have the large wing patches of buff and chestnut that distinguish them immediately from the dark-winged Green Heron (which is a larger chunkier bird). Also hides by freezing. A rare dark phase is rich chestnut in color. Call, about 4 identical soft, low *coos.*

roosting

im.

BLACK-CROWNED NIGHT HERON
L 20″ W 44″

ack-crowned ight Heron

im.

ad

im.

YELLOW-CROWNED NIGHT HERON
L 21″ W 44″

im.

Yellow-crowned Night Heron

im.

bittern "freezing"

im.

LEAST BITTERN
L 11″ W 17″

AMERICAN BITTERN
L 23″ W 45″

WOOD IBIS
Myctéria americána

This only American stork is locally common in southern swamps, marshes, and ponds. The bill is long and thick; adult's dark head is unfeathered. Immature has a paler head and neck; yellow bill. Flies with neck and legs extended; often soars. Wingbeats are slow and powerful. It feeds on fish, reptiles, and amphibians. Nests in colonies in trees. Call is of humming notes.

WHITE-FACED IBIS
Plégadis chihí

Uncommon. Can be told from Glossy Ibis, only in the breeding season, by the broad white line around the eye and under the chin of the adult. Immatures are identical to the Glossy. Flies in lines or V-formation; alternates flapping and gliding. Call of low quacks.

GLOSSY IBIS
Plégadis falcinéllus

Uncommon but extending its range. Feeds in small flocks in fresh or salt marshes. Adult is a uniform bronze brown, which appears black at a distance. The immature resembles immature White Ibis but has a light neck and dark rump. The thin decurved bill, outstretched neck, rapid wingbeats, and alternately flapping and gliding flight distinguish it from herons.

WHITE IBIS
Eudócimus álbus

Locally abundant, but more confined to coastal locations than other ibises. Adult has red face and bill. The small black wing tips are usually hidden when at rest. Young birds show white rump when flying, and from below the dark neck contrasts with the white belly. Often seen in large flocks that fly in long lines or in V-formation. Calls are low and harsh.

ROSEATE SPOONBILL
Ajáia ajája

Rare and local in shallow salt water. Bill, flattened at the tip, is unique. Adult is mostly pink; faint pink on immature intensifies with age. Flies with neck outstretched. Feeds on small marine life. Usually silent.

AMERICAN FLAMINGO
Phoenicópterus rúber

A rare straggler on mudflats of southern Fla.; most are probably escapees. Neck and legs extremely long, bill thick and hooked, plumage variable from light pink to rose. Feeds on small marine life. Call, gooselike honks.

IBISES AND SPOONBILLS

WOOD IBIS
L 35" W 66"

im.

WHITE-FACED IBIS
L 19" W 37"

GLOSSY IBIS
L 19" W 37"

im.

WHITE IBIS
L 22" W 38"

im.

im.

AMERICAN FLAMINGO
L 42" W 55"

½ scale

ROSEATE SPOONBILL
L 28" W 53"

CRANES AND THEIR ALLIES (Order Gruiformes) are a diversifie
group. All are wading birds with long legs, but other features suc
as size, body outline, bill shape, and neck length are variable.

FAMILIES OF CRANES AND THEIR ALLIES

WHOOPING CRANE   *Grús americáne*

Extremely rare; population totals about 50. Breeds i
northern fresh-water bogs, winters in coastal prairie
Note the adult's white head and body, and bare ree
face and crown, and the black primaries of all birds
Young are reddish-brown, lighter below. Black and whit
pattern of flying birds is more like that of Snow Goos
than that of White Pelican or Wood Ibis. Very long nec
and white tail of Whooping Crane are diagnostic. Call, «
vibrant trumpet note.

SANDHILL CRANE   *Grús canadéns*

Locally common in prairies and fields, and occasion
ally in open pinelands and marshes. Both the gray adu
and the brown immature can be recognized by thei
very large size and uniform coloration. Note the bare
red cap of the adult. The flight is an alternation of glid
ing and flapping; the rapid upstroke of the wings is «
good field mark. Often seen in large flocks except dur
ing the breeding season. Small rodents, frogs, and in
sects are its food. The voice is a low, loud, musical rattle

LIMPKIN   *Arámus guaraún*

Locally common in wooded swamps; uncommon i
marshes. The long slender bill, slightly decurved, wi
distinguish the Limpkin from the night herons (p. 96)
Each feather on the dark brown body plumage has «
large white crescent. The long neck is usually held erec
and is extended in flight. Active by day and by night
Snails are its favorite food. Its call, a carrying *krr-oww*
is heard most often at night.

duck

coot

rail

ibis

egret

crane

rails and Limpkin in marsh

Whooping Crane dance

coots take off

Purple Gallinule

SANDHILL CRANE
L 37" W 80"

im.

im.

WHOOPING CRANE
L 45" W 90"

LIMPKIN
L 22" W 42"

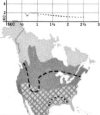

VIRGINIA RAIL
Rállus limícolo

A common but elusive rail of fresh and brackish marshes. It is half the size of the King and Clapper Rails (p. 104), though similar in plumage except for the gray cheeks. Like other rails, it runs silently through the grass when pursued, seldom resorting to its weak, fluttering flight. When in the air its long legs dangle limply below. The Virginia Rail is best identified by the voice: a metallic two-syllable note often written as *kid-ick, kid-ick*, a descending Mallard-like series of quacks, and several other less characteristic calls.

SORA
Porzána carolína

Most common of the rails, but seldom seen. It frequents marshes, especially fresh, with dense vegetation. The best field mark is the short, sturdy, chicken-like bill. The immature lacks the black facial pattern of the adult, but is told from other small rails by the white undertail coverts. The Sora is easier to flush than other rails, but, like them, has a short weak flight. Call is a whistled *ker-wee*, also a musical descending whinny.

CORN CRAKE
Créx créx

Casual on East Coast. A large European rail found in hay and other crop fields. Told by the large rusty wing patch and buffy body. Rasping call is seldom heard.

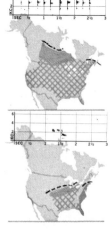

YELLOW RAIL
Cotúrnicops noveboracénsis

A very small rail, rare and extremely shy. It inhabits fresh and salt marshes, also meadows and even grainfields. The yellowish plumage is interrupted by black striping on the back. The bill is small and yellow. In flight the best field mark is the white wing patch, but this bird can rarely be flushed. The voice, heard mostly at dusk, is clicking notes in alternating groups of 2 and 3, imitated by tapping two pebbles together.

BLACK RAIL
Laterállus jamaicénsis

This smallest rail is locally rather common, usually in salt marshes amid cordgrasses, rarely in fresh. The tiny size, the black coloration, and the white spots on the back identify it. The black bill of the adult is diagnostic. The chicks of all rails are black. Call, *kickee-doo*, the last note softer and much lower; heard late at night.

SMALL RAILS

VIRGINIA RAIL

L 7½"
W 14"

im.

chick

SORA
L 6¾" W 12½"

im.

CORN CRAKE
L 9"

YELLOW RAIL
L 5"

BLACK RAIL
L 4½"

chick

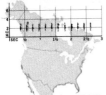

CLAPPER RAIL   *Rállus longiróstris*

An abundant, large, gray or gray-brown, salt-marsh rail. The neck is short, the bill long and slightly down-turned. The very short tail is cocked upward. Immatures are dark above (see Va. Rail, p. 102). Southern and western Clapper Rails resemble King Rails but are grayer at bend of wing and less plainly marked on belly. As in other rails, the body, deep in profile, is compressed laterally. The voice is a series of loud unmusical ticks.

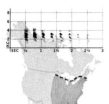

KING RAIL   *Rállus élegans*

This common large rust-colored rail of fresh-water marshes occasionally occurs with the Clapper in brackish marshes. Similar in plumage and habits but browner, and with stronger barring. The chicks are black with the entire bill pale white. Call is like Clapper's, but shorter and more musical and resonant.

COMMON GALLINULE   *Gallinula chlóropus*

Common in fresh-water marshes and along the edges of lakes. Its resemblance to ducks is countered by the bright red frontal plate of the head and the yellow-tipped chicken-like bill. Feeds along the edges of open water and, when disturbed, seeks cover in dense vegetation. It swims well. Call, hen-like clucks.

PURPLE GALLINULE   *Porphýrula martínica*

Less widespread and less common than the Common Gallinule, which it resembles closely in habits. The adult is unmistakable, with green back and purple head and underparts. The white plate on the front of the head marks this species. The immature is browner and paler than the immature Common Gallinule and lacks the white side stripe. Calls are similar to Common Gallinule's.

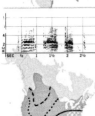

AMERICAN COOT   *Fúlica americána*

Common. In nesting season found on fresh water and in winter on both fresh and salt. The dark plumage contrasts with the high white bill and the white marking underneath the short tail. Feeds on shore, on the surface of the water or under it, diving with an upward jump before submerging. Swims buoyantly, nodding its head and paddling with its lobed toes. Flight is heavy, with trailing legs. Call, short rough notes.

LARGE RAILS

CLAPPER RAIL
L 12″ W 20″

KING RAIL
L 14″ W 24″

GALLINULES

im.

**COMMON
GALLINULE**
L 10½″ W 21″

im.

**PURPLE
GALLINULE**
L 10½″ W 21″

im.

chick

AMERICAN COOT
L 12″ W 25″

● **SHOREBIRDS, GULLS, AND ALCIDS** (*Order* Charadriiformes) form a large and diverse group of wading or swimming birds with ten families in North America. Most are white and gray or brown, with long pointed wings and long legs or webbed feet. Sexes are similar in most species. Shorebirds fall into six families (p. 107), but four of these are minor ones. Shorebirds typically have long legs and pointed wings. They are highly migratory. Most feed along shores, a few inland. Gulls and terns (*Family* Laridae) and their relatives the skimmers (*Family* Rynchopidae), and the jaegers and skuas (*Family* Stercorariidae) are short-legged, web-footed birds, more aquatic than all shorebirds except the phalaropes. The auks, murres, and puffins (*Family* Alcidae) are short-winged pelagic birds.

jaeger   gull   tern   alcid

BEHAVIOR OF SHOREBIRDS

Many of these birds, so varied in form and habits, have behavior traits that are characteristic either of shorebirds in general or of individual species.

1. Dowitcher probing in sand or mud for worms and small crustaceans.

2. Avocet skimming the surface of ponds for insects and their larvae.

3. Spotted Sandpiper tipping up tail. Often seen on rocks rather than sand.

4. Killdeer feigning wing injury to lead intruder away from its nest.

5. Oystercatchers bowing in courtship.

6. Willet showing wing stripe. Many shorebirds have a less conspicuous stripe.

7. Snipe "winnowing" in flight, making a whistling sound with its wings and tail.

8. Phalarope spinning in shallow water to stir up insect larvae.

9. Dunlin standing on one foot, a typical resting posture of shorebirds.

JACANAS (*Family* Jacanidae) are tropical birds with long legs and very long toes. They walk on lily pads, eat insect larvae. Eggs, 4.

OYSTERCATCHERS (*Family* Haematopodidae) are large chunky shorebirds with bright red bills and black heads. The long bill, which is compressed laterally, is used to open bivalves. Eggs, 2-3.

PLOVERS, TURNSTONES, AND SURFBIRDS (*Family* Charadriidae) are small to medium-sized shorebirds, shorter billed and shorter necked than most sandpipers. The heads of most are strongly marked. Backs are plain or speckled. Food is small marine life. Eggs, usually 4.

SANDPIPERS (*Family* Scolopacidae) A large and varied group of shore and wading birds; some upland, some fresh-water, but most seen along ocean shores. Size ranges from 5″ to 19″. Plumage is mainly dull gray, buff, or brown, mottled or streaked. Many are identified by their tail, rump, and wing markings. Legs and bills are long and slender. Feed mainly on small invertebrates. Often seen in flocks. Sexes are alike or nearly so. Eggs, 2 to (usually) 4.

AVOCETS (*Family* Recurvirostridae) are medium-large slender-legged waders with long thin bills that are straight or curved upward. They feed on insects and small marine invertebrates. Eggs, usually 4.

PHALAROPES (*Family* Phalaropodidae) have lobed toes. Males are duller than females. Food, small marine life. Eggs, usually 4.

DARK-BACKED SHOREBIRDS are grouped here for convenience because their plumage, silhouettes and behavior are so different from those of other shorebirds. The heavy-bodied oystercatchers, the extremely long-legged avocet and stilt, and the long-toed Jacana are in families by themselves; the rounded-winged, crested Lapwing is in a different subfamily from the other plovers.

AMERICAN OYSTERCATCHER   *Haemátopus palliátus*

Uncommon; on coastal mudflats and sandy beaches, where it feeds on shellfish. Usually seen in very small flocks well apart from other shorebirds. Its black and white plumage, large white wing stripe, and red bill identify it. Call is a shrill, loud *kleep*.

BLACK OYSTERCATCHER   *Haemátopus báchmani*

Uncommon. Prefers rocky shores. Note the black body, red bill, and pink legs. In courting, both American and Black males display by walking up to the female with bowed head. The flight is strong, and flocks fly in lines in V-formation. Calls are short peeping notes.

AMERICAN AVOCET   *Recurviróstra americána*

Rather common, breeding on the shores of marshes and lakes. Legs and neck are long and thin; the needle-like bill curves upward. In flight the black bar on the white inner wing is an excellent field mark. The legs are blue-gray. Call, a loud *wheet*.

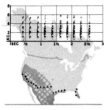

BLACK-NECKED STILT   *Himántopus mexicánus*

Common, breeding in both fresh- and salt-water habitats. Note the long thin legs and neck, and the thin straight bill. The plumage is black above, white below. In flight the wings are an unrelieved black; the red legs trail far behind the white tail. Call is a monotonous series of loud piping notes.

LAPWING   *Vanéllus vanéllus*

A Eurasion plover, casual on the Northeast coast. The crest is present in all plumages. The wings are broad and rounded at tip, face white, head and back dark. Call is a high pitched, sad *weep*.

JACANA   *Jacána spinósa*

Casual on ponds in south Texas. Note long toes, long greenish legs, yellow flight feathers. Very active, feeding constantly; occasionally raises wings. Flight is rail-like, close to water. Call, a shrill whistle.

display   probing

AMERICAN OYSTERCATCHER
L 16"

BLACK OYSTERCATCHER
L 15"

summer

AMERICAN AVOCET
L 15"

BLACK-NECKED STILT L 13"

winter

LAPWING L 11"

ACANA
L 7"
⅔ scale

⅔ scale

PLOVERS (*Family* Charadriidae, *Subfamily* Charadriinae) are medium sized to small shorebirds. The bill is rather short and has a noticeable swelling near the tip. The neck is short; so is the tail, which is carried horizontally, not drooping. The wings are pointed, almost narrow, flight is direct and fast. Plovers are active feeders, walking or running swiftly on shore or grassland, foraging for insects or small marine animals. The nests are on the ground. Typical plovers fall into two groups: the medium-sized unbanded plovers (this page) and the smaller ringed plovers (p. 112). Surfbirds and Turnstones (*Subfamily* Arenariinae) are shown with rock-inhabiting sandpipers on p. 120.

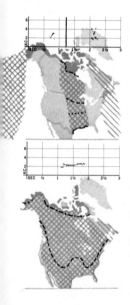

DOTTEREL　　　　　　　　　　　*Eudrómias morinéllus*

Casual in western and northern Alaska, but may breed there. Winters in Asia. Adult with its cinnamon underparts is unmistakable. Female is like male. In fall could be mistaken for Golden Plover, but the broad white eye stripes meet on the nape, and at close range the pale breast line is visible and diagnostic.

MOUNTAIN PLOVER　　　　　　　　*Eúpoda montána*

Common, breeding in dry short-grass prairie and sage-brush; otherwise found in small flocks in cactus deserts or on high plains. The plumage is drab, and the white face pattern is lost in fall. The thin white wing stripe and the black tail band with the white border are the best field marks. This is a fast runner that seldom flies. When it does, it flies low, with down-curved wings. Call is a low drawling whistle.

AMERICAN GOLDEN PLOVER　　　*Pluviális dominica*

Common on the arctic tundra; winters in southern South America. Seen in spring in fields, pastures, and mudflats; in fall, most migrate offshore. The spring plumage is golden above and black below with a dark rump and tail and no wing stripe. In fall compare with Black-bellied. Call is a clear, short, whistled *oodle-oo*.

BLACK-BELLIED PLOVER　　　　*Squatárola squatárola*

A common plover that nests on the arctic tundra and winters along both coasts to central South America. It is larger than the Golden Plover, from which it can always be told by the white rump and striking black axillars under the wing. It is grayer above than the Golden and larger billed. Does not migrate in large flocks, as the Golden does. Call is a plaintive, slurred whistle.

knot

turnstone

unbanded plover

Spotted Sandpiper

Dunlin

banded plover

merican olden over

Semipalmated Plover for comparison

summer

winter

DOTTEREL
L 7"

MOUNTAIN PLOVER
L 7½"

winter

summer

AMERICAN GOLDEN PLOVER
L 9"

winter

summer

BLACK-BELLIED PLOVER
L 9½"

winter

summer

BANDED PLOVERS *(Genus Charadrius)* are similar to the larger un-banded plovers (p. 110), but have one or two black neck bands.

PIPING PLOVER
Charádrius melódus

Uncommon; on the drier portions of sandy beaches. Note the pale back, single (usually partial) neck band, yellow legs and feet. In spring the bill is yellow; in winter it is dark. Piping Plovers are seen singly or in small flocks. The call is two-noted and organ-like.

SNOWY PLOVER
Charádrius alexandrínus

Locally common on sand flats and alkali ponds. Paler than the Piping, with one incomplete dark band, dark bill, and legs. At close range the bill appears to be longer and thinner than that of the Piping. Call is a low-pitched *chu-wee*.

SEMIPALMATED PLOVER
Charádrius semipalmátus

Common on beaches and mudflats. Note the dark back, prominent white collar, white face markings, black and orange bill, and orange legs. In immature and adult winter plumage the band on the neck is brown and the legs yellow. Call, *chur-wee*. Ringed Plover *(Charádrius hiaticula,* L 6") breeds in Greenland and Baffin Island, winters in the Old World. Not safely separable from Semipalmated except by lack of webs on toes.

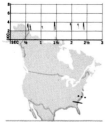

WILSON'S PLOVER
Charádrius wilsónia

Uncommon and rather local. Prefers sandy beaches and mudflats. It is noticeably larger than the Semi-palmated, with a longer and broader eye stripe, a heavier black bill, and a wider neck band. The feet are a dull pink. Female is much paler than male. Call, *wheet*. Mongolian Plover *(Charádrius mongólus,* L 6"), a rare breeder of western Alaska, has a brown breast-band and strong facial markings in summer; in winter, gray indistinct breastband and pale facial markings.

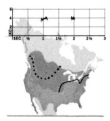

KILLDEER
Charádrius vocíferus

Very common in fields and pastures, often far from water. Adult Killdeer has two neck bands, juvenal only one. The tail is longer than in other plovers. Note the orange on the upper tail and lower back. Seldom occurs in large flocks. Feigns injury near its nest to distract intruders. Repeats its name as a call.

PIPING PLOVER
L 5½"

winter   summer

SNOWY PLOVER
L 5¼"

im.

♂ summer

SEMIPALMATED PLOVER
L 5¾"

winter   summer

NGOLIAN
VER

RINGED PLOVER
L 6"

♀   ♂

WILSON'S PLOVER
L 6¼"

KILLDEER
L 8"

feigning

● **SANDPIPERS** (*Family* Scolopacidae) differ from plovers in having bills that are longer, more slender, and in several species distinctly curved. Necks tend to be longer than in plovers, and backs are cryptically patterned in most species by pale edging on feathers.

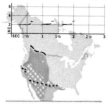

LONG-BILLED CURLEW — *Numénius americánus*

Rather common. Nests in meadows and pastures, and is also found in marshes, mudflats, and beaches. The very long bill is a good field mark, but varies greatly. The cinnamon underwing linings should be seen to clinch identification. Crown is unstreaked. Call is a plaintive *curlew* with rising inflection.

WHIMBREL — *Numénius phaéopus*

Common in marshes, mudflats, shores, and prairies. Smaller than Long-billed, with distinct striping on crown, a shorter bill, and pale underparts. In good light the back appears grayer than the Long-billed's. Call is a short mellow whistle, repeated rapidly 6-7 times. Bristle-thighed Curlew (*Numénius tahitiénsis*, L 15″) is a rare breeder in western Alaska, winters on central Pacific islands. It resembles the Whimbrel, but has a bright rusty tail contrasting with a somber brown back.

ESKIMO CURLEW — *Numénius boreális*

Nearly extinct; since 1959 seen in spring on Galveston Island, Tex. Smaller than Whimbrel, with comparatively shorter, more slender bill, and cinnamon wing linings.

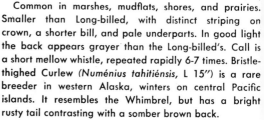

MARBLED GODWIT — *Limósa fédoa*

Rather common in West, rare in East. Breeds on prairies, meadows, and pastures, and winters along the coasts. The brown plumage is mottled above and barred below. The very long bill turns up. Note the cinnamon wing linings. Call is a whistled *godwit*.

HUDSONIAN GODWIT — *Limósa haemástica*

Uncommon; in marshes, meadows, shores, and mud-flats. The bold black and white tail pattern is distinctive. In flight axillars are black, wing linings sooty. Call is like Marbled Godwit's, but higher.

BAR-TAILED GODWIT — *Limósa lappónica*

Nests in arctic Alaska, winters in western Pacific. Note barring on tail, no barring on underparts.

LARGE SANDPIPERS

BRISTLE-THIGHED CURLEW L 15"

Long-billed Curlews

LONG-BILLED CURLEW L 19"

Whimbrel

WHIMBREL L 14"

ESKIMO CURLEW L 11"

Marbled

MARBLED GODWIT L 16"

Marbled

Hudsonian

summer

HUDSONIAN GODWIT L 13"

winter

BAR-TAILED GODWIT L 13"

winter

summer

● **UPLAND SANDPIPERS** are an arbitrary group of sandpipers that typically breed in inland locations high above sea level.

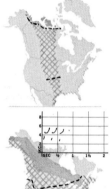

UPLAND PLOVER *Bartrámia longicaúda*
Local and uncommon in grass country. Has a distinctive silhouette—long neck, small head, short bill, and relatively long tail. The crown and outer wings are much darker than the rest of the plumage. Flies stiffly, as a Spotted Sandpiper does, and briefly holds its wings erect after it lands. Call is a mellow whistle.

BUFF-BREASTED SANDPIPER *Tryngites subruficóllis*
Rare and local in short-grass habitats such as golf courses, airports, and short-grass prairies. This buffy bird has the slender-necked profile of the Upland Plover, but is much smaller. The white eye ring, broad buffy feather edging on the back, and pale legs are good field marks. Wing linings in flight appear white. When flushed, it twists and turns like a snipe. Call, a low trill.

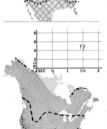

SOLITARY SANDPIPER *Tringa solitária*
Common along streams, lakes, and swamps. Often seen with Spotted Sandpiper, from which it is told by the barred outer tail feathers, by the longer darker legs, and in flight by the plain dark wings. Dark rump distinguishes it from Stilt Sandpiper and yellowlegs. The white eye ring is seen at close range. It flies buoyantly, almost swallow-like. Call like Spotted's, but higher.

SPOTTED SANDPIPER *Actitis maculária*
A very common sandpiper that breeds along fresh water, winters along southern coasts. Its characteristic stance is with body tilted forward, head held low. It bobs the tail up and down almost continuously. In flight the wings are held stiffly downward with very shallow rapid beats. The breast spots of the summer plumage are lacking in winter. Usually seen singly. Call is a shrill 2- or 3-toned piping.

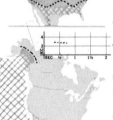

WANDERING TATTLER *Heteróscelus incánum*
This uncommon sandpiper nests along mountain streams and winters almost exclusively on rocky seashores and coral reefs. It is very dark above and occasionally bobs its tail like the Spotted. The bill is longer and the legs yellow. Call, 4-8 rapid tinkling notes.

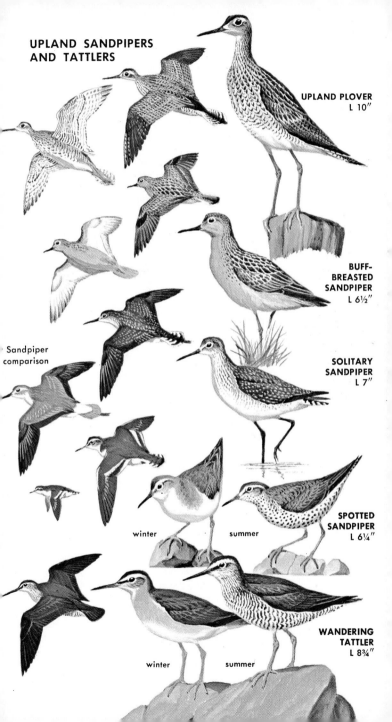

UPLAND SANDPIPERS AND TATTLERS

UPLAND PLOVER
L 10"

BUFF-BREASTED SANDPIPER
L 6½"

Sandpiper comparison

SOLITARY SANDPIPER
L 7"

winter   summer

SPOTTED SANDPIPER
L 6¼"

winter   summer

WANDERING TATTLER
L 8¾"

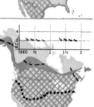

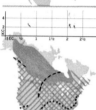

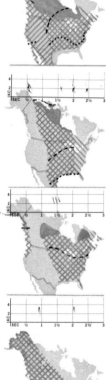

WILLET   *Catoptróphorus semipalmátus*

Common; eastern birds breed along the coast, western ones on lakes. Both winter in salt marshes. Best identified in flight by the diagnostic wing pattern. Standing birds are plump, with a thicker bill than yellowlegs'. Seen in small flocks or pairs. Call, *pill-will-willet.*

GREATER YELLOWLEGS   *Tótanus melanoleúcus*

Common on muskeg and tundra in summer and in marshes in winter. Noticeably slimmer than Willet and with thinner bill. Among the tall long-legged sandpipers, only the two yellowlegs have bright yellow legs. Greater is distinguished from Lesser Yellowlegs by size, longer bill (sometimes barely upturned), and the sharp 3- to 5-note whistle.

LESSER YELLOWLEGS   *Tótanus flávipes*

Fairly common. Similar to the larger Greater Yellowlegs, but bill is much shorter and more slender. Call is a soft 1- to 3-note whistle that lacks the loud ringing quality of the Greater's. Often seen in loose flocks.

STILT SANDPIPER   *Micropálama himántopus*

Uncommon; in fresh and salt marshes and mudflats. The rusty cheek and crown and the barred flanks are present only in breeding plumage. The long greenish legs, clear white rump, and dark trailing edges of wings are fall field marks. Often feeds with dowitchers, but is more slender and has longer legs and a shorter bill. Call, a low *querp,* softer, hoarser than Lesser Yellowlegs'.

SHORT-BILLED DOWITCHER   *Limnódromus gríseus*

Common, especially along coasts. Notice long bill, the tip of which is usually out of sight when the birds are feeding. The white rump patch extends farther up the back than on other shorebirds. Legs are short, the body chunky. Call, a low mellow 3-note whistle.

LONG-BILLED DOWITCHER   *Limnódromus scolopáceus*

This common western dowitcher averages larger and longer billed than the Short-billed, and in summer plumage has rusty lower belly, barred flanks, and blacker bars on the white tail. At close range look for Long-billed's paler, more finely barred tail in winter plumage. Call is a single, thin, peeping note or a series of same.

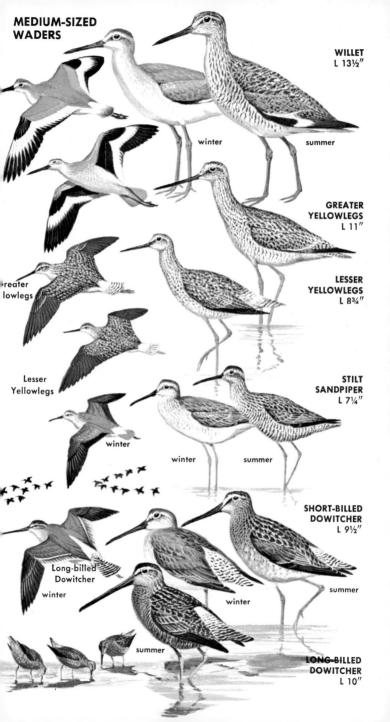

MEDIUM-SIZED WADERS

WILLET
L 13½"

winter   summer

GREATER YELLOWLEGS
L 11"

Greater legs

LESSER YELLOWLEGS
L 8¾"

Lesser Yellowlegs

STILT SANDPIPER
L 7¼"

winter   winter   summer

SHORT-BILLED DOWITCHER
L 9½"

Long-billed Dowitcher

winter   winter   summer

summer

LONG-BILLED DOWITCHER
L 10"

SURFBIRD
Aphríza virgáta

Common along rocky Pacific shorelines in winter; breeds in mountains above timberline. Dark and plump, with short yellow legs; told in flight by the black triangle at the tip of the white tail. The Tattler (p. 116), found in the same habitat, has a dark rump and lacks the wing stripe. Call, a plaintive 3-note whistle.

RUDDY TURNSTONE
Arenária intérpres

Turnstones have slender pointed bills, slightly upturned at the tip. Ruddy is common along coast, rare inland. It prefers rocky tidal shores, feeding in the seaweed. Note the head and breast pattern and short orange-red or yellow legs and in flight the striking black, brown, and white pattern of the wings, rump, and tail. Call, 1-8 fast, low, slurred whistles.

BLACK TURNSTONE
Arenária melanocéphala

Common on rocks along the Pacific Coast. All plumages appear darker and more uniform than in the Ruddy Turnstone, though the wing and back patterns are much the same. Note the white speckling on the side of the breast of the breeding adult. Immatures are grayer-headed than winter adult and have buffy edgings on back feathers. Calls are slightly higher pitched than Ruddy Turnstone's.

PURPLE SANDPIPER
Erólia marítima

Common, but restricted to rocky coasts and jetties; winters farther north than other shorebirds. This darkest sandpiper on the East Coast has a thin yellow-based bill and yellow legs. Usually in small flocks, often with turnstones or sanderlings. Call, *wit* or *weet-wit.* This, the Rock Sandpiper, and the smaller species on pp. 122-124 are collectively known as peeps.

ROCK SANDPIPER
Erólia ptilocnémis

Common locally. Breeds on the tundra; winters along rocky shores with turnstones and surfbirds. A plump bird with short neck and greenish legs. The dark breast patch (summer) is higher up than the black belly of the Dunlin (p. 122). In flight Rock shows a broad white wing stripe, but a dark tail; other western rock-inhabiting shorebirds have white on the tail except the dark-winged Tattler. Call is flicker-like.

ROCK SHOREBIRDS

SURFBIRD
L 8″

winter

summer

RUDDY TURNSTONE
L 7″

winter

summer

BLACK TURNSTONE
L 7″

winter

summer

PURPLE SANDPIPER
L 7½″

winter

summer

ROCK SANDPIPER
L 8″

Purple Sandpipers and turnstones

winter

summer

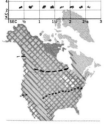

PECTORAL SANDPIPER   *Erólia melanótos*

Uncommon; in grassy marshes and wet fields. Note the abrupt border between the streaked breast and white underparts, erect stance, short bill, and greenish legs. When flushed, its flies zigzag, as the Snipe does; wings are uniformly dark. Call, a low *prrrp*. Sharp-tailed Sandpiper (*Erólia acumináta*, L 7″), a regular fall visitor to Alaska, irregular along West Coast, is like Pectoral, but in fall its breast is buffy, narrowly streaked at sides.

KNOT   *Calidris canútus*

A medium-sized, short-necked, stocky, locally common bird along sandy shores, rocks, and mudflats. The short bill and lack of a white streak up the back will distinguish it from dowitchers. In spring the gray back and Robin-like breast are distinctive. In flight note the light rump and tail. Call is a low buzzy whistle, *tlu-tlu*.

RUFF (female, Reeve)   *Philómachus púgnax*

A regular fall (rarely spring) visitor from Eurasia. Resembles Lesser Yellowlegs, but is much browner, with no barring on the body under the wings. The bill is slightly thicker and yellow at the base. Legs are dull yellow. Posture is erect. In flight the large white oval patches at the base of the tail are diagnostic. Call, a low *tu-whit*.

CURLEW SANDPIPER   *Erólia ferrugínea*

Dunlin

A casual fall visitor on East Coast. Similar in winter to Dunlin, but bill is curved throughout its length. Dunlin lacks the white rump. Call is a soft whistled *chirrup*.

DUNLIN   *Erólia alpína*

Common along coast in winter; less common inland. A stout short-necked shorebird with a long, slightly downcurved bill, heavy at base. In spring note the bright rusty back and black belly. In winter it is plain gray above. Call, a rapid, low, grating trill.

SANDERLING   *Crocéthia álba*

Common along sandy beaches at the water's edge. Reddish in spring, very light gray in winter plumage. When with Least or Semipalmated, the larger size is apparent. In flight note the broad white wing stripe and black wrist. Flight call is a sharp, distinctive *plick*.

Sanderling

SHARP-TAILED SANDPIPER L 7″

winter

PECTORAL SANDPIPER L 7½″

Knot

summer

winter

KNOT L 9″

♂

♀

Reeve

RUFF L 10″

Curlew

summer

winter

CURLEW SANDPIPER L 7″

winter

summer

DUNLIN L 7″

SANDERLING L 6½″

summer

winter

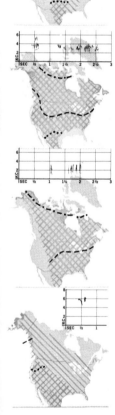

WHITE-RUMPED SANDPIPER
Erólia fuscicóllis

Uncommon; inland and along coast. Usually flocks with other peeps. The best field mark is the white rump. The only other short-legged sandpiper with a white rump is the rare Curlew Sandpiper (p. 122) which is larger and has a longer bill. Feeds by probing. Call, a thin *jeet.*

BAIRD'S SANDPIPER
Erólia báirdii

Uncommon; in drier short grassy marshes; sometimes found on shores and mudflats. Pale feather edgings give the back a scaly appearance. The body seems longer and slimmer than that of most peeps. The body is held more horizontal; the long wings extend well beyond the tail. The plumage is buffy even in fall. Rather tame. In feeding, Baird's picks rather than probes. Call, *kreep.*

LEAST SANDPIPER
Erólia minutilla

Very common. Prefers salt marshes and muddy shores of rivers and estuaries. The bill is thin and short; no other small peep has yellow legs. It feeds both by probing into the mud and by picking food from the surface. Browner and more streaked on the breast than other sandpipers. Call, a high *breep.*

SEMIPALMATED SANDPIPER
Ereunétes pusillus

Probably the most abundant shorebird; found on both fresh and salt water, often with Least and Western Sandpipers. Told from the Least by black legs and grayer body with less streaking on the breast, from Western by shorter slimmer bill. Feeds by picking. Often seen in very large flocks with other peeps. Call, a short *krip,* lower pitched than Least's. The Rufous-necked Sandpiper (*Erólia ruficóllis,* L 5¼") of western Alaska is much like the Semipalmated, but with russet on the neck in spring. Not separable in fall. Head is illustrated.

WESTERN SANDPIPER
Ereunétes maúri

Common on sandbars and mudflats, where it probes in deeper water than the similar Semipalmated; it sometimes submerges its head. Told from the Semipalmated by longer bill with a definite droop at the tip. In summer, back and crown are rusty; in fall the plumage is gray above, sometimes with a trace of rust on the scapulars. Call, *cheep,* much higher pitched than Semipalmated's.

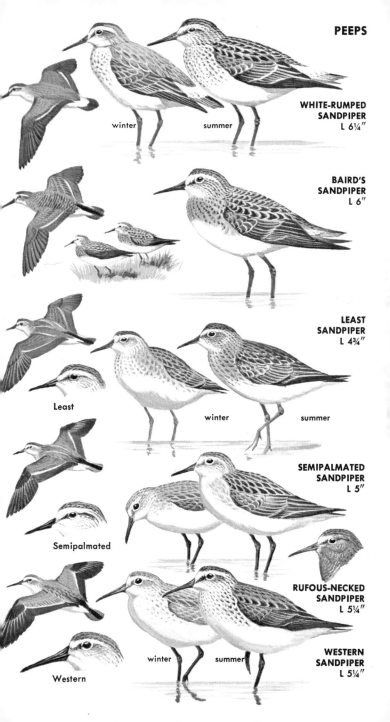

PEEPS

WHITE-RUMPED SANDPIPER L 6¼"

winter   summer

BAIRD'S SANDPIPER L 6"

LEAST SANDPIPER L 4¾"

Least

winter   summer

SEMIPALMATED SANDPIPER L 5"

Semipalmated

RUFOUS-NECKED SANDPIPER L 5¼"

Western

winter   summer

WESTERN SANDPIPER L 5¼"

PHALAROPES (*Family* Phalaropodidae) look like sandpipers, but have lobed toes and swim readily. The neck and legs are long. Two species are pelagic. Females are larger and more colorful than the males. Phalaropes spin in circles in shallow water to stir up food.

WILSON'S PHALAROPE
Steganopus tricolor

Uncommon and the landlubber of the family; nests on prairie sloughs and ponds. The bill is very thin and much longer than the head. With its white rump and dark wings it looks like a yellowlegs or Stilt Sandpiper. Call is low, gallinule-like.

RED PHALAROPE
Phalaropus fulicarius

An uncommon pelagic species most often seen during storms along the coast. The yellow bill is short and much stouter than in other phalaropes. In gray winter plumage the black eye line of phalaropes is characteristic. Call suggests turnstone's.

NORTHERN PHALAROPE
Lobipes lobatus

Common on the breeding grounds and in flocks at sea; uncommon to rare inland. The slender bill is intermediate in length between those of other two phalaropes. The legs are dark. Flying birds in winter plumage resemble Sanderlings, but are darker backed and slenderbilled and have a black line through the eye. Its call is of low, short, scratchy notes.

WOODCOCK AND SNIPE (*Family* Scolopacidae) are primarily inland sandpipers of moist woodlands, marshes, and river banks. Neck and legs are short, and the bill is extremely long.

AMERICAN WOODCOCK
Philohela minor

Rather common, but nocturnal; lives in moist woodlands, swamps, and thickets. Stocky, with short legs, short neck, and very long bill. Permits close approach, then explodes with whistling wings. Call, a nasal *peent.*

COMMON SNIPE
Capella gallinago

Common in marshes and bogs and along river banks. The size and shape of dowitchers, it is told by the browner, more streaked head and back, and in flight by the brown rump and orange tail. Flies in a rapid zigzag. Generally stays close to cover, while dowitchers prefer to feed in the open. Call, a low, rasping *kzrrt.*

WILSON'S PHALAROPE
L 7½"

winter

♀ summer

♂ summer

RED PHALAROPE
L 6½"

♀ summer

winter

♂ summer

NORTHERN PHALAROPE
L 6"

winter

♀ summer

♂ summer

AMERICAN WOODCOCK
L 8¼"

COMMON SNIPE
L 9"

display flight

dowitcher for comparison

Knot p. 122

Rock Sandpiper p. 120

Pectoral Sandpiper p. 122

Baird's Sandpiper p. 124

Least Sandpiper p. 124

Semipalmated
Sandpiper p. 124

Wilson's Phalarope p. 126

Red Phalarope p. 12

Knot—Chunky, gray with light rump; in flocks on beaches
Rock Sandpiper—Dark bird of West; small flocks on rocks
Pectoral Sandpiper—Rusty; heavily streaked breast; greenish legs
Baird's Sandpiper—Buffy, scaly back; long wings; black legs
Least Sandpiper—Very small, brown; short thin bill; yellow legs
Semipalmated Sandpiper—Very small, gray; sturdy bill; black legs
Wilson's Phalarope—Long thin bill; phalarope eye mark; gray
Red Phalarope—Small, gray; sturdy yellow bill; eye mark; oceanic

Purple Sandpiper p. 120

Sanderling p. 122

White-rumped Sandpiper p. 124

Curlew Sandpiper p. 122

Western Sandpiper p. 124

Dunlin p. 122

Northern Phalarope p. 126

Spotted Sandpiper p. 116

Purple Sandpiper—Small flocks on rocks in East; dark; yellow legs
Sanderling—Small flocks on beach; wide white wing stripe
White-rumped Sandpiper—Small, gray; white rump patch; dark tail
Curlew Sandpiper—Medium size; curved bill; white rump patch; rare
Western Sandpiper—Very small, brown; drooping bill; coastal
Dunlin—Medium size; curved bill, dark rump; common, coastal
Northern Phalarope—Small, gray; short thin bill; eye mark
Spotted Sandpiper—Small, brownish; teeters; common inland

● **JAEGERS AND SKUAS** (*Order* Charadriiformes, *Family* Stercorariidae) look like dark gulls with elongated central tail feathers, but their silhouette, flight, and feeding habits are very different. Their slender wings are sharply bent at the "wrist" and their tails are frequently fanned as they suddenly change course. Wingbeats are powerful and rapid. Light bases of primaries distinguish these birds from gulls and terns. Jaegers and skuas are most often seen robbing other seabirds of fish. They seldom come ashore except to nest and generally are silent. Late afternoon is the best time to see them from shore. Dark phases are rare in East. Immatures lack the long tail feathers. Eggs, 2-3.

PARASITIC JAEGER   *Stercorárius parasíticus*
The most common jaeger, frequently seen pursuing terns. Adult is told from the larger heavier Pomarine by the short, flat, pointed, central tail feathers; from the Long-tailed by tail length alone. Immature is browner than Long-tailed and has more white in the wing.

POMARINE JAEGER   *Stercorárius pomarínus*
The largest of the jaegers; nearly the size of Herring Gull. The bill is proportionately larger than those of other jaegers. The flight is heavier and more steady. The long central tail feathers are broad and twisted. In the light phase the sides are barred and the breast band is more distinct than in other jaegers.

LONG-TAILED JAEGER   *Stercorárius longicaúdus*
Common on breeding grounds, rare in migration. The smallest bodied and slimmest of the jaegers and the least inclined to rob other seabirds. The central tail feathers of the adult extend 5-8 inches behind the others. On nesting ground it often hovers over its chief prey, the lemming. The dark phase is almost unknown. Light phase is grayer than other jaegers'. Immature also is gray rather than brown. Flight is more graceful and ternlike than other jaegers'.

SKUA   *Cathorácta skúa*
This, the only bird that breeds both in the Arctic and in the Antarctic (different populations), is common on breeding grounds. At other seasons, rare along our coasts but a regular offshore visitor. At a distance it looks like a dark short-tailed Herring Gull, but can be told by the large white patches at the base of the primaries. More of a scavenger than the jaegers, it often soars with gulls.

shearwater   falcon   gull   tern   jaeger

im.

light phase

PARASITIC JAEGER
L 16″

dark phase

Parasitic

POMARINE JAEGER
L 17″ W 48″

Pomarine chasing gull

LONG-TAILED JAEGER
L 18″

Long-tailed hovering

SKUA
L 17½″ W 16″

GULLS (*Order* Charadriiformes, *Family* Laridae, *Subfamily* Larinae) are sturdy robust birds with webbed feet, long pointed wings, a stout hooked bill, and generally a square tail. They are primarily scavengers. Some species gather by thousands at garbage dumps and fish docks. They rarely dive from the air, but alight on the water to seize food. Flight is deliberate and powerful; some species soar frequently. Sexes are alike; immatures of the larger species take several years to·acquire adult plumage. They nest in colonies. Eggs, 2-5.

IVORY GULL   *Pagóphila ebúrnea*
Rarely encountered outside the Arctic. In breeding season it is found along the coast, otherwise over open water in the Arctic Ocean. The Ivory is much smaller than the other all-white gulls; it is easily told by the black legs and black bill (yellow-tipped in the adult). Its flight is more pigeon-like than that of other gulls.

GLAUCOUS GULL   *Lárus hyperbóreus*
Uncommon; when seen is generally with Herring Gulls along the coast. Told from Iceland Gull by its size (larger than Herring Gull) and heavier bill and by its tail, which extends beyond the wing tips when at rest. Immature can be told from all other "white-winged" gulls by more flesh color at base of bill. In all plumages of Glaucous and Iceland note in flight the translucent "windows" at base of primaries. Glaucous is predatory.

ICELAND GULL   *Lárus glaucoídes*
Uncommon; along coast; rare on Great Lakes, Slightly smaller than Herring Gull, Iceland has white wing tips in all plumages. When sitting, its folded wings protrude beyond the tail. The head looks small for the body, and the bill seems still smaller. First- and second-year plumages also resemble those of the Glaucous Gull but bill of the Iceland is all dark and much smaller. The feet are always flesh-colored in both species.

GLAUCOUS-WINGED GULL   *Lárus glaucéscens*
Abundant, especially in harbors and garbage dumps. In all plumages Glaucous-winged lacks the paler primaries of the Glaucous and the dark wing tips of the other gulls with which it might be confused. Second-year plumage is lighter than first-year. Bill is black the first year, with a flesh-colored base the second year. Flight, behavior, and call are similar to Herring Gull's.

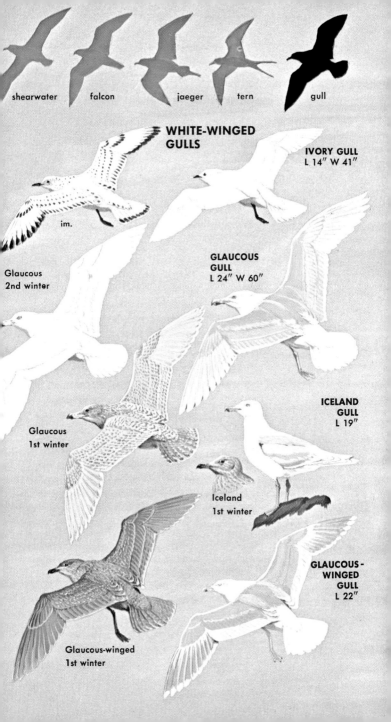

shearwater falcon jaeger tern gull

WHITE-WINGED GULLS

IVORY GULL
L 14″ W 41″

im.

Glaucous
2nd winter

**GLAUCOUS
GULL**
L 24″ W 60″

Glaucous
1st winter

**ICELAND
GULL**
L 19″

Iceland
1st winter

Glaucous-winged
1st winter

**GLAUCOUS-
WINGED
GULL**
L 22″

GREAT BLACK-BACKED GULL   *Lárus marínus*

Common and increasing in numbers and range. A coastal species, rarely found inland. This and the Lesser are the only black-backed gulls in the East. Immature, which goes farther south in winter than adult, can be confused only with Herring Gull; note shape and extent of black band on tail, contrast between light head and dark back, and heavy bill of Black-backed. Predatory, especially in nesting colonies. Call, a low-pitched *kow-kow-kow*. Lesser Black-backed Gull (*Lárus fúscus*, L 18″), casual on the East Coast, is similar to Great Black-backed, but is much smaller with yellow, not pink, legs.

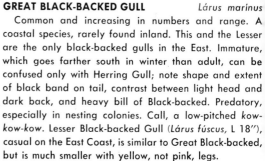

WESTERN GULL   *Lárus occidentális*

Common along the outer beaches, vagrant inland. Replaces the Great Black-backed in the West. Smaller in size but almost identical in behavior and plumages. The darkest gull south of Alaska except for the smaller Heermann's. Call is low and resembles Great Black-backed's. Slaty-backed Gull (*Lárus schistisagus*, L 22″), intermediate in size between Great Black-backed and Western, is not easily separable. Casual Asiatic visitor to the Aleutians, where the others do not occur.

HERRING GULL   *Lárus argentátus*

Abundant along the coast, particularly in harbors and garbage dumps; common on lakes and rivers. Adults are told from the very similar California and Ring-billed (p. 136) by larger size, heavier build, and pink legs. First- and second-year Herrings are much darker tailed than Ring-billed, and are darker headed and smaller billed than Great Black-backed. First-year Herring is told from immature California by all-dark bill. Primarily a scavenger, the Herring Gull will also break mollusks by dropping them. Commonly seen high overhead soaring like hawks. Call, loud, clear, and bugle-like.

CALIFORNIA GULL   *Lárus califórnicus*

Common along the Pacific Coast in winter and inland in breeding season, nesting in large colonies on the prairies. Slightly smaller than the Herring Gull, but resembles it in all plumages. Note that the bill of the first-year bird is largely pinkish (not all black), and the legs begin to turn greenish by the second year (pink in Herring). See also Ring-billed Gull (p. 136).

LARGE WHITE-HEADED GULLS

Great Black-backed
1st winter

Herring Gulls feeding

Herring
2nd winter

1st winter

1st winter

GREAT BLACK-BACKED GULL
L 24″ W 65″

WESTERN GULL
L 21″ W 55″

HERRING GULL
L 20″ W 55″

CALIFORNIA GULL
L 17″ W 52″

RING-BILLED GULL — *Lárus delawarénsis*

Common, especially inland. Complete black ring on yellow bill of adult is diagnostic. Adult has greenish-yellow legs. The other large eastern gulls have flesh-colored or black legs. Adult is most similar to California (p. 132), which has a small red spot as well as a black one on the lower mandible. Underside of wing tip has larger dark area than Herring Gull's. Immature is told from Herring and California by the narrow black tail band, from Mew by the larger bill and whiter body plumage. Calls are similar to Herring Gull's.

MEW GULL — *Lárus cánus*

Common along the coast in winter, inland in breeding season. At close range adult is told from all other gulls except kittiwakes by its unmarked, short, thin, yellow bill. Immature most closely resembles Ring-billed Gull. Calls are higher pitched than Herring Gull's.

HEERMANN'S GULL — *Lárus heérmanni*

Common along West Coast except in spring, when confined to its breeding islands. Rare inland; often found offshore. The darkest of the gulls, it is the only species that is uniformly dark below. The white head of the adult is mottled in winter. In flight the black tail and red bill of the adult are diagnostic, as are the narrow white terminal band and blackish underparts of the immature.

BLACK-LEGGED KITTIWAKE — *Ríssa tridáctyla*

Abundant on breeding cliffs, wintering well offshore. The adult is recognized by its sharply defined triangular black wing tips (no trace of white spot). The more commonly seen immature resembles several of the dark-headed gulls (p. 138), but is told by the combination of dark neck band, short black legs, and black wing tips, and very slightly forked tail. Often flies low over water.

RED-LEGGED KITTIWAKE — *Ríssa breviróstris*

Common breeder on Pribilof Islands, winters to Aleutians. Red legs; shorter bill, darker underwing than Black-legged. Immature like adult, but has dark bill, nape line and forewing.

ROSS' GULL — *Rhodostéthia rosea*

Rare visitor to northern Alaska and northern Canada from Siberia. The only gull with a wedge-shaped tail. Adult is rosy at all seasons; no neck band in winter. Flight is pigeon-like.

SMALL WHITE-HEADED GULLS

im.

RING-BILLED GULL L 16" W 49"

im.

MEW GULL L 14" W 42"

im.

HEERMANN'S GULL L 15"

im.

winter

summer

BLACK-LEGGED KITTIWAKE L 13½" W 36"

ROSS' GULL L 11"

RED-LEGGED KITTIWAKE L 15"

Ross' Gull

im.

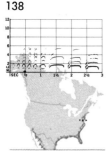

LAUGHING GULL   *Lárus atricilla*

A very common coastal species; seldom found far from salt water, though it occasionally feeds on insects and earthworms in plowed fields. Adult is told from adult Franklin's by solid dark wing tips. First-winter bird is very dark above; it is told from immature Franklin's by the dark breast and dark head. One-year-old bird like immature Franklin's. This is the largest and darkest of the black-headed gulls. Winter adult has a mottled head and darker bill. Calls; a variety of low chuckles.

FRANKLIN'S GULL   *Lárus pipixcan*

The common gull of the prairies, wintering mostly south of U.S. Adult is told from adult Laughing by the white spots on the primaries. The immature is not separable from the one-year-old Laughing Gull. Feeds largely on insects, following the plow, hawking in the air, and fishing in ponds. Call is higher pitched than Laughing's.

BONAPARTE'S GULL   *Lárus philadélphia*

This small gull is common inland in the breeding season, on the coasts and larger lakes in winter. The flashy white wing tips are shared only by the rare Black-headed Gull. The black bill and the dark spot behind the eye are good field marks in winter. Flies buoyantly and tern-like, with the bill held down. Call, a low quacking.

SABINE'S GULL   *Xéma sábini*

Common on breeding grounds, elsewhere alone or in small flocks. Probably winters at sea. Casual in early fall and late spring along East Coast and inland. Note the forked tail and the bold pattern of triangles on the wings of both adult and young. Compare wing and tail pattern with immature kittiwake's (p. 136). Very tern-like in flight.

BLACK-HEADED GULL   *Lárus ridibúndus*

A rare but regular European straggler on the East Coast. Resembles Bonaparte's, but larger. Bill larger and dark red. Adult's primaries are dark below. Usually seen with Bonaparte's. Call, *kwuririp*.

LITTLE GULL   *Lárus minútus*

European straggler and rare breeder. This smallest gull is tern-like in flight, but has rounded wings. Note dark underwing of adult and black tail band of immature. Hood more extensive than on Bonaparte's with which it usually flocks. Call, *kek-kek-kek*.

2nd winter

winter

winter

winter

winter

ck-
aded

summer

inter

inter

LAUGHING GULL
L 13″ W 41″

summer

im.

summer

FRANKLIN'S GULL L 11″ W 35″

im.

summer

BONAPARTE'S GULL L 11″ W 32″

im.

summer

SABINE'S GULL L 11″

im.

summer

BLACK-HEADED GULL L 13″

im.

summer

LITTLE GULL L 9″

im.

IMMATURE GULLS are very difficult to identify. Only typical plumages are shown here. The time it takes to acquire adult plumage differs from species to species. In general small gulls take two years, larger ones four. For example, Bonaparte's Gull acquires adult plumage the second winter, after partial molts in the fall and spring.

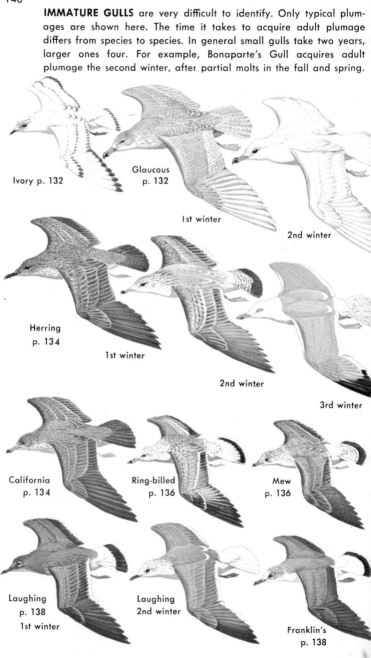

Ivory p. 132

Glaucous
p. 132

1st winter

2nd winter

Herring
p. 134

1st winter

2nd winter

3rd winter

California
p. 134

Ring-billed
p. 136

Mew
p. 136

Laughing
p. 138
1st winter

Laughing
2nd winter

Franklin's
p. 138

The larger Herring Gull acquires adult plumage in the fourth autumn, after two partial molts the first year and one complete and one partial each following year. This sequence of molt is important in understanding the intermediate plumages, not shown here.

Glaucous-winged
p. 132

1st winter

2nd winter

Great
Black-backed
p. 132

1st
winter

2nd
winter

3rd
winter

Little
p. 138

Heermann's
p. 136

Black-legged
Kittiwake
p. 136

Ross'
p. 136

Black-headed
p. 138

Bonaparte's
p. 138

Sabine's
p. 138

● **TERNS** (Order Charadriiformes, Family Laridae, Subfamily Sterninae) are slender birds with long narrow wings, forked tails, and a pointed bill. Their flight is buoyant, with bill pointed downward as they search for small fish or insects. They dive from the air. Eggs, 1-4.

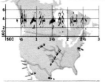

LEAST TERN
Stérna álbifrons

Common along sandy beaches, rare inland. Note the rapid wingbeat, white forehead, yellow bill (spring), and yellow or yellowish (fall) legs. Immature has contrasting wing pattern. Call, a rapid series of paired notes.

ARCTIC TERN
Stérna paradisáea

Abundant, but migrates far offshore. At close range adult can be told from Common Tern by the white streak below the black cap, the longer tail (extending to wing tips), the short legs, the blood-red bill (no black tip), and a translucent spot near the wing tip. Immature has white upper-wing coverts (gray on immature Common). Calls like those of the Common, but more nasal and rasping.

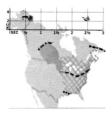

COMMON TERN
Stérna hirúndo

Abundant coastally and over large inland lakes; the commonest U.S. tern. Flocks with Arctic, Roseate, or Forster's. Wing tips are noticeably darker than in Roseate and Forster's, tail is shorter, and bill bright red orange (black tip varies in extent). Fall and immature head is like Arctic's; also compare with Forster's. Call, a harsh *kee-urr*.

ROSEATE TERN
Stérna doúgalli

Locally common along coast. Paler above than Common and Arctic terns. Tail whiter, longer, more deeply forked, wing tips paler and bill black (red only at base). Note also its deep wingbeat and distinctive calls: a soft *chivy* and a less frequent rasping *z-a-a-p*.

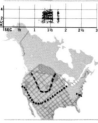

FORSTER'S TERN
Stérna fórsteri

Common in fresh and salt marshes, rare on coastal beaches. Strongly resembles Common Tern, but primaries are lighter than rest of wing, tail is pale gray with white outer margin (reversed in the Common), bill and legs are more orange, and wingstroke is faster and more shallow. Winter birds are best told from the others on this page by the narrow black eye-patch. Feeds on insects as well as fish. Call, a low toneless *zrurrrr*.

LIGHT-WINGED TERNS

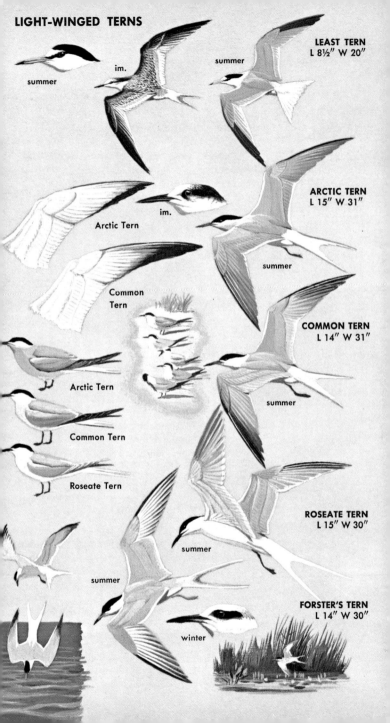

summer

im.

summer

LEAST TERN
L 8½″ W 20″

Arctic Tern

im.

ARCTIC TERN
L 15″ W 31″

summer

Common
Tern

Arctic Tern

COMMON TERN
L 14″ W 31″

Common Tern

summer

Roseate Tern

summer

ROSEATE TERN
L 15″ W 30″

summer

summer

FORSTER'S TERN
L 14″ W 30″

winter

SANDWICH TERN
Thalásseus sandvicénsis

Uncommon; on sandy beaches, often with Royal Terns. No other North American tern has a black bill tipped with yellow. Note also the long slender bill, the black legs, and the slight crest. Forehead of immature is mostly black, but adult has white on forehead and crown in winter. Fishes far offshore. Call, a loud grating *kirrik*.

GULL-BILLED TERN
Gelochelídon nilótica

Uncommon; over salt marshes. This whitest of North American terns is larger bodied than the Common Tern. Recognized in all plumages by the short, thick, black, gull-like bill and the broad, very white wings. The tail is less forked than in most terns and the legs are black and long. The flight is more gull-like than other terns'. Rarely dives, but hawks for insects over marshes. The nasal 2- or 3-syllable call is characteristic.

ELEGANT TERN
Thalásseus élegans

Regular visitor along southern California coast in fall from breeding grounds in Mexico. Similar to the larger Royal Tern, but has a slimmer bill and a longer crest. Bill of immature, blackish. Call, *karr-reek*.

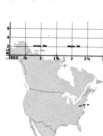

ROYAL TERN
Thalásseus máximus

This large tern is quite common but is strictly limited to salt water. The Royal Tern has a crest in all plumages, can be told at a distance from the smaller terns by the thick orange bill and slower wingbeat. Told from Caspian by the white forehead (solid black cap is of very short duration in breeding season), orange bill, lighter wing tips from beneath, shorter legs (obvious when standing together), more deeply forked tail of adult in spring, and voice. It feeds almost entirely on fish. Usually fishes offshore. Call, *chirrip*.

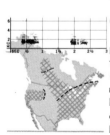

CASPIAN TERN
Hydroprógne cáspia

Rather common both coastally and inland. The Caspian closely resembles the Royal Tern, but can always be told by its blood-red bill, loud raucous call, and other comparisons noted above. The wider wings give it a more gull-like appearance than most terns, and its behavior also is more gull-like. It alights on the water, occasionally soars, robs other sea birds, and eats eggs. Fish is its chief diet. Call, a very loud harsh *kraaa*.

im.

summer

SANDWICH TERN
L 15″ W 34″

Sandwich Tern

Gull-billed Tern

summer

winter

GULL-BILLED TERN
L 13″ W 35″

summer

ELEGANT TERN
L 17″ W 43″

ROYAL TERN
L 18″ W 43″

Elegant
Tern

winter

early summer

Royal
Tern

winter

CASPIAN TERN
L 20″ W 53″

winter

summer

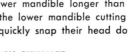

BLACK TERN
Chlidónias níger

Locally common breeder on lakes and fresh marshes; also migrates along coast. All other dark-backed terns are coastal. Adult is unmistakable. Fall birds are told from young Least Terns (p. 142) by the very plain wings; underparts may be blotched with black. Black Terns dive little; eat mostly insects. Flight is erratic. Call is nasal. White-winged Black Tern (*Chlidónias leucópterus*, L 9″), a casual Old World visitor, is similar, but has white tail and forewings, black back and wing linings.

SOOTY TERN
Stérna fuscátc

Breeds abundantly on Dry Tortugas, Fla. Seen on Atlantic and Gulf coasts only during hurricanes. No other tern is jet black above. Immature is dark brown with white undertail coverts; its all-dark head and forked tail distinguish it from noddies. Does not dive; catches surface fish in flight. Call, a nasal *wide-a-wake*.

ALEUTIAN TERN
Stérna aleútica

Breeds very locally in coastal Alaska from Norton Sound to Yakutat. The pale Arctic (p. 142) is the only other tern in its U.S. range.

BRIDLED TERN
Stérna anaethétus

Casual on East Coast during hurricanes. Compare face pattern, back color with Sooty's. Note pale neck ring, pale underwing tips.

NODDY TERN
Ánoüs stólidus

Common breeder at Dry Tortugas, Fla.; accidental elsewhere in U.S. In all plumages noddies show a pattern opposite of other terns—dark body, white cap, and wedge-shaped rather than forked tail. Highly pelagic, feeds without diving. Call, a soft low-pitched *k-a-a-a*.

BLACK NODDY TERN
Ánoüs tenuiróstris

In U.S. seen only at Dry Tortugas, Fla., where it is rare but regular visitor. Told from Noddy by small size, black color, and slender bill.

SKIMMERS (*Order* Charadriiformes, *Family* Rynchopidae) are the only birds with the lower mandible longer than the upper. They fly low over the water, the lower mandible cutting the surface. On contact with food, they quickly snap their head down and close the bill.

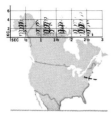

BLACK SKIMMER
Rýnchops nígra

Locally common in flocks in coastal bays. The large red bill is distinctive. Young are brown above, speckled with white. Call is a loud, low-pitched, resonant *auw*.

DARK-WINGED TERNS

im.

BLACK TERN
L 9" W 35"

im.

SOOTY TERN
L 16" W 34"

ALEUTIAN TERN
L 13"

BRIDLED TERN
L 14"

NODDY TERN
L 15"

BLACK NODDY TERN
L 12"

BLACK SKIMMER
L 17"

ALCIDS (Auks and relatives, *Order* Charadriiformes, *Family* Alcidae), black and white pelagic birds with short tails and rapid wingbeats, are usually silent. They come ashore only to breed. Swim underwater, using wings. Immatures are usually like adults. Eggs, 1-3.

RAZORBILL
Alca tórda

Locally common, breeding on offshore cliffs. Winters at sea; sometimes is seen singly off rocky coasts. When swimming, its thick bill and tail are usually uptilted. In flight the back is more arched than in murres.

COMMON MURRE
Úria aálge

Very common in large breeding colonies on cliffs. Winters at sea; rare within sight of land. Murres are told in all plumages from other alcids by the combination of long slender bills and white sides. The bill of the Common Murre is longer than, but barely half as thick as, the Thick-billed Murre's; at close range the narrow black streak back from the eye in winter plumage is diagnostic.

THICK-BILLED MURRE
Úria lómvia

Strongly resembles the Common Murre and is about equally common. Note the shorter thicker bill and the narrow white streak at the base of mouth. In winter plumage there is no white above the black eye line.

DOVEKIE
Plaútus álle

This smallest East Coast alcid is abundant at nesting sites in summer, far offshore in the North Atlantic in winter. Appears along coast but rarely inland during Nov. storms. The short body, whirring wingbeats, and very small bill are distinctive.

BLACK GUILLEMOT
Cépphus grýlle

Rare and local in winter within sight of land. Not as gregarious as other alcids nor as pelagic. The very large white wing patch of adult is diagnostic. In the immature the wing patch is usually mottled. Compare the adult with White-winged Scoter (p. 58). Wingbeats fast.

PIGEON GUILLEMOT
Cépphus colúmba

Common. Resembles Black Guillemot in plumage and behavior. Usually distinguished from it by the black bars on the white wing patch, but immature Black Guillemot sometimes has black on the white wing patch.

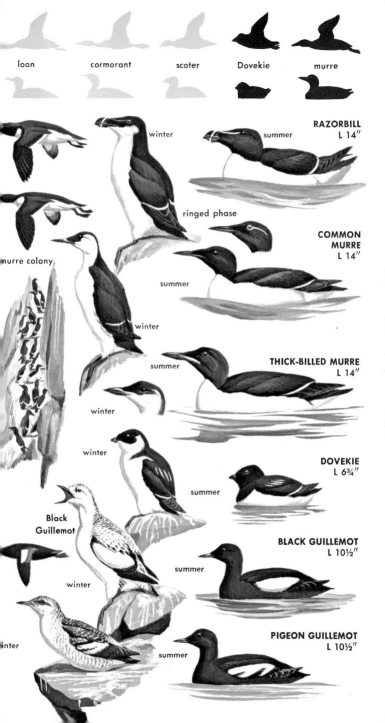

loon   cormorant   scoter   Dovekie   murre

winter

RAZORBILL
L 14″

summer

ringed phase

murre colony

winter

summer

COMMON
MURRE
L 14″

summer

THICK-BILLED MURRE
L 14″

winter

winter

summer

DOVEKIE
L 6¾″

Black
Guillemot

winter

summer

BLACK GUILLEMOT
L 10½″

summer

inter

summer

PIGEON GUILLEMOT
L 10½″

COMMON PUFFIN
Fratércula árctica

Locally common in nesting colonies. Winters at sea. Outer layers of the bill are shed in late summer, so winter adults and especially the immatures have small bills (rectangular at base). Although the face is largely dark in winter, the characteristic facial pattern is still present. No other puffin occurs in North Atlantic.

HORNED PUFFIN
Fratércula corniculáta

Common; similar to the Common Puffin, but ranges do not overlap. The tiny erectile horn over the eye is seen only at close range. Winter puffins are told from other western alcids by the heavy rectangular (immature) or triangular (adult) bills and large chunky bodies.

TUFTED PUFFIN
Lúnda cirrháta

Common, but very local in southern part of its range. The summer adult with its white face and jet-black body is unique. Winter birds can be told from the Horned Puffin by their dusky rather than pure white sides and at close range by the light line over the eye.

RHINOCEROS AUKLET
Cerorhínca monoceráta

Auklets are small, short-billed, dark-backed, western alcids that nest in burrows or rock slides. Rhinoceros, the largest, is common along the Pacific Coast in winter. It is nearly puffin size but much more slender-billed. It is twice as large as the short-billed Cassin's (p. 152), the only other dark-breasted alcid within its range.

CRESTED AUKLET
Aéthia cristatélla

Common resident in southwest Alaska (Aleutian, Pribilof and Shumagin islands). Often nests under rocks with Parakeet Auklets. The quail-like crest is shared only with the small rare Whiskered, which has 3, not 1, white facial plumes all year. The immature is separable from immature Whiskered and Cassin's only by direct comparison of size and face pattern at close range; the belly is sooty in Crested, whitish in Whiskered.

WHISKERED AUKLET
Aéthia pygmaéa

Uncommon and local. Seldom wanders far from its limited range in the Aleutians (Kiska to Akutan). Adult always has the quail-like crest and three facial plumes. Compare immature with Cassin's (p. 152).

winter summer

COMMON PUFFIN
L 11"

at nest burrow

im.

winter summer

HORNED PUFFIN
L 11½"

im. winter summer

TUFTED PUFFIN
L 12½"

im. winter summer

RHINOCEROS AUKLET
L 11½"

im. winter summer

CRESTED AUKLET
L 7"

im.

WHISKERED AUKLET
L 6½"

152

CASSIN'S AUKLET　　　　　*Ptychorámphus aleútica*
Common, especially offshore. This is the only small alcid south of Alaska that is dark to the waterline. Compare with the much larger Rhinoceros Auklet and Tufted Puffin (p. 150), both of which have much heavier bills.

LEAST AUKLET　　　　　*Aéthia pusílla*
Locally common resident in Bering Sea and Aleutians. White throat patch is diagnostic. In winter plumage compare the head pattern and bill with those of the next two species. These three are the only alcids with the white scapulars. Neck is short; flight rapid.

MARBLED MURRELET　　*Brachyrámphus marmorátum*
Murrelets are uniformly small alcids with short, generally thin bills. Marbled is told in summer by its plain brown back and long slender bill. In winter it is the only alcid south of Alaska that has white scapulars.

KITTLITZ'S MURRELET　　*Brachyrámphus breviróstre*
Locally common breeder near glacial waters on west and south coasts of Alaskan mainland (Cape Prince of Wales to Glacier Bay). Winters in Asia. In summer, paler and grayer backed than other alcids. In winter entire face is white. Bill half as long as Marbled's.

XANTUS' MURRELET　　*Endomychúra hypoleúca*
Uncommon and irregular. Looks like a miniature murre. In summer note the white underparts. In winter (same plumage) the slender bill, all-dark back, and white underparts clinch identification. Craveri's Murrelet (*E. cravéri,* L 8"), a casual fall visitor north to Monterey, California, is similar but has dark underwing coverts.

ANCIENT MURRELET　　*Synthliborámphus antíquum*
Uncommon within sight of land, but stragglers occur far inland. Note the pale bill, the contrast between black throat and white neck and between black head and gray back. The white plume is present in summer.

PARAKEET AUKLET　　　*Cyclorrhýnchus psittácula*
Fairly common offshore; seldom seen from land except when nesting. The almost circular red bill is the best field mark. This is the only red-billed auklet south of Alaska. Bill of immature may be dark.

CASSIN'S AUKLET
L 7″

winter   summer   **LEAST AUKLET**
L 5¼″

winter   summer   **MARBLED MURRELET**
L 8″

winter   summer   **KITTLITZ'S MURRELET**
L 7½″

XANTUS' MURRELET
L 8″

winter   summer   **ANCIENT MURRELET**
L 8″

winter   summer   **PARAKEET AUKLET**
L 7¼″

● **PIGEONS AND DOVES** (*Order* Columbiformes, *Family* Columbidae) are small-headed, short-legged, swift-flying birds with pointed wings and fanned or tapered tails. Females are duller than males. All species coo; bob heads when walking. Eat grains, small seeds, acorns (Band-tailed) and fruit. Nests are generally in trees; eggs, usually 2, are white (except olive-buff for White-fronted).

BAND-TAILED PIGEON *Colúmba fasciáta*

Locally common in western oak and pine woods, especially in summer. The large size and the broad gray tip on the fanned tail distinguish this bird from all others. Note the yellow bill and white neck band. Frequents waterholes and salt licks in large numbers. The call is a low-pitched, owl-like coo-coo.

ROCK DOVE (domestic pigeon) *Colúmba lívia*

This common introduced pigeon of farmyards and city parks has a white rump and (except in white birds) a dark terminal tail band. Wing tips collide on takeoff. Glides with wings raised at an angle. Nests on buildings.

WHITE-WINGED DOVE *Zenáida asiática*

Locally abundant; our only dove with large white wing patches. In flight note the large, white corners of the tail. Nests in colonies in citrus groves, mesquite, and open woods. Call, a low hhhooo-hoooo-hoo-hoooo.

MOURNING DOVE *Zenaidúra macroúra*

At all seasons the commonest native dove in suburbs and farmlands. Note the slim body and long tapered tail. Flight is swift and direct, without coasting; the whistling of the wings is diagnostic. Nests singly, feeds in flocks. Call, ooah-ooo-oo-oo, 4-6/min.

WHITE-CROWNED PIGEON *Colúmba leucocéphala*

Common in its limited range in the Fla. Keys, where the only other doves are the Mourning Dove and Ground Dove. Adult's white crown contrasts sharply with dark body. Immature lacks the white crown. Call is a very low-pitched co-woo (about 5 times).

RED-BILLED PIGEON *Colúmba flaviróstris*

Uncommon in summer (rare in midwinter); in woodlands and brush along the lower Rio Grande River (west to Falcon Reservoir) in southern Texas. A large all-dark bird, the size and shape of a Rock Dove; note its red bill. Call, hoo-hoohoohoohooo.

falcon   Killdeer   Mourning Dove   Rock Dove   cuckoo

Rock Doves feeding

BAND-TAILED PIGEON L 13½″

ROCK DOVE L 11″

WHITE-WINGED DOVE L 10″

White-winged Dove

MOURNING DOVE L 10½″

Mourning Dove on nest

WHITE-CROWNED PIGEON L 11″

RED-BILLED PIGEON L 11½″

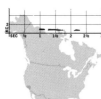

SPOTTED DOVE
Streptopélia chinénsis

Introduced. Locally common resident in Los Angeles Co., Calif.; occurs from Santa Barbara to San Diego. Heavier bodied than Mourning Dove; its tail is rounded and more broadly tipped with white. No other dove has the "lace-neck" pattern, present only in the adult. Found in agricultural lands, parks, and suburbs. Call is a low, harsh whistle: *hoo-hoooo-hoo.*

RINGED TURTLE DOVE
Streptopélia risória

A common cage bird that has become a local resident in central downtown Los Angeles, in Tampa and Miami. Told by its sandy plumage and black crescent on the back of its neck. Slimmer than brown Rock Dove and lacks white rump. Call, *hoo-hrrooo.*

GROUND DOVE
Columbigallina passerina

Common in brush and farmlands in the Far South. Bluebird size, its wings flash bright rufous in flight. On the ground it looks like a miniature Mourning Dove, but in flight the rapid wingbeats, bright rufous wing patches, and short rounded dark tail identify it. Nest usually on ground. Call a series of identical low soft whistles, each with a rising inflection: *hooah,* 40-60/min.

INCA DOVE
Scardafélla inca

A tiny-bodied, long-tailed dove resident in fields and pastures in the arid Southwest. The body is distinctly gray, without a brownish cast; the rufous area in primaries may show only in flight. Scaly back is diagnostic when the bird is on the ground. In flight the white margin to the long gray tail will immediately distinguish the Inca Dove from the smaller chunkier Ground Dove. Call is a monotonous repetition suggesting the call of the Ground Dove, but the coos are in pairs.

WHITE-FRONTED DOVE
Leptótila verreaúxi

An uncommon resident of the lower Rio Grande Valley, Texas. Similar in size and shape to White-winged Dove (p. 154), but white is restricted to forehead, belly, and tip of the tail. Wings are uniform brown above with bright chestnut linings below. Feeds on the ground near brush or wooded areas. Call is 2 soft, very low-pitched *hoos,* dropping in pitch at the end.

INTRODUCED
AND
SMALL DOVES

im.

SPOTTED DOVE L 11"

RINGED TURTLE DOVE L 10"

♂

♀

♂

GROUND DOVE L 5½"

INCA DOVE L 6½"

WHITE-FRONTED DOVE L 10"

● **CUCKOOS, ANIS, AND ROADRUNNERS** (Order Cuculiformes, Family Cuculidae) are slender birds with rounded wings, curved upper mandibles and long "graduated" tails, the outer tail feathers shortest. Sexes are alike. Cuckoos are sluggish birds of forest and brush; they eat hairy caterpillars. The coal-black anis resemble large grackles except for their weak flight, thick bills, and heavy tails. Roadrunners are large, crested ground birds of the arid Southwest. Eggs, 2-12.

MANGROVE CUCKOO
Coccýzus minor

Rare and local resident in mangroves and hammocks of Keys and southwest coast of Florida north to Tampa Bay. Usually outnumbered by Yellow-billed Cuckoos. Note the bright buffy underparts and black mask. Call is harsher and slower than Yellow-billed's.

YELLOW-BILLED CUCKOO
Coccýzus americánus

The commonest nesting cuckoo south of the Missouri and Ohio rivers and the only one west of the Rockies. Told from Black-billed by large white spots contrasting with black undertail surface, also by the bright rufous flash in the open wing and by the yellow lower mandible. Found in woods and brush, especially during outbreaks of tent caterpillars. Song, guttural and toneless in comparison with Black-billed's, is never in series of 3 or 4.

BLACK-BILLED CUCKOO
Coccýzus erythrophthálmus

Common in eastern North America. Tail spots are indistinct and the bill is all black. Has little or no rufous in spread wing. Bare skin around eye of adult is red. Like Yellow-billed, it is most common at caterpillar outbreaks. Song is 3 or 4 coos, 35-52 series/min.

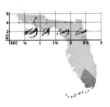

SMOOTH-BILLED ANI
Crotóphaga áni

Local resident in southern Florida (Belleglade south into Keys). Feeds in small flocks on the ground in brush and farmland. Likely to be overlooked because of resemblance to grackles. Groove-billed Ani (Crotóphaga sulciróstris, L 14"), resident in southern Texas, has grooves on bill, visible at close range.

ROADRUNNER
Geocóccyx califórnianus

Large, crested, terrestrial bird of arid Southwest. Wings are short and rounded. Runs rapidly, trailing its long white-tipped tail. Seldom flies. Eats lizards, snakes, insects. Song, dove-like, each note lower pitched.

falcon   Killdeer   Mourning Dove   Rock Dove   cuckoo

MANGROVE CUCKOO
L 11"

Yellow-billed

YELLOW-BILLED CUCKOO
L 11"

Black-billed

im.

GROOVE-BILLED ANI
L 14"

im.

BLACK-BILLED CUCKOO
L 11"

SMOOTH-BILLED ANI
L 12"

ROADRUNNER
L 22"

OWLS (Order Strigiformes, *Families* Tytonidae—the Barn Owls—and Strigidae—all other owls), large-headed, short-necked birds of prey, are mostly nocturnal and best seen and more frequently heard at dusk. The large eyes are fixed in their sockets, so the entire head moves as owls shift their gaze. The flat, round, or heart-shaped "facial disk" conceals the large external ear flaps. All owls on this page and some on p. 166 have erect ear tufts. All fly silently, hunting for rodents and other small mammals. Females are like males, but larger; immatures resemble adults. Calls are distinctive hoots, wails, or whistles. Most small owls and some large ones are cavity nesters. Eggs are round, white, 2-8 in a clutch.

SCREECH OWL Ótus ásio

This is the common small "eared" owl of towns, orchards, and small woodlots. Its plumage is bright rusty, brown, or gray; the facial disk is the same color as the head. In the East all other "eared" owls are distinctly larger. In the West and Southwest, Flammulated and Whiskered Owls (p. 166) are similar. Nests in cavities and occasionally in flicker boxes. Song is a quavering whistle (monotone or descending) or series of short notes.

GREAT HORNED OWL Búbo virginiánus

This common large "eared" owl is twice the size of the crows that often harass it. Color pattern is similar to the smaller slimmer Long-eared Owl's; Horned Owl's ear tufts are larger and farther apart; its belly is finely barred horizontally, whereas the Long-eared is more boldly streaked lengthwise. Call is typically 4 to 7 low hoots.

LONG-EARED OWL Ásio ótus

Locally common in deciduous or coniferous woods near open country. All owls with which it may be confused, especially the Great Horned Owl, are on this page. Looks larger in flight because of its very long wings. Generally silent except near its nest, where it makes a variety of low hoots, whistles, and shrieks.

SHORT-EARED OWL Ásio flámmeus

Locally common in open country over plains, sloughs, and marshes. The "ears" are hard to see. Note the black patch near bend of the underwing and the large buffy area on upper wing surface. Active before dark; flight is irregular. Wings are tilted upward like Marsh Hawk's (p. 68). Usually silent.

buteo

owl

nighthawk

crow

SCREECH OWL
L 8″ W 22″

gray phase

brown phase

red phase

GREAT HORNED OWL
L 20″ W 55″

LONG-EARED OWL
L 13″ W 39″

Long-eared Owl

Short-eared Owl

SHORT-EARED OWL
L 13″ W 41″

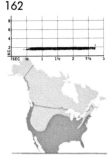

BARN OWL
Týto álba

This large light-colored uncommon owl is known by its heart-shaped face, small dark eyes, and long legs. All other owls except the Snowy are heavily marked below. It is strictly nocturnal; hunts rats and mice in farmyards, marshes, and fields. It has a peculiar habit of lowering its head and moving it back and forth. It nests in barns, abandoned buildings, and tree cavities. Does not hoot, but has a soft ascending wheezy cry. At the nest it gives a toneless hiss.

SNOWY OWL
Nýctea scandiaca

A diurnal arctic owl that winters irregularly in the U.S. Most adult birds are almost pure white. Immatures, which are darker, go farther south than adults in winter. The large size, pale plumage, and lack of ear tufts are diagnostic. It perches near the ground in open country and often allows birders to approach closely. Feeds on lemmings and other rodents and rabbits. Silent south of its breeding grounds.

BARRED OWL
Strix vária

Common in southern swamps and river bottoms; less common, but widespread, in northern woods. Has dark eyes; the only other eastern owl with dark eyes is the unstreaked heart-faced Barn Owl. In flight the Barred Owl resembles the Great Horned (p. 160). Usually nests in cavities. Typically hoots 8 times; 4-7 series/min.

SPOTTED OWL
Strix occidentális

This rare western counterpart of the Barred Owl is identified by the horizontal barring of its underparts. The dark-eyed Flammulated Owl (p. 166) of the West is similar, but is much smaller and has short ear tufts. Common call of Spotted is suggestive of Barred Owl's, but consists of only 3 or 4 hoots.

GREAT GRAY OWL
Strix nebulósa

Rare and local at high elevations in north and central Sierra Nevada and Rockies, where it is found in pine and spruce forests. Common only in the Far North. Note the long tail and the prominent gray concentric circles on the facial disk. The only other large owl with yellow eyes and no ear tufts is the Snowy. Voice is a deep, booming series of *whoos*, each lower in pitch.

LARGE EARLESS OWLS

Barn
Owls

BARN OWL
L 14″ W 44″

**SNOWY
OWL**
L 20″ W 55″

im.
♀

**BARRED
OWL**
L 17″ W 44″

SPOTTED OWL
L 16″ W 42″

**GREAT GRAY
OWL**
L 22″ W 60″

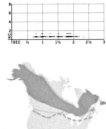

HAWK-OWL   *Súrnia úlula*

A tame diurnal owl of the muskegs of northern Canada, rarely moving south in winter into northern U.S. No other owl except the little Pygmy (p. 166) has the long slender tail that gives this bird a falcon-like appearance. Told from Boreal and Saw-whet Owls by the fine horizontal barring of its underparts. Perches in the open on treetops, where it raises its tail and slowly lowers it. Sometimes sits with its tail cocked up at an angle. Flight is straight and swift, usually very low, with alternate flapping and gliding. It also hovers, as a Sparrow Hawk does. Calls are series of whistles, 10-15 groups/min.

BURROWING OWL   *Speótyto cuniculária*

A small long-legged diurnal owl of the plains, locally common, usually nesting in prairie dog "towns." The permanent residents in Fla. inhabit prairies and airports. Frequently bobs up and down by quick bending motion of legs. Perches on the ground or on a fencepost. Hovers when hunting. Distinguished from all other owls except Barn by sandy color and long legs. Nests in burrows. Calls are a cackling alarm note and, at night, a 2-note coo-c-o-o.

BOREAL OWL   *Aególius funéreus*

A very tame, nocturnal, earless owl of the Far North, irregular in northern U.S. in winter. Told from Saw-whet by its light bill, black facial border, and chocolate streaking of its underparts. Told from the Screech Owl (p. 160) by the lack of ear tufts and from the Hawk-Owl by streaked underparts, short tail, and more erect posture. Lives in coniferous forests. Only during the arctic summer does it feed by day. Call is a series of whistles like sound of water dripping; 12-15 groups/min.

SAW-WHET OWL   *Aególius acádicus*

The only tiny tuftless owl likely to be seen in the central and eastern states. Commoner than generally believed, but nocturnal and seldom seen unless found roosting in dense young evergreens or in thickets. In the West it overlaps the range of Flammulated (p. 166), which has dark eyes and ear tufts, and the Pygmy (p. 166), which is slender and long-tailed with dark brown streaks on flanks. Common call is a long series of short whistles.

SMALL OWLS

HAWK-OWL
L 14" W 33"

BURROWING OWL
L 8" W 22"

Burrowing Owls
with prairie dogs

Chickadees scolding
Saw-whet Owl

BOREAL OWL
L 10" W 24"

SAW-WHET OWL
L 7" W 17"

juv.

WHISKERED OWL   Ótus trichópsis

Common in Southwest canyons. Closely resembles Screech Owl, whose range it overlaps; can be distinguished only at exceedingly close range. Watch for long whiskers and large white spots on scapulars. Generally found in dense oak or oak-pine woods. Distinctive call, 4 to 9 high-pitched boos slowing at the end, is best means of identification.

FLAMMULATED OWL   Ótus flamméolus

Rare and local. The only small owl with dark eyes. Like the Screech Owl, it occurs in gray and rusty phases, but the facial disk of Flammulated is redder than the rest of its head. Only in southeast Ariz. do Screech, Whiskered, and Flammulated Owls occur together. Prefers pine woods. Call is a single or double low-pitched hoot, repeated for long periods, 40-60/min.

PYGMY OWL   Glaucídium gnóma

A small, common, tame, long-tailed owl of coniferous and deciduous woods. Partly diurnal. No other small "earless" owl has blackish-streaked flanks. Entire tail extends beyond the wing tips and is usually cocked at an angle. Flight is undulating like a shrike's, with rapid wingbeats. Black patch at the side of its hind neck separates it from all owls but the rust-colored Ferruginous Owl. Call is a long repetition of single or double dove-like notes, 60-80/min.

ELF OWL   Micrathéne whitneyi

A nocturnal owl common in southwestern deserts. The underparts are buffy with indistinct streaking. No ear tufts. This tiny slim owl has a short tail that separates it from the Pygmy and Ferruginous Owls. Best seen at dusk in saguaro deserts, as it roosts by day in holes in the giant cactus. Call is a rapid high-pitched series of 6 or more cackling notes.

FERRUGINOUS OWL   Glaucídium brasiliánum

This small, uncommon, rusty relative of the Pygmy Owl is typical of wooded river bottoms and saguaro deserts near the Mexican border. Told from Pygmy Owl by its plain rusty back, rusty streaks on the sides, and a tail faintly barred with black on rust. Call is a long series of single notes.

SMALL OWLS

WHISKERED OWL
L 6½″ W 16″

Screech Owl
for comparison

FLAMMULATED
OWL
L 6″ W 14″

PYGMY OWL
L 6″ W 15″

ELF OWL
L 5¼″ W 15″

FERRUGINOUS
OWL

L 6″ W 15″

GOATSUCKERS (Order Caprimulgiformes, Family Caprimulgidae) are nocturnal insect eaters with large flat heads, small bills, enormous mouths, and distinctive white patches in wings or tail. Eyes are a mere slit by day, huge and round at night. All except nighthawks are named for their call. Eggs (2) are laid on ground or rooftop.

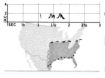

CHUCK-WILL'S-WIDOW   *Caprimúlgus carolinénsis*

Common in Southeast pine woods. Told from nighthawks by lack of white in wing, from Whip-poor-will by much larger size, more buffy body, and by the call. Narrow throat band is buffy in female. Song, 25-40/min.

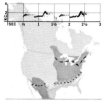

WHIP-POOR-WILL   *Caprimúlgus vocíferus*

This common round-winged goatsucker is seen only at dusk unless flushed from nest or ground roost in woods. Its eyes glow red in a light beam. Prefers woods near fields. Female has buffy throat band, no white on tail. Song, 50-65/min. Ridgway's Whip-poor-will (*Caprimúlgus rídgwayi* L 8½"), of Guadalupe Canyon, N. Mex., is told from the Whip-poor-will by the buff collar across back of neck. Song very different.

POOR-WILL   *Phalaenóptilus núttallii*

This small relative replaces the Whip-poor-will in the West. White in tail of both sexes is quite limited; young have buffy collar. Song is repeated 30-40/min.

PAURAQUE   *Nyctídromus albicóllis*

This large species of southern Texas brush country has white patches in its wings and tail. Call, 10-12/min.

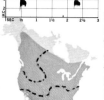

COMMON NIGHTHAWK   *Chordeiles minor*

Nighthawks differ from other goatsuckers in their long pointed wings, slightly forked tails, and white wing patches. They become active before dark, flying above treetops and houses. They sit lengthwise on limbs, diagonally on wires. In cities this common species nests on flat-topped buildings. On breeding grounds when the bird dives, the wing feathers produce a peculiar musical hum. Call is a nasal *peent* like a woodcock's, 25-35/min.

LESSER NIGHTHAWK   *Chordeiles acutipénnis*

Common in the Southwest, where it is told from Common Nighthawk by its smaller size, position of white in wings, its habit of flying very low, and by its low trilling call.

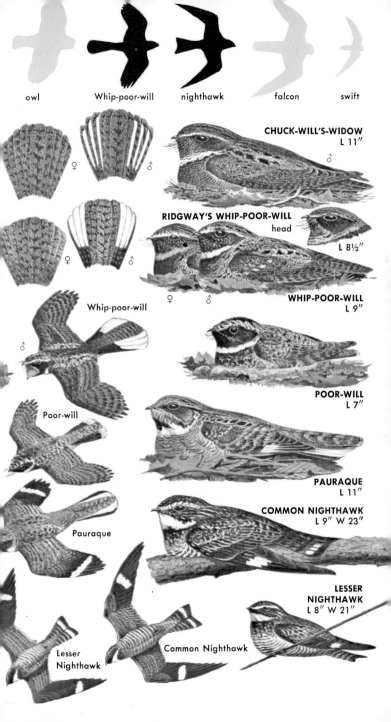

owl

Whip-poor-will

nighthawk

falcon

swift

♀ ♂

♀ ♂

CHUCK-WILL'S-WIDOW
L 11″
♂

RIDGWAY'S WHIP-POOR-WILL
head
L 8½″

Whip-poor-will

♀ ♂

♂

WHIP-POOR-WILL
L 9″

Poor-will

POOR-WILL
L 7″

Pauraque

PAURAQUE
L 11″

COMMON NIGHTHAWK
L 9″ W 23″

**LESSER
NIGHTHAWK**
L 8″ W 21″

Lesser
Nighthawk

Common Nighthawk

SWIFTS (*Order* Apodiformes, *Family* Apodidae), like goatsuckers, feed almost exclusively on flying insects caught on the wing with their wide mouths. Swifts fly continuously all day except in heavy rain. Their wings, built for speed, are long, stiff, slender, and slightly decurved. In contrast to swallows, with which they are often found, swifts appear to beat their wings alternately. Sexes are alike. Swifts nest on cliffs, in chimneys, and in hollow trees. Eggs are white, 3-6 (1 by Black Swift).

BLACK SWIFT *Cypseloídes níger*

This uncommon swift has solid black underparts and a slightly forked tail. When seen with Vaux's, its larger size is obvious. The adult male Purple Martin (p. 206) is similar, but has broad wings bent at the "wrist." The Black Swift's "wrist" is so close to the body that the wing angle is barely visible. It cruises many miles from its high-altitude nesting cliffs. Unlike Vaux's and Chimney Swifts, it seldom is heard away from the nest site.

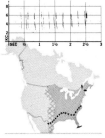

CHIMNEY SWIFT *Chaetúra pelágica*

Normally the only swift east of the Missouri and Mississippi rivers. Common, usually in flocks of flittering dark birds. Tail is stiff, slightly rounded, and never forked or fanned; bristles that support the tail when clinging to a vertical surface are not visible in the field. Noisy chatter of chipping notes generally discloses Chimney Swifts overhead. During migration they roost by the hundreds in tall chimneys, entering in a huge funnel formation at dusk. Call, rapid short chips.

VAUX'S SWIFT *Chaetúra vaúxi*

Replaces Chimney Swift west of Rockies. Told from swallows by typical body shape, from White-throated Swift by slightly rounded tail and uniformly pale underparts. Smaller and paler below than the almost identical Chimney Swift. It nests in hollow trees in dense forests; rarely in chimneys. Voice is like Chimney Swift's.

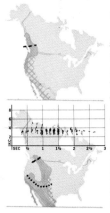

WHITE-THROATED SWIFT *Aëronaútes saxátalis*

Common. Only North American swift with bold black and white pattern. Most likely to be confused with Violet-green Swallow, with which it associates. Violet-green also has white flank patches, visible from above and below, but its entire underparts are white. White-throated is found near cliffs and canyons. Call, a shrill twitter.

falcon   nighthawk   swift   swallow

SWIFTS

BLACK SWIFT
L 7″

CHIMNEY SWIFT
L 5″ W 12½″

VAUX'S SWIFT
L 4½″

White-throated Swift

Violet-green Swallow
for comparison

WHITE-THROATED SWIFT
L 6½″ W 14″

HUMMINGBIRDS (*Order* Apodiformes, *Family* Trochilidae) are the smallest of North American birds, all with long slender bills adapted for reaching deep into tubular flowers. Wingbeat is so rapid it produces a humming sound. All species feed while hovering and can also fly backward. Throat feathers look black when light does not reflect the brilliant iridescent colors. Young birds resemble females; some are difficult to identify. All are fearless and pugnacious. Males have a "pendulum" courting flight, with distinctive patterns for some species. Migrate by day, flying low. Eggs, 2, are small, white.

RUBY-THROATED HUMMINGBIRD

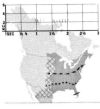

Archílochus cólubris

Common. Only hummingbird east of Great Plains except Rufous, which is rare in Gulf and South Atlantic states in late fall and winter. Only the adult male has the bright red throat. Often detected by rapid, squeaky, chipping made in flight or by the hum of the wings. Found near tubular flowers in gardens or woods.

BROAD-TAILED HUMMINGBIRD

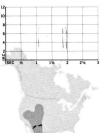

Selásphorus platycércus

This is the common breeding hummer of the Rockies. Male, which is similar to Ruby-throated, is more readily told by the distinctive shrill metallic wing whistling than by its wider rounded tail and rose-colored throat. No other western hummer has a green crown and tail and a solid red throat. Females are similar to several other hummers. Calliope is much smaller, with wings extending beyond the tail. Broad-tailed female cannot safely be separated from Rufous and Allen's (p. 174).

CALLIOPE HUMMINGBIRD

Stéllula calliope

Smallest U.S. hummer; common in western mountains. Male is only hummer whose colored throat feathers form streaks against a white background. The purple feathers can be distended. Female is much smaller than Broad-tailed; smaller, slimmer, and shorter-tailed than Rufous and Allen's (p. 174), with less rufous on sides and tail.

ANNA'S HUMMINGBIRD

Calýpte ánna

Common resident west of Sierras. Forehead as well as throat is red. Female's green tail is broadly tipped with white; throat usually has a few red feathers. Female is larger and stouter than Black-chinned; larger and darker below than Costa's. Male is the only Calif. hummer with a real song (sung when perched).

HUMMINGBIRDS

flight display

RUBY-THROATED
HUMMINGBIRD
L 3"

♀

im.
♂

♂

♂ Broad-tailed

♀

♀

BROAD-TAILED
HUMMINGBIRD
L 3¾"

oad-tailed
ummingbird

♀

♂

♂

distended bib

CALLIOPE
HUMMINGBIRD
L 2¾"

Calliope Hummingbird
flight display

♂

♂

♀

ANNA'S
HUMMINGBIRD
L 3½"

BLACK-CHINNED HUMMINGBIRD

Archilochus alexándri

Common in western mountains, this is the only North American hummer with a truly black throat; throats of other species may look black in poor light. White below the purple stripe confirms this species. Often captures insects flycatcher-fashion. Female has no rufous on sides and tail and is not safely separable from Costa's. Female Anna's (p. 172), which is restricted to Calif. and southern Ariz., is larger and plumper.

COSTA'S HUMMINGBIRD

Calýpte cóstae

Common in Southwest deserts. Male is unmistakable with its violet cap and throat, the latter with long side feathers. Female is not safely told from Black-chinned. Female Anna's (p. 172) is larger and slightly darker below and often has red flecks on throat. Immature Calliope and other species commonly found in Costa's range have rufous sides and tail base.

RUFOUS HUMMINGBIRD

Selásphorus rúfus

Abundant migrant through western U.S.; the common breeding hummer of western Wash., western Oreg., and western Canada. Adult male has unmistakable solid rufous back. Female and immature are similar to Allen's, the larger Broad-tailed, and smaller Calliope (folded wings of Calliope extend beyond tail). Female Allen's is separable only at extremely close range when its narrow outer tail feather can be seen. Aerial display of male is a rapid dive to within inches of female. Air moving through the feathers produces a loud whine as the male suddenly checks its descent. In normal flight the male produces only a subdued humming.

ALLEN'S HUMMINGBIRD

Selásphorus sásin

Common only in coastal Calif. The male is our only red-throated hummer with a solid rufous tail and a green cap and back. The female can be identified in the breeding season when migrants of similar species are absent, but during migration it is practically impossible to tell female and immature from the closely related Rufous Hummingbird. Even the call notes of the two species are the same: a sharp *bzee*. The courtship pendulum flight of the male (a 25' arc) is followed by a dive from about 100'.

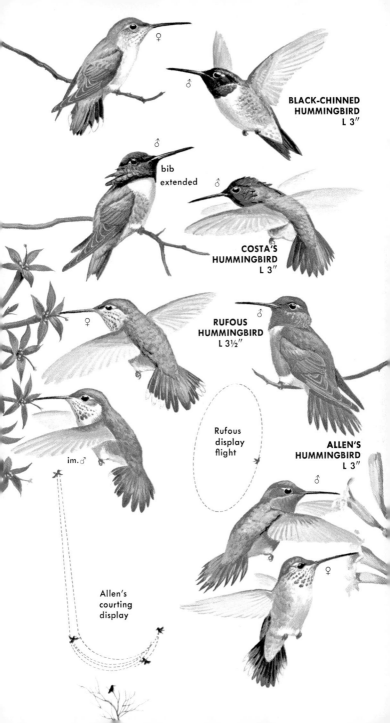

♀

♂

BLACK-CHINNED HUMMINGBIRD
L 3″

♂

bib extended

♂

COSTA'S HUMMINGBIRD
L 3″

♀

♂

RUFOUS HUMMINGBIRD
L 3½″

im. ♂

Rufous display flight

ALLEN'S HUMMINGBIRD
L 3″

♂

Allen's courting display

♂

♀

SOUTHWEST HUMMINGBIRDS include species found in summer along U.S.-Mexican border. Those that breed in U.S. are mapped below. Four species have bright red or orange bills with black tips.

LUCIFER HUMMINGBIRD   *Calothórax lúcifer*
Male is only violet-throated hummingbird with green crown; also has a deeply forked tail. Female is the only one with a buff throat and decurved bill. Casual, possibly breeds, in Chisos Mts., Tex.

RIVOLI'S HUMMINGBIRD   *Eúgenes fúlgens*
Male is told by its large size, green throat, and violet-blue crown; female is recognized by its large size, dark bill, and narrow grayish tail edging. Breeds from southeastern Ariz. mountains to Chisos Mts., Tex.

BLUE-THROATED HUMMINGBIRD
Lampórnis cleménciae
Recognized by its large size, the very broad white tip to its long black tail, and double white line on the face. Blue throat of male is obvious at close range.

VIOLET-CROWNED HUMMINGBIRD *Amazília verticális*
No other North American hummingbird has violet crown and white throat. Female and immature have lighter and greener crowns. Breeds in Guadalupe Canyon, Chiricahau Mts., Ariz.; recorded in Huachuces.

BUFF-BELLIED HUMMINGBIRD   *Amazília yucatanénsis*
Bright orange bill, large size, and green throat separate this species from other Texas hummers. Sexes are alike. Breeds and rarely winters in the lower Rio Grande Valley, in wood margins and thickets.

BROAD-BILLED HUMMINGBIRD   *Cynánthus latiróstris*
Male is told by its dark body, long orange bill, and forked tail; female by its orange bill and sooty underparts. Compare carefully with the paler-breasted White-eared. Breeds from south central Ariz. and southwest N. Mex. southward, rarely in western Texas

WHITE-EARED HUMMINGBIRD   *Hylocháris leucótis*
Only small hummingbird with long "ear" stripe. Male may appear all dark, like Broad-billed, but tail is square-tipped. Note green flanks, spotted throat of female. Casual summer species in southeast Ariz. mts.

SOUTHWEST HUMMINGBIRDS

LUCIFER HUMMINGBIRD
L 3¼″

RIVOLI'S HUMMINGBIRD
L 5″

BLUE-THROATED HUMMINGBIRD
L 5¼″

VIOLET-CROWNED HUMMINGBIRD
L 3½″

BUFF-BELLIED HUMMINGBIRD
L 3¾″

BROAD-BILLED HUMMINGBIRD
L 3¼″

WHITE-EARED HUMMINGBIRD
L 3″

● **PARROTS** (*Order* Psittaciformes, *Family* Psittacidae) are brightly colored tropical birds with strongly hooked beaks and short legs; 2 toes in front, 2 behind. Several species have escaped from captivity.

THICK-BILLED PARROT   *Rhynchopsitta pachyrhýncha*
A casual visitor in southeast Ariz. and southwest N. Mex. No recent U.S. records. A bright yellow patch on the underwing coverts is conspicuous in flight. Note red forehead and thick bill.

● **TROGONS** (*Order* Trogoniformes, *Family* Trogonidae) are short-billed, long-tailed, tropical fruit eaters represented in extreme southern U.S. by a single species. Nest in tree cavities. Eggs, 2-4.

COPPERY-TAILED TROGON   *Trógon élegans*
Rare summer resident in mountains of southeast Ariz.; casual in lower Rio Grande Valley, Texas. Male is unmistakable; all plumages have black band at tip of long square-cut tail and rose on belly. Call, 4-6 low croaks.

● **KINGFISHERS** (*Order* Coraciiformes, *Family* Alcedinidae) are large-headed, short-tailed birds that dive for fish, which they catch with their long sharp beaks. They perch motionless in the open, over water. Their legs are very short. Usually lay 3-8 white eggs in a deep burrow in a steep bank.

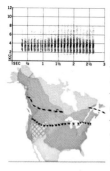

BELTED KINGFISHER   *Megacéryle álcyon*
The most common kingfisher in North America and the only one north of Texas and Ariz. Seen singly or in pairs along streams and ponds. Except for terns, kingfishers are the only small birds that dive headlong from air into water. Recognized in flight by its deep, irregular wingbeats, its big-headed appearance, and its loud rattling call. Often hovers before diving. Ringed Kingfisher (*Megacéryle torquáta*, L 15½″), casual in Rio Grande Valley, Tex., and common farther south, is told in all plumages by its much larger size and bright rusty belly. Both species are crested in all plumages.

GREEN KINGFISHER   *Chlorocéryle americána*
Rare in southeast Ariz. and lower Rio Grande Valley. Its small size, green back, and lack of a crest distinguish it immediately from the other kingfishers. Rattle is higher pitched and less harsh than Belted's. Female has greenish breast bands; male has a rusty one.

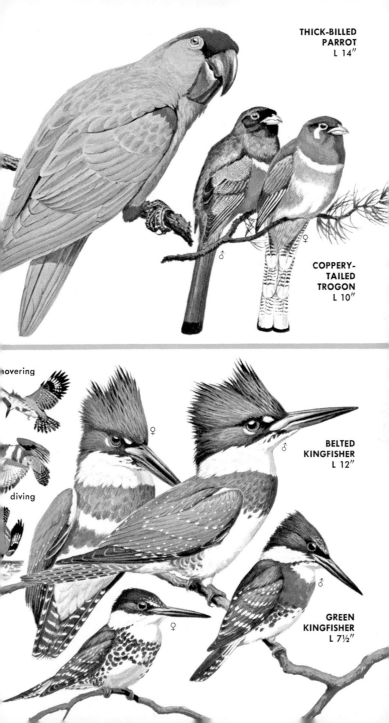

THICK-BILLED PARROT L 14"

COPPERY-TAILED TROGON L 10"

♂

♀

hovering

diving

BELTED KINGFISHER L 12"

♀

♂

GREEN KINGFISHER L 7½"

♀

♂

WOODPECKERS (Order Piciformes, *Family* Picidae) have a strong bill, sharply pointed for chipping and digging into tree trunks or branches for wood-boring insects. The stiff tail is used as a prop. Most species "drum" on resonant limbs, poles, or drainpipes. Flight is usually undulating, with wings folded against the body after each series of flaps. Nest is in a cavity chiseled deep into a large branch or trunk. Eggs, 4-8, are white.

Flickers are jay-sized woodpeckers with brown back, no white on wings, and a black breast band. In flight note white rump, yellow or salmon under wings and tail. Often seen on ground eating ants.

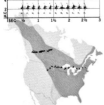

YELLOW-SHAFTED FLICKER — Coláptes aurátus

Common in open country near large trees. Undersurface of wing and tail feathers is golden, grading to orange or salmon in hybrids. Black "mustache" present except in adult female. Nape of neck is always red. Call of all flickers is a loud repeated *flick* or *flicker*; series repeated 2-7/min. Also a shrill descending *kee-oo*.

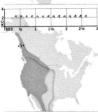

RED-SHAFTED FLICKER — Coláptes cáfer

Common. Crown is brown, face gray; mustache of the male is red, not black, as in Yellow-shafted. The red nape is lacking. Wing and tail linings salmon.

GILDED FLICKER — Coláptes chrysoïdes

Common resident in the giant-cactus region of the Southwest, where it digs a nest hole in the saguaro. Told from Yellow-shafted by its brown crown, gray face, and lack of a red nape; from Red-shafted by its yellow wing and tail linings.

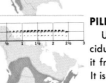

PILEATED WOODPECKER — Dryócopus pileátus

Uncommon and local; a wary bird of extensive deciduous or mixed forests. Solid black back distinguishes it from other large birds except crows and some hawks. It is conspicuously crested in all plumages. Flight is strong with irregular flaps of wings. Drumming is distinctive: loud, slow, softer at end. Call is a series, never single.

IVORY-BILLED WOODPECKER — Campéphilus principális

On verge of extinction. Last reported in deep forests of southeast Texas, central La., northwest Fla., and S.C. Extensive white on wing, folded and in flight, and white bill are diagnostic. Male has red crest, female black. Call is a high-pitched single note.

woodpecker

nuthatch

creeper

warbler

YELLOW-SHAFTED FLICKER L 10½″

flight of flicker

♀

♂

GILDED FLICKER L 10″

♂

RED-SHAFTED FLICKER L 11″

♂

IVORY-BILLED WOODPECKER L 18″

♂

Pileated

Ivory-billed

PILEATED WOODPECKER L 15″

● **LADDER-BACKED WOODPECKERS** fall into two groups: medium-sized birds with light rumps, colored or pale napes, and white wing patches that show in flight; and small birds with dark rumps, black napes, and spotted sides. All are non-migratory. Juvenal is like adult, but juvenal heads are browner in *Centurus*.

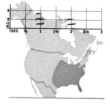

RED-BELLIED WOODPECKER   *Centúrus carolínus*
Common in southeastern woodlands. Red-headed (p. 184) is same size and has a similar call, but note the ladder back and red cap and hind neck (not head) of the Red-bellied. Immature has brown head. May occur with Red-cockaded in longleaf pine woods. Calls are low, short, and hoarse; also a rattle.

GOLDEN-FRONTED WOODPECKER *Centúrus aúrifrons*
Common in deciduous woodlands. Note the large gold spot on hind neck (duller in immature) and yellow above bill in adult. Voice is like Red-bellied's.

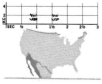

GILA WOODPECKER   *Centúrus uropygiális*
Common around giant cactus. Note that only the male has a red cap. White wing patches, as in Red-bellied, tell it from all ladder-backed woodpeckers in its range. Compare with immature sapsuckers (p. 184).

LADDER-BACKED WOODPECKER *Dendrócopos scaláris*
Fairly common in deciduous woods and mesquite, less common in cactus. Note the distinct black and white on side of head. Told from Gila and Golden-fronted by the dark rump, finely spotted sides, and lack of white wing patch in flight. Call is like Hairy Woodpecker's.

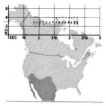

RED-COCKADED WOODPECKER
Dendrócopos boreális
Rare and local in longleaf pine woods. Told from Red-bellied by solid black nape and cap; from Hairy and Downy by ladder back and large white cheek patches. Nest hole, in pine trunks, is recognized by oozing gum.

NUTTALL'S WOODPECKER   *Dendrócopos núttallii*
Common, especially in live oaks and chaparral west of the Sierras. Face is blacker than Ladder-backed Woodpecker's. See also Williamson's Sapsucker (p. 184) and Downy and Hairy Woodpeckers (p. 186). Call is a series of high-pitched squeaks.

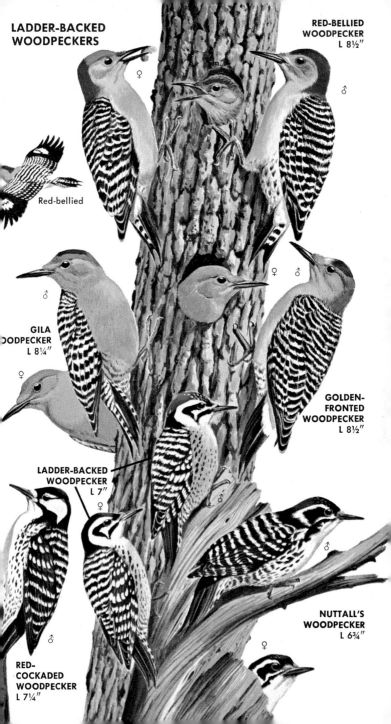

LADDER-BACKED WOODPECKERS

RED-BELLIED
WOODPECKER
L 8½"

♀

Red-bellied

♂

GILA
WOODPECKER
L 8¼"

♂

♀

♀ ♂

GOLDEN-
FRONTED
WOODPECKER
L 8½"

LADDER-BACKED
WOODPECKER
L 7"

♀

♂

♂

NUTTALL'S
WOODPECKER
L 6¾"

♀

RED-
COCKADED
WOODPECKER
L 7¼"

♂

RED-HEADED WOODPECKER
Melanérpes erythrocéphalus

Uncommon in much of its range; prefers open deciduous woods. Adult head is entirely red. Large white wing area separates it from other species. The similar red-breasted sapsucker (below) has a narrow white wing stripe. Often perches in the open. Call is a raucous *kwrrk*.

ACORN WOODPECKER
Melanérpes formicivorus

Common, especially in oaks, and gregarious. Its black chin, white rump, and small but conspicuous white wing patch separate it from all other dark-backed woodpeckers except sapsuckers. Its flight is undulating. Call is of high, sharp, fussing notes.

LEWIS' WOODPECKER
Asyndésmus léwis

Locally common in large trees in open country. Red face and light collar and underparts contrast with the rest of its dark greenish plumage. The rump is black. Flight is slow, with even, crow-like flapping. Gregarious. Catches flying insects. Call is of soft short notes.

WHITE-HEADED WOODPECKER
Dendrócopos albolarvátus

Locally common in pines and firs. The only white-headed woodpecker. Also note white wing patch at rest and in flight. May alight sideways or upside down.

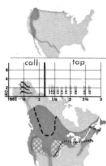

YELLOW-BELLIED SAPSUCKER
Sphyrápicus várius

Common (but quiet, retiring, and easily overlooked) in woods and orchards. Plumage is variable, but the narrow longitudinal wing stripe and finely mottled back are diagnostic. Red-breasted races occur on the Pacific slope. Sapsuckers tap in distinctive rhythms (2 or 3 series /min.), but do not drum. They drill parallel rows of small holes in live trees, then return to feed on sap and small insects. Calls are weak.

WILLIAMSON'S SAPSUCKER
Sphyrápicus thyroídeus

Uncommon; in pine forests, at higher elevations in summer. Sexes are entirely different. Male has two white stripes on solid black head and a solid black breast. Female has a more uniformly brown head and more black on the breast than female Yellow-bellied Sapsucker. It is also more distinctly marked on the back.

ACORN WOODPECKER
L 8"

RED-HEADED
WOODPECKER
L 7½"

Red-headed

Acorn

im.

Lewis'

WHITE-
HEADED
WOODPECKER
L 7¾"

White-
headed

LEWIS'
WOODPECKER
L 9"

juv.

Yellow-bellied

Yellow-bellied

YELLOW-
BELLIED
SAPSUCKER
L 7¾"

♂

Williamson's

WILLIAMSON'S
SAPSUCKER
L 8¼"

♀

♂

im.
♀

red
race

ARIZONA WOODPECKER
Dendrócopos arizónae

Fairly common resident in its limited range on pine-oak slopes, 4,500-7,000'. No other brown-backed woodpecker has a dark rump, unbarred back, or white on the face. Female lacks red on the back of the neck. Call, *beep*, similar to Downy's, but longer and louder.

HAIRY WOODPECKER
Dendrócopos villósus

Fairly common, especially in mature deciduous or mixed woods. Recognized by its medium size, the vertical white stripe on the back, and its long bill. Sexes are similar, but the female does not have a red patch on the back of its head. Easily confused with Downy Woodpecker, which is smaller and has a much smaller bill, and Northern Three-toed, which has barred sides and a much narrower white eye stripe. Call is a loud *peek*, also a loud kingfisher-like rattle.

DOWNY WOODPECKER
Dendrócopos pubéscens

Commonest eastern woodpecker; also common in parts of West. Seen in suburbs, orchards, shade trees, and woods. Looks like a miniature Hairy Woodpecker; is best told by its short slender bill and by its calls. Barred outer tail feathers when visible are diagnostic (they are rarely unbarred like Hairy's). May be mistaken for a sapsucker, whose white stripe is on the wing, not the back. Call, *pik*, is much softer than Hairy's; rattle call descends in pitch toward end.

BLACK-BACKED THREE-TOED WOODPECKER
Picoídes árcticus

An uncommon woodpecker even in its preferred habitat—coniferous forests. Note barred sides and black back. In the East, no other woodpecker except the much larger Pileated has a solid black back. In the West only Lewis' and White-headed have black back and rump. Only the male has the yellow crown. Call is a sharp *pik*.

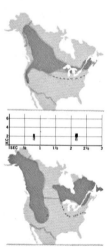

NORTHERN THREE-TOED WOODPECKER
Picoídes tridáctylus

Locally common in western coniferous forests; rare in the East. Note the black wings, rump, and tail, the barred sides and back, and the yellow cap. No other woodpecker except the Black-backed (and, very rarely, the Hairy) has a yellow crown. Female has barred sides, no crown patch. Calls are similar to preceding species.

ARIZONA WOODPECKER L 7¼"

♂

♀

Hairy

Downy

HAIRY WOODPECKER L 7½"

♂

♀

DOWNY WOODPECKER L 5¾"

♂

♂

♀

BLACK-BACKED THREE-TOED WOODPECKER L 8"

♂

♀

NORTHERN THREE-TOED WOODPECKER L 7½"

PERCHING BIRDS (*Order* Passeriformes) are medium to small land birds. All have feet well adapted for perching: 3 toes in front and 1 long one behind. Most are fine singers. Bill shape, feather colors, and habits are most useful for family identification. Most insectivorous species and some fruit and seed eaters are highly migratory.

1. **FLYCATCHERS** have broad flat bills; plumage mostly olive or gray; catch flying insects with a loud snap of the beak. p. 190

2. **LARKS** walk; they are generally in flocks in large open fields, never in trees. p. 204

3. **SWALLOWS** have long pointed wings, often notched or forked tails. They catch insects in flight; most nest in colonies. p. 204

4. **JAYS AND CROWS** are large, noisy, omnivorous birds, mostly blue or green (jays) or all black (crows); gregarious. p. 208

5. **CHICKADEES AND TITMICE** are small friendly long-tailed birds, mostly gray, white, and black; stubby bill; in small flocks. p. 214

6. **WRENTITS** are long-tailed dark brown birds of dense thickets; West Coast only. Illustrated on p. 218

7. **BULBULS** have long tails, crests. Illustrated on p. 218

8. **DIPPERS** are plump gray birds of western mountain streams; short tails. p. 218

9. **NUTHATCHES** are slender-billed short-tailed birds that crawl over trunks and branches, usually in small flocks. p. 220

10. **CREEPERS** creep up tree trunks, then fly to base of another; use tail as prop. p. 220

11. **WRENS** are brown, generally solitary, with finely barred tails cocked upward, and slender bills; loud songs, scolding rattles. p. 222

12. **MOCKINGBIRDS AND THRASHERS** are long-tailed brush-loving birds, either brown or gray, with loud repetitious songs. p. 228

13. **THRUSHES,** medium-sized birds, typically are brown with spotted breasts; bills shaped like Robin's; eat worms, fruit; fine singers. p. 230

14. **GNATCATCHERS AND KINGLETS** are tiny very active gray or olive birds with eye ring or line over eye; body unstreaked. p. 236

15. **PIPITS** walk; slender-billed, sparrow-like birds; in flocks in large fields. p. 238

16. **WAXWINGS** are crested flocking birds with yellow fringe at tip of tail. p. 240

17. **PHAINOPEPLAS** are slender, crested birds of Southwest deserts; black or dark gray. p. 240

18. **SHRIKES** have heavy hooked bill, black mask, black wing with white patch. p. 242

19. **STARLINGS** look like short-tailed blackbirds; noisy, in large flocks. p. 242

20. **VIREOS** glean insects from leaves of deciduous trees and brush with their slightly hooked bills; plain olive backs. p. 244

21. **WARBLERS** are mostly brightly colored insect eaters of woods and brush; slender bills; very active; many have white tail spots. p. 250

22. **WEAVER FINCHES** are introduced Old World sparrows, common in towns, farms. p. 278

23. **BLACKBIRDS AND ORIOLES** represent a large family of Robin-sized birds, some all black, others with bright orange or yellow. p. 278

24. **TANAGERS** are brilliant arboreal Robin-sized insect and fruit eaters; heavy bills; unstreaked plumage; most with no wing bars. p. 288

25. **GROSBEAKS, FINCHES, AND SPARROWS** have heavy conical seed-cracking bills. Mostly brown, red, yellow, or blue, seldom olive. p. 290

COTINGAS (Family Cotingidae) are a large family of tropical fly-catchers, but only one species enters our area. These large-headed treetop birds with large beaks often hover. Nests are bulky. 3-6 eggs.

ROSE-THROATED BECARD   *Platypsáris aglaiae*
Rare and local along U.S.–Mexican border in Ariz., N. Mex., and Texas. Male has distinctive rose throat; female and young are brown with broad buffy neck band and black crown. Call is a thin sputtering whistle.

TYRANT FLYCATCHERS (Family Tyrannidae) are large-headed, broad-billed, short-legged birds that perch on bare branches or wires waiting for flying insects. Many of the small species flip their tails. Sexes similar (except Vermilion); young are only slightly different. Most nest in trees or shrubs. Eggs, 2-6.

SCISSOR-TAILED FLYCATCHER   *Muscivora forfic*
Common in open country. Note long streaming tail of adult. Young similar to the Western Kingbird (p. 192), but have pink sides and a whiter tail. Calls suggest Western Kingbird's. Fork-tailed Flycatcher (*Muscivora tyrán-nus*, L 15") is similar, with long streaming tail, but underparts are white and crown is black. Immature is brownish. A casual visitor in eastern U.S.

KISKADEE FLYCATCHER   *Pitángus sulphurátus*
Locally common in lower Rio Grande Valley. Easily recognized by its bold black and white face pattern. In flight notice the rufous wings. Named for its call.

VERMILION FLYCATCHER   *Pyrocéphalus rubinus*
Common near streams in arid Southwest. Decidedly smaller than Cardinal and tanagers, it is readily recognized by its small bill and flycatching habit. Male is unmistakable. Finely streaked sides and strawberry wash on flanks identify the female. Say's Phoebe has longer tail and no streaks. Song, rapid, high, sputtering notes.

SULPHUR-BELLIED FLYCATCHER
Myiodynástes luteiventris
Fairly common locally in canyons at 5,000-7,500'. Noisy, but hard to see high in the foliage. The only North American flycatcher with bold streaking below. Call resembles Western Flycatcher's, but is much louder.

shrike

flycatcher

vireo

warbler

sparrow

uebird

♀

throated
card

im.

♂

**ROSE-
THROATED
BECARD**
L 5½″

♂

**SCISSOR-
TAILED
FLYCATCHER**
L 13″

Kiskadee

**KISKADEE
FLYCATCHER**
L 9″

**VERMILION
FLYCATCHER L 5″**

♂

**SULPHUR-
BELLIED
FLYCATCHER**
L 6¾″

KINGBIRDS are aggressive, usually gray-headed flycatchers of open or semi-open country. Their posture is less erect than most flycatchers'. Crown patches are generally concealed, but a black mask identifies most kingbirds.

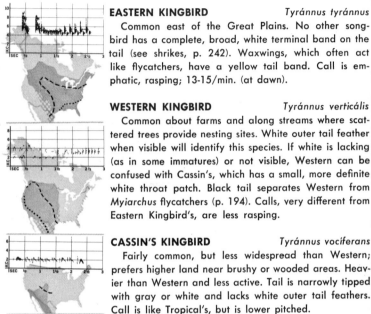

EASTERN KINGBIRD
Tyránnus tyránnus

Common east of the Great Plains. No other songbird has a complete, broad, white terminal band on the tail (see shrikes, p. 242). Waxwings, which often act like flycatchers, have a yellow tail band. Call is emphatic, rasping; 13-15/min. (at dawn).

WESTERN KINGBIRD
Tyránnus verticális

Common about farms and along streams where scattered trees provide nesting sites. White outer tail feather when visible will identify this species. If white is lacking (as in some immatures) or not visible, Western can be confused with Cassin's, which has a small, more definite white throat patch. Black tail separates Western from *Myiarchus* flycatchers (p. 194). Calls, very different from Eastern Kingbird's, are less rasping.

CASSIN'S KINGBIRD
Tyránnus vociferans

Fairly common, but less widespread than Western; prefers higher land near brushy or wooded areas. Heavier than Western and less active. Tail is narrowly tipped with gray or white and lacks white outer tail feathers. Call is like Tropical's, but is lower pitched.

TROPICAL KINGBIRD
Tyránnus melanchólicus

Common in chaparral near Mexican border. Fall vagrant along Calif. coast. The breast, as well as the belly, is bright yellow; back is olive. There is no white on the pale notched tail. Call is a loud *chi-queer*.

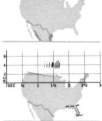

GRAY KINGBIRD
Tyránnus dominicénsis

Common on utility wires in Fla. Keys; local elsewhere near the coast. Note its huge bill, pale upper parts, and lack of white on the notched tail. Call, *pe-cheerrry*.

THICK-BILLED KINGBIRD
Tyránnus crassiróstris

Rare; in Guadalupe Canyon, Ariz.–N. Mex. Brownish upper parts and pale underparts suggest flycatchers on next page, but facial mask, white throat, dark tail, lack of wing bars, and actions identify this as a kingbird.

KINGBIRDS

chasing crow

Eastern

Western

EASTERN
KINGBIRD
L 6¾"

WESTERN
KINGBIRD
L 7"

CASSIN'S
KINGBIRD
L 7"

TROPICAL
KINGBIRD
L 7"

GRAY
KINGBIRD
L 7½"

THICK-BILLED
KINGBIRD
L 7¼"

194

● **MYIARCHUS FLYCATCHERS** are characterized by their large size, olive head and back, yellowish belly, and (except in Olivaceous) bright rusty tail; all have wingbars. Their posture is more erect than kingbirds', and they are more inclined to perch in the shade. All nest in cavities in trees and posts; also in bird, mail, or newspaper boxes.

GREAT CRESTED FLYCATCHER   *Myiárchus crinítus*
Common in deciduous and mixed woods. This is the only *Myiarchus* to be expected east of the Rockies and central Texas. Identified as a flycatcher by its broad bill, large head, and flycatching habits. No other eastern flycatcher has a long rusty tail. Note similarity to Western Kingbird (p. 192), which is rare but regular along the Atlantic Coast from Sept. to Oct. Western Kingbird perches in the open and has a black tail with white outer feathers. Call is a harsh ascending *wheep*, 30-45/min.

WIED'S CRESTED FLYCATCHER   *Myiárchus tyránnulus*
Fairly common in deciduous woods and desert saguaros in the Southwest. Larger and yellower below, with a longer brighter tail than the similar Ash-throated and Olivaceous flycatchers. Migrants in southern Texas can be distinguished from the Great Crested by their heavy solid black bill and much paler throat and breast. Call much like Great Crested's, but separable.

ASH-THROATED FLYCATCHER   *Myiárchus cineráscens*
Common in western deciduous woods, mesquite, and saguaros. Palest of the *Myiarchus* group, it is decidedly smaller than Great Crested and Wied's and more slender billed. The white throat is a good field mark. Ash-throated is the only *Myiarchus* north of southern Nev. and southwest N. Mex. Call of short sharp notes has quality of Western Kingbird's.

OLIVACEOUS FLYCATCHER   *Myiárchus tubercúlifer*
Fairly common, especially below 6,000' in scrub-oak thickets. Adult shows little it any rusty color in the tail. Barely larger than the phoebe, it is not likely to be confused with Wied's and lacks throat contrast of Ash-throated. Unlike other birds on this page, if often picks insects from foliage while hovering. The other *Myiarchus* flycatchers eat flying insects almost exclusively. Call is a long slightly descending whistle; imitating sound will often bring the bird into view.

nesting in mailbox

MYIARCHUS FLYCATCHERS

GREAT CRESTED FLYCATCHER
L 7"

WIED'S CRESTED FLYCATCHER
L 7¼"

ASH-THROATED FLYCATCHER
L 6½"

OLIVACEOUS FLYCATCHER
L 5¾"

PHOEBES are medium-sized flycatchers that differ from the others in their habit of leisurely jerking their longish tail downward. Phoebes do not have an eye ring. Adults lack conspicuous wingbars, but young may have quite conspicuous ones. Typically they are found near water, although all species, especially Say's, occur and even nest far from water. Also, unlike other flycatchers, phoebes nest under overhanging cliffs or banks, under bridges and eaves, or inside farm buildings. Quite tame and easily seen as they perch in the open, usually less than 20′ off the ground. Eggs, 4-5, are usually plain white.

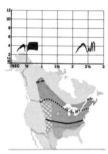

EASTERN PHOEBE
Sayórnis phoébe

Common near farm buildings and bridges. The dark head, solid black bill, and tail-wagging habit provide the best identification in all plumages. Although adult phoebes lack wingbars, immatures have conspicuous buffy ones and can be mistaken for pewees (p. 202); pewees as well as the small *Empidonax* flycatchers always have wingbars and usually a pale lower mandible. Head of Eastern Phoebe is darker than the back; head of pewee is the same shade as the back. Phoebes do not whistle, but say *fee-be* and *fee-blee*, 20-40 times/min.

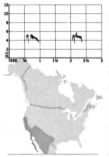

BLACK PHOEBE
Sayórnis nígricans

Common about western farmyards and along streams, generally below 6,000′. This is our only black-breasted flycatcher, and also the only flycatcher with a sharp color break between breast and belly. Its color pattern suggests a junco, but the erect posture, tail-wagging, and flycatching habits do not. As in the other phoebes, the head is darker than the body. A solitary species; usually perches in shady places. Food is almost entirely flying insects. Song is a high thin *ti-wee, ti-wee;* alternate calls descend gradually at the end, 20-30 pairs/min.

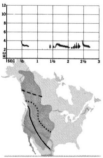

SAY'S PHOEBE
Sayórnis sáya

Common on the plains in the vicinity of ranch buildings, bluffs, and cliffs; prefers dry sunny locations more than the other phoebes. From the front it is recognized by the rusty belly and undertail coverts, from behind by the contrast between the pale back and the black tail, which it frequently wags. The female Vermilion Flycatcher is much the same color, but is decidedly smaller, with a white throat and finely streaked sides. Say's song is a slurred *chu-weer* (30-40/min.) and *pippety-chee*.

shrike flycatcher vireo warbler sparrow

PHOEBES

im.

**EASTERN
PHOEBE**
L 5¾"

BLACK PHOEBE
L 5¾"

Traill's
Flycatcher
for comparison

Eastern Wood
Pewee for
comparison

im.

SAY'S PHOEBE
L 6¼"

● **THE GENUS EMPIDONAX,** the most difficult genus of North American flycatchers, is commonly referred to by its Latin name. Species are frequently impossible to identify in the field. All are small short-tailed flycatchers with eye rings and wingbars. Wingbars of immature are more buffy than adult's. They flip their tails up and then down with rapid jerky motions. Size differences are slight and overlapping. With experience most can be identified on the breeding ground when singing and when habitat provides a clue. The eastern species and some western ones also have distinctive chips.

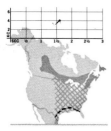

YELLOW-BELLIED FLYCATCHER *Empidonax flavivéntris*
Common on its breeding ground in spruce-fir forests, but rarely seen on migration. The only eastern *Empidonax* with a yellow throat. Acadian has yellow on flanks, especially in the immature, but its throat is white. No other eastern *Empidonax* has a whistled song—an ascending *per-wee* suggestive of Semipalmated Plover's call; also a single leisurely *che-bunk* similar to the oft-repeated *che-bek* of the Least Flycatcher.

ACADIAN FLYCATCHER *Empidonax viréscens*
Common in moist woodlands, especially deciduous floodplain forests, where it usually stays below the canopy. During migration, Acadian and Yellow-bellied Flycatchers can be seen in the same habitat; Acadian can be told by its white throat. Acadian is larger and heavier billed than Least, slightly greener above than Traill's, but not safely distinguishable except by its calls. Song is an explosive *peet-suh*, 2-4 times/min.

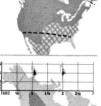

TRAILL'S FLYCATCHER *Empidonax trailli*
Common. Larger than Least, with greater contrast between white throat and olive sides. Browner backed than Acadian, Yellow-bellied, and the western species (p. 200). Songs and call note are distinctive—a whistle superimposed on a buzz. Northern birds in alder swamps sing a 3-syllable *fee-bee-o*; southern birds in dry brush a 2-syllable *fitz-bew*; 12-30/min. May be two species.

LEAST FLYCATCHER *Empidonax minimus*
Common in scrub growth, wood margins, and unsprayed orchards. This smallest eastern *Empidonax* has less contrast between throat and side of breast than the Traill's, and little or no greenish on back. Told by its song, a dry *che-bek,* repeated 50-70/min.

EASTERN *EMPIDONAX* FLYCATCHERS

YELLOW-BELLIED
FLYCATCHER
L 4½"

im.

ail wag

ACADIAN
FLYCATCHER
L 4¾"

TRAILL'S
FLYCATCHER
L 4¾"

LEAST FLYCATCHER
L 4½"

200

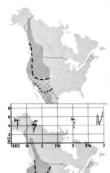

HAMMOND'S FLYCATCHER   *Empidonax hammondi*
Common in firs, spruces, and pines; nests up to 11,000'. Avoids dense forests; prefers openings and edge. On returning to its high exposed perch, it flicks its tail a few times, then sits motionless. Often impossible to tell from Dusky by sight or songs. Note the olive-brown back, gray breast, and pale yellow belly. Song very low pitched, often of 3 parts: *seput*, a burry *pzrrrt*, and *treeip*.

DUSKY FLYCATCHER   *Empidonax oberhólseri*
Common on brushy slopes. Found below 2,000' in Wash., but at 7,000-9,000' in N. Mex. Similar to Hammond's, but has less contrast between breast and belly, and tail is slightly longer. Note that its back is more gray, underparts less yellow. Song low pitched, no particular sequence: *cheepit, chuwee, cheepit, pseet*.

GRAY FLYCATCHER   *Empidonax wrightii*
Fairly common in sagebrush and junipers of the Great Basin. Slightly larger than Hammond's; with distinctly grayer crown, back, and underparts than Hammond's and Dusky. Basal two-thirds of lower mandible is yellowish; little or no yellow on underparts. Song is typically of 2 elements: a vigorous rapid low *churweeoo* and a faint higher *cheeip*.

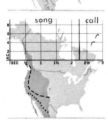

WESTERN FLYCATCHER   *Empidonax difficilis*
Common in moist deciduous on coniferous woods or on mixed slopes with tall trees, where it seeks an inconspicuous perch. The only western *Empidonax* with a yellow throat. Much yellower below than Hammond's, Dusky, or Traill's. Song very high: *pchip, ee, pcheewee*, call, *whee-see*.

BUFF-BREASTED FLYCATCHER   *Empidonax fúlvifrons*
Rare and local on steep canyon slopes with scattered tall pines, small oaks, and shrubby undergrowth, 5,000-8,500'. May be recognized by its small size and bright buff-colored breast, flanks, and belly.

BEARDLESS FLYCATCHER   *Camptóstoma imbérbe*
Rare; in dense low deciduous growth, sea level to 4,000'. Told from kinglets by buffy wingbars and by lack of bold eye ring and crown striping. Behavior and call notes resemble Verdin's (p. 218), but Verdin lacks wingbars. Told from *Empidonax* by its tiny bill, dusky throat and breast. Call, shrill descending *pier pier pier*

WESTERN *EMPIDONAX* FLYCATCHERS

im.

HAMMOND'S FLYCATCHER
L 4½"

GRAY FLYCATCHER
L 4¾"

DUSKY FLYCATCHER
L 4¾"

WESTERN FLYCATCHER
L 5"

BEARDLESS FLYCATCHER
L 3½"

BUFF-BREASTED FLYCATCHER
L 4"

COUES' FLYCATCHER *Contópus pértinax*

Fairly common at 7,000-10,000' on steep pine-oak slopes. This large tropical pewee is separated from other pewees and the *Empidonax* species by its lack of wing-bars and its larger size. Its large head and large bill resemble the Olive-sided Flycatcher's, which, however, always has a vertical white streak separating the olive sides. Note that Coues' has a grayer cast on the sides and breast and a yellow lower mandible. A slight crest gives it a different head shape from other pewees'. It differs also in giving short jerks of its tail. Call is a sad, whistled *ho-say mari-a*.

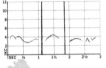

EASTERN WOOD PEWEE *Contópus vírens*

Common in deciduous and mixed woods. Told from Eastern Phoebe (p. 196) by light lower mandible, prominent wingbars, and the lack of contrast between head and back. Told from all *Empidonax* species by lack of eye ring, shorter legs, more deeply notched tail, and longer wings (extending nearly halfway down the tail). Pewees usually do not wag their tails. In fall immature Eastern Phoebes have buffy wingbars, but their breasts are lemon yellow. Song is a plaintive, whistled *pee-oo-wee, pee-oo* (6-11/min.). Twilight song (25-33/min.) also includes a third call, *pee-widdi*.

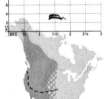

WESTERN WOOD PEWEE *Contópus sordídulus*

Common in deciduous and coniferous woods and in tall trees along streams. Seldom separable in the field from Eastern Wood Pewee except by song. The western species tends to be darker on the sides, breast, lower mandible, and underwing surface. The nasal song (9-12/min.), a descending burry call, is entirely different from Eastern Wood Pewee's and is occasionally given even during fall migration.

song | call

OLIVE-SIDED FLYCATCHER *Nuttallórnis boreális*

Fairly common in northern coniferous woods, locally in aspens, birch, maple, and eucalyptus. Resembles Eastern Phoebe, but the head and bill are much larger and the tail is shorter. The white throat and breast streak contrast with the dark olive sides. White tufts under wings often protrude. Habitually returns to the same perch at the top of a dead snag. Song is a loud melodious whistle, *whip-three-beers*, 6-10/min.; call, *pip-pip-pip*.

OLIVE-SIDED FLYCATCHERS

COUES'
FLYCATCHER
L 6"

im.

EASTERN
WOOD
PEWEE
L 5¼"

im.

WESTERN
WOOD
PEWEE

L 5¼"

im.

OLIVE-SIDED
FLYCATCHER
L 6¼"

LARKS (*Family* Alaudidae), slender-billed birds of large fields with sparse or low vegetation, usually walk; seldom alight in trees or shrubs. If flushed, they return to the ground. They sing in flight, high above the ground; outside the breeding season are seen in loose flocks. Eat insects and small seeds. Nest on the ground; eggs, 3-5.

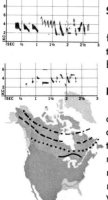

SKYLARK
Alaúda arvénsis

Resident (introduced) on Vancouver Island, B.C. Told from sparrows by slender bill, from pipits by shorter tail and heavier build, from Horned Lark by streaked breast. Long aerial song, sweet liquid notes.

HORNED LARK
Eremóphila alpéstris

Common in large fields, at the shore, and in other open places. Recognize adults by the black breast mark and facial design; immature shows these marks less distinctly. In normal flight, low and slightly undulating, notice the black tail feathers. Feeds in winter in freshly manured fields. Song, weak, high-pitched, is repeated many times (9-13/min.) in a single flight high overhead. Winter call, faint tinkling notes.

SWALLOWS (*Family* Hirundinidae) have long pointed wings and most species have notched or deeply forked tails. All are strong elegant fliers. Legs and bills are short, but mouths are wide for capturing flying insects. Commonly perch on wires. Often seen in large mixed flocks. Most nest in colonies. Eggs, 4-7, are white or spotted.

BARN SWALLOW
Hirúndo rústica

Common near farms, where it builds a mud nest on timbers of barns and other buildings. The only swallow with a deeply forked tail; others with rusty underparts have orange rumps. Song, long and twittering.

CLIFF SWALLOW
Petrochélidon pyrrhonóta

Cliff Swallow

Locally common. Note the orange rump, square tail, broad martin-like wings, and buffy forehead. Soars more than other swallows. The bulb-shaped nests are built under eaves or in the shelter of cliffs, dams, or bridges. Call is a single melodious note.

CAVE SWALLOW
Petrochélidon fúlva

Very local in spring and summer near Carlsbad Caverns, N. Mex., and in south-central Texas. Like Cliff Swallow except for buffy throat. Nests in limestone caves.

Killdeer   nighthawk   swift   lark   Barn Swallow   Cliff Swallow

SKYLARK
L 6¼"

m.
Horned
Lark

HORNED LARK
L 6½"

prairie race

northern race

im.

BARN SWALLOW
L 6"

CLIFF SWALLOW
L 5"

CAVE SWALLOW
head
L 4¾"

Cliff Swallow
at nest

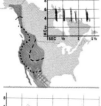

VIOLET-GREEN SWALLOW   *Tachycinéta thalassína*

Common in mountains and locally in towns. Best told by large white flank patches, which nearly meet over the tail. Adult is confused only with the Tree Swallow or White-throated Swift (p. 170). Young are brown above and have a less conspicuous eye patch, but the white flank patch is like the adult's. In flight Violet-green flaps more rapidly than Tree Swallow and glides less. Song is a rapid twitter.

TREE SWALLOW   *Iridoprócne bícolor*

Common nester in tree cavities or nest boxes, especially near water. It is the only green-backed swallow regularly seen in the East. Brown-backed young may be confused in fall and winter with Rough-wing or Bank, but white of flanks extends above tail, the throat is always white, and the breast band is not clean-cut. Flocks of thousands of Tree Swallows gather along the Atlantic Coast in fall. In cold weather they eat bayberries. Song is of separate liquid notes.

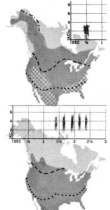

BANK SWALLOW   *Ripária ripária*

Locally common near steep river banks and gravel pits. Told from all other swallows by narrow brown breast band contrasting with white throat. Nests in colonies, burrowing into banks. Call is a low unmusical buzz.

ROUGH-WINGED SWALLOW   *Stelgidópteryx ruficóllis*

Fairly common, especially near water. Brown back and brown throat and breast separate it from all but the much larger martins, which show a purplish tinge on the back and head. Nests, usually single, are in burrows in banks or in small drainpipes at highway bridges. Call is like Bank Swallow's, but separable with practice.

PURPLE MARTIN   *Prógne súbis*

Locally common where proper multicelled nesting boxes or gourds are provided. No other North American swallow is dark all over. Females, young, and first-year males are light-bellied and could be confused with smaller swallows. Watch for purple iridescence on head and top of wings. Note the broad wings and more soaring flight of martins. In late summer flocks of thousands roost together in shade trees of some cities. Song and calls are a distinctive, low-pitched, liquid, rolling twitter.

arn

Cliff

Violet-
green

Tree

Bank

Rough-
wing

Purple
Martin

im.

**VIOLET-GREEN
SWALLOW**
L 4¾"

im.

TREE SWALLOW
L 5"

**ROUGH-
WINGED
SWALLOW**
L 4¾"

ANK SWALLOW
L 4¾"

♂

♀

1st year
♂

**PURPLE
MARTIN**
L 7"

martin house

208

JAYS, MAGPIES, AND CROWS (*Family* Corvidae) are medium to large, gregarious, omnivorous birds with heavy bills. Wings of jays and magpies are short and rounded, reaching only to the base of the long rounded tail. Wings of crows and ravens are long and rounded, extending nearly to the tail tip. Sexes are similar. Often scolded and chased by smaller birds in nesting season. Songs are poor, mostly raucous. Eggs, 3-6 (magpies, 5-9), are colored and speckled.

BLUE JAY — Cyanocitta cristáta

Common in oak and pine woods. The only eastern jay except in central Fla. and Far North, and the only blue-winged jay with white on wings and tail. Conspicuously crested in all plumages. Migrates by day in loose flocks of 5-50. Common call is a loud *jay, jay,* 10-20 pairs/min.

STELLER'S JAY — Cyanocitta stélleri

Common in coniferous forests. The only crested jay in and west of the Rockies; dark crest is always present. Calls are low-pitched, raucous, and varied, often in series of 3. Like the Blue Jay, Steller's imitates hawks expertly.

SCRUB JAY — Aphelócoma coeruléscens

Locally common, especially in scrub oaks, where it skillfully remains out of sight. This crestless jay is best told by its white throat, outlined in blue. The sharp contrast between blue crown and olive-gray back also separates it from the other jays. Flights are short, ending with a sweeping glide. Calls, similar to Steller's, are higher and often in ones or twos.

MEXICAN JAY — Aphelócoma ultramarina

Common in oak and oak-pine forests, 2,000-8,000'. Looks like a faded Scrub Jay with a uniformly gray throat and breast. Calls, less raucous than other jays', are slurred upward; frequently repeated.

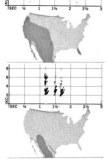

PINYON JAY — Gymnorhinus cyanocéphalus

Short-tailed, crow-like in flight and habits; common in arid regions. Nests in pinyon pines and junipers; is often seen on the ground around sagebrush. In winter it wanders erratically to farmlands. Told from other jays by its uniform steel-blue color, short tail, and long beak. Compare with Mountain Bluebird (p. 234). Has a high mewing call in flight; when perched, a *queh queh queh.*

fisher   jay   Cardinal   magpie   crow   grackle   shrike

BLUE JAY
L 10″

Scrub Jay

STELLER'S JAY
L 11″

SCRUB JAY
L 10″

MEXICAN JAY
L 10¾″

PINYON JAY
L 9″

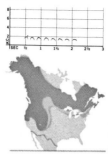

GRAY JAY   *Perisóreus canadénsis*

Locally common in northern coniferous woods, especially about lumber camps, where it is very tame. Adult is recognized by the black and white pattern of head and nape; lacks the black and white wing and tail pattern of Clark's Nutcracker. A Blue Jay flying overhead, with its blue feathers appearing gray against the sky, may be mistaken for a Gray Jay. The dusky juvenal can be identified in midsummer by its short rounded wings, long rounded tail, and lack of a crest. Call is a whistled *wheeoo;* also many other jay-like notes.

GREEN JAY   *Cyanocórax yncas*

Locally common resident in woods along lower Rio Grande west to Laredo, Texas. Normally the only jay in that area, it is unmistakable, with brilliant green body and golden outer tail feathers. Has various jay-like calls, especially a long call followed by 3 short ones.

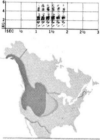

BLACK-BILLED MAGPIE   *Pica pica*

Common and conspicuous in open country near heavy brush or occasional trees that support its huge nest. Long streaming tail and white wing patches characterize magpies. No other North American land birds except Scissor-tailed and Fork-tailed Flycatchers have tails longer than the body. Ranges of this and Yellow-billed do not overlap. Black-billed Magpie wanders erratically in winter. Call is an ascending whine or a rapid series of loud harsh notes.

YELLOW-BILLED MAGPIE   *Pica núttalli*

Common in the farming areas of Calif. valleys and nearby hills. Easily recognized in all plumages by its typical magpie form and its bright yellow bill. Calls are similar to Black-billed Magpie's.

CLARK'S NUTCRACKER   *Nucifraga columbiána*

Locally common in conifers near timberline, where it nests. Flashy white wing and tail patches and the even gray body suggest a stub-tailed Mockingbird, but Mockingbirds are not found at high elevations. Long sharply pointed bill and white face confirm the identification at a distance. Its flight and general body form are crow-like. It wanders irregularly to low country in winter. Call is a drawn-out grating *kr-a-a-a.*

juv.

GRAY JAY
L 10"

GREEN JAY
L 9¾"

**ELLOW-
ILLED
AGPIE**
16"

Black-billed

**BLACK-BILLED
MAGPIE**
L 18"

Black-billed

Yellow-billed

CLARK'S NUTCRACKER
L 11"

● **RAVENS AND CROWS** are large flocking birds recognized by their solid black plumage, their cawing or croaking notes, and their fondness for open country. They post a sentinel while feeding and walk rather than hop. They fly in long lines to and from their communal roosts which may contain hundreds of birds.

COMMON RAVEN   Córvus córax

Common only in the Far North and in the West, especially near heavy timber. Rare and local in the Appalachians. Our largest "songbird," it can be mistaken only for a hawk or for other birds on this page. The heavy bill and the wedge shape of the tail are diagnostic. It flaps less and soars more than crows and is more of a carrion feeder. Call is a low hoarse croak.

WHITE-NECKED RAVEN   Córvus cryptoleúcus

Common in arid open farmland near the Mexican border. The white neck is seldom visible, so in the narrow zone of overlap with the Common Crow one must rely upon the voice. Note that this raven glides more in flight and has a slightly wedge-shaped tail. The raven-like croak is higher pitched than Common Raven's.

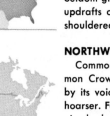

COMMON CROW   Córvus brachyrhýnchos

Well known, easily recognized, and abundant in the East and locally in the West except in arid regions. Told from a distant hawk by its frequent steady flapping. Seldom glides more than 2 or 3 seconds except in strong updrafts or when descending. Barely smaller than Red-shouldered Hawk. Call is a distinctive *caw.*

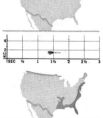

NORTHWESTERN CROW   Córvus caurinus

Common near tidewater. Slightly smaller than Common Crow; with practice can generally be recognized by its voice, which typically is lower pitched and a bit hoarser. Feeds some in croplands, but more easily recognized when scavenging along shorelines (especially on Olympic Peninsula).

FISH CROW   Córvus ossífragus

Locally common. Scavenges on shore; inland feeds with Common Crows. It is slightly smaller and thinner billed. Identified best by its voice, a short nasal *car* which may be confused with the *caw* of a young Common Crow; also a more distinctive *cuh-cuh.*

gfisher   jay   Cardinal   magpie   crow   grackle

shrike

COMMON RAVEN
L 21"

WHITE-NECKED RAVEN
L 17½"

white neck
exposed

crows chasing
Red-tailed Hawk

**COMMON
CROW**
L 17"

kingbirds
attacking crow

FISH CROW
L 15"

**NORTHWESTERN
CROW**
L 14½"

● **CHICKADEES** (*Family* Paridae, part) are black-bibbed, dark-capped acrobats, tame and friendly. Only in the mountains of the Northwest do more than two species occur together. Sexes are similar and young are like adults. Chickadees nest in cavities in trees and nest boxes, and most are easily attracted to feeding stations.

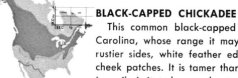

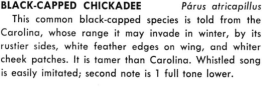

BLACK-CAPPED CHICKADEE   *Párus atricapíllus*
This common black-capped species is told from the Carolina, whose range it may invade in winter, by its rustier sides, white feather edges on wing, and whiter cheek patches. It is tamer than Carolina. Whistled song is easily imitated; second note is 1 full tone lower.

CAROLINA CHICKADEE   *Párus carolinénsis*
Fairly common. Smaller than Black-capped, sides paler. Has narrow gray edging on wing feathers, smaller bib, shorter tail. Non-migratory. Calls are faster than corresponding calls of the Black-capped; whistled song is an octave higher, of 4 or 5 notes, 8-12/min.

MOUNTAIN CHICKADEE   *Párus gámbeli*
Common in conifers. The only chickadee with a white eye stripe; see Bridled Titmouse (p. 216). Nests in mountains, may wander to valleys in winter. Call hoarser, song nearly same as Black-capped's, 8-10/min.

MEXICAN CHICKADEE   *Párus scláteri*
Note the large black throat patch and gray sides. This is the only chickadee found in its limited range in southern Ariz. and N. Mex. Call is low and rasping.

Boreal Chickadee

BOREAL CHICKADEE   *Párus hudsónicus*
Fairly common in northern coniferous forests. Only chickadee with brown cap, back, and sides. No whistled song; *chick-a-dee* call is slow and hoarse.

Chestnut-backed Chickadee

CHESTNUT-BACKED CHICKADEE   *Párus ruféscens*
Common in Pacific lowlands, local in mountains; prefers conifers. Note the bright chestnut back and sides, sooty cap. Has no whistled song; calls are hoarse, rapid.

GRAY-HEADED CHICKADEE   *Párus cínctus*
Larger and paler than Boreal and lacks brown sides. Found in spruce, aspen, and willow at edge of Alaskan and w. Canadian tundra. Call resembles Boreal's.

chickadee   titmouse   nuthatch   creeper   wren

CHICKADEES

CAROLINA
CHICKADEE
L 4¼″

BLACK-CAPPED
CHICKADEE
L 4½″

MOUNTAIN
CHICKADEE
L 4¼″

MEXICAN CHICKADEE
L 4¼″

BOREAL
CHICKADEE
L 4¼″

CHESTNUT-BACKED
CHICKADEE
L 4¼″

GRAY-
HEADED
CHICKADEE
L 4¾″

● **TITMICE** (*Family* Paridae, part) are crested birds that act like chickadees, but are larger. Only Bridled has a bib. Other birds with conspicuous crests are larger, crests usually longer. Sexes are similar. Often flock with chickadees, warblers, and kinglets except in nesting season. Do not migrate. Nest in cavities; 5-8 eggs.

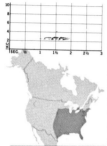

TUFTED TITMOUSE
Párus bícolor

This largest North American titmouse is common in deciduous woodlands of the Southeast, especially along streams. Told from chickadees (with which it usually associates) by the crest, the larger size, and the lack of a black bib. Usually found in flocks of 3-8 birds. No other titmouse occurs east of Texas. Visits feeding stations near woods. Whistled song is 2 notes (or one slurred one) repeated 2 to 4 times, 14-22/min. Other calls are chickadee-like but distinctive.

BLACK-CRESTED TITMOUSE
Párus atricristátus

Common in deciduous woodlands, scrub oaks, and shade trees. Adults with the black crest are unmistakable. Young are very similar to those of other titmice, but there are very few places where more than one species occurs. Young Black-cresteds are told from Tufteds by the whitish forehead (gray in young Tufted) and from young Plain Titmice by the rusty tinge on the flanks. Songs and calls are like those of the Tufted.

PLAIN TITMOUSE
Párus inornátus

This is the common plain gray titmouse of the West. Its range overlaps only with the Bridled. It is told from all chickadees by its white throat. Prefers oaks, also pinyon-juniper. The Plain Titmouse repeats a whistled 2-note song, accented on the first note (its form similar to Tufted Titmouse's). Unlike other titmice, it also has a *chick-a-dee-dee* call that sounds much more like the call of a chickadee than of a titmouse.

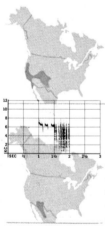

BRIDLED TITMOUSE
Párus wollwéberi

This distinctively marked titmouse is common in stands of Scrub Oak and junipers in the Southwest mountains at elevations of 5,000-7,000' (occasionally to 8,500'). It can be confused only with the uncrested Mountain Chickadee, whose range it overlaps. Young Bridled Titmice always show enough face pattern to separate them from other titmice and chickadees.

chickadee   titmouse   nuthatch   creeper   wren

juv.

TITMICE

**TUFTED
TITMOUSE**
L 5½"

juv.

**BLACK-CRESTED
TITMOUSE**
L 4½"

juv.

**PLAIN
TITMOUSE**
L 5"

juv.

**BRIDLED
TITMOUSE**
L 4½"

Mountain
Chickadee
for comparison

VERDIN AND BUSHTITS (*Family* Paridae, part) are small, slim, long-tailed relatives of chickadees, which they resemble in habits.

VERDIN
Aurìparus flàviceps

Common in mesquite and other desert scrub. Note yellow head and throat, gray body, and chestnut shoulders. Juvenals resemble young bushtits until late Aug., but are told by their shorter tails and high thin whistles.

COMMON BUSHTIT
Psaltrìparus mínimus

Abundant in large flocks in scrub habitats, open woodlands, and residential shrubbery. Told by its nondescript plumage, lack of wingbars, very long tail, and very short bill. Call, high, thin, fussing notes.

BLACK-EARED BUSHTIT
Psaltrìparus melanótis

Rare; usually seen above 5,000'. Male has the black face. Female and immature are told from Common Bushtit by whiter throat, darker flanks, and grayer face. Habitat is similar to Common Bushtit's; call much lower pitched.

WRENTITS (*Family* Chamaeidae) are small, non-migratory, wren-like birds. Weak fliers, they prefer to hop through vegetation.

WRENTIT
Chamaéa fasciáta

Common in dense chaparral, but usually stays out of sight. Told from wrens by the white eye, longer unbarred tail, and short bill. Song is a loud clear monotone.

BULBULS (*Family* Pycnonotidae) are Old World birds with a patch of hairlike feathers on the nape. They lay 2-5 eggs.

RED-WHISKERED BULBUL
Pycnonótus jocósus

Locally common. Liberated August, 1960, south Miami (Kendall), Fla. Told by its black crest and red ear patch and undertail coverts. Sexes are similar.

DIPPERS (*Family* Cinclidae), with their strong legs and special oil glands, are uniquely adapted to a watery habitat. Solitary birds, they build large moss nests near water; lay 3-6 eggs.

DIPPER
Cínclus mexicánus

Fairly common along mountain streams. Told by sooty plumage and short tail. Bobs entire body up and down. Walks under water. Song suggests that of Bewick's Wren.

VERDIN
L 3½"

juv.

♀

♂

**COMMON
BUSHTIT**
L 3½"

Rocky Mt. race

♀

♂

WRENTIT
L 5¼"

**BLACK-EARED
BUSHTIT**
L 3½"

DIPPER
L 5¾"

**RED-
WHISKERED
BULBUL**
L 7"

220

● **NUTHATCHES** (*Family* Sittidae) are large-headed, short-tailed, short-legged, tree-climbing birds that glean insects from the bark of trunks and limbs. Acrobatic, equally at home climbing up, around, or down a trunk head first. Often flock with chickadees and titmice. Wings extend nearly to tip of tail. Sexes differ only slightly. Migrate by day. Flight is jerky. Lay 4-9 eggs in cavities.

WHITE-BREASTED NUTHATCH   *Sitta carolinénsis*
Common in deciduous woodlands. Except for the white throat, resembles chickadee in plumage, though not in shape and actions. Note the white face and solid black cap of male (gray in female). Call, a low *yank-yank*. Song, 8-15 low rapid notes, given 6-15/min.

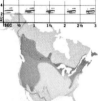

RED-BREASTED NUTHATCH   *Sitta canadénsis*
Common in conifers within its wide range. This is the only nuthatch with white stripe above and black stripe through the eye. Migrates irregularly, often in alternate years. The call is more nasal and less loud than the White-breasted's.

BROWN-HEADED NUTHATCH   *Sitta pusilla*
Occurs in large flocks with chickadees and warblers. This small nuthatch is the only eastern one with a brown cap. Feeds along outer branches and cones of southern pines. Its calls are soft and twittering, with no resemblance to the calls of other eastern nuthatches.

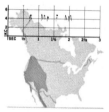

PYGMY NUTHATCH   *Sitta pygmaéa*
Western counterpart of Brown-headed, which it resembles in plumage and habits. Pygmy's cap is grayer. Partial to pines, especially Yellow Pines, at 3,500-10,000'; leaves high elevations in winter. Calls are similar to Brown-headed Nuthatch's.

● **CREEPERS** (*Family* Certhiidae) are short-legged, small, brown-backed birds that creep spirally up trees searching for insects. Bill is decurved. Solitary. Lay 6-7 eggs in oval nest behind loose bark.

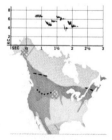

BROWN CREEPER   *Cérthia familiáris*
A common but inconspicuous small woodland bird. The stiff points on its long tail feathers are used as props as it works up and around a trunk. Song is high, faint, rarely heard outside its breeding grounds, 6-12/min. Call is a single very high note.

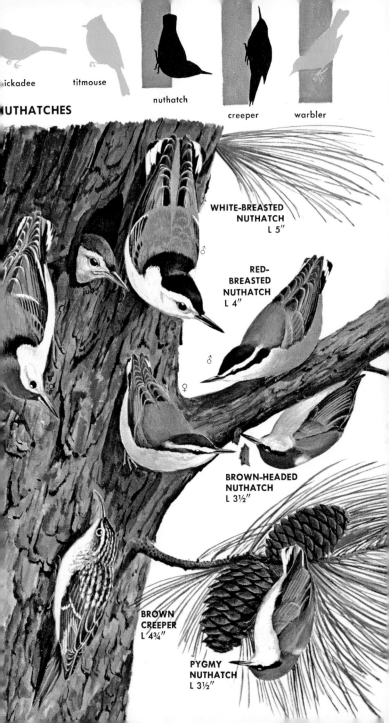

chickadee titmouse nuthatch creeper warbler

NUTHATCHES

WHITE-BREASTED
NUTHATCH
L 5″
♂

juv

♀

RED-
BREASTED
NUTHATCH
L 4″
♂

♀

BROWN-HEADED
NUTHATCH
L 3½″

BROWN
CREEPER
L 4¾″

PYGMY
NUTHATCH
L 3½″

WRENS (*Family* Troglodytidae) are small, restless, brownish birds with finely barred, narrow, rounded tails that are often cocked upward. Females and immatures resemble males. With their long slender bills they feed mainly on insects. Eggs, 4-9, are laid in a cavity or globular nest, usually within 12′ of the ground. Wrens have loud songs and dry scolding rattles.

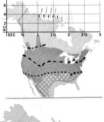

HOUSE WREN *Troglódytes aédon*

Common in shubbery and brush. The plainest wren and the commonest one in the East. Told from marsh wrens by its unstreaked back, from other wrens by the indistinct eye stripe and lack of a dark belly. It is aggressive, driving other birds from nest boxes. Also nests in natural cavities. Song is loud and bubbling.

BROWN-THROATED WREN *Troglódytes brunneicóllis*

Uncommon; resident at 7,000-8,000′ in southeast Ariz. mountains. Song and habits like House Wren's. Note buffy eye stripe, buffy throat and breast.

WINTER WREN *Troglódytes troglódytes*

Sonagram on p. 11   Uncommon; in brush piles or thick undergrowth in moist forests. A very short tail, bobbing action, and dark brown barring on the belly separate this bird from the larger House Wren, which it barely overlaps in range and migration dates. Note the inconspicuous eye stripe. Song is a rapid succession of very high clear notes and trills; it lasts about 5 sec. and is repeated 4-6/min.

BEWICK'S WREN *Thryómanes béwickii*

Common and widespread in the West, uncommon and local in the Appalachians, in farmyards, brush, and fencerows. Distinguished from other wrens by its eye stripe, white underparts, and unstreaked brown back. Note also the characteristic sideways jerking of its long white-fringed tail. The song is higher and thinner than House Wren's, 2-5 notes followed by a trill, 6-12/min.

CAROLINA WREN *Thryóthorus ludoviciánus*

Common in thick underbrush in Southeast except after severe winters. This largest eastern wren is identified by its broad white eye stripe, rufous back, and bright buffy underparts. Prefers moist areas. Song consists of very loud triplets repeated 4-6 times, 8-13/min.

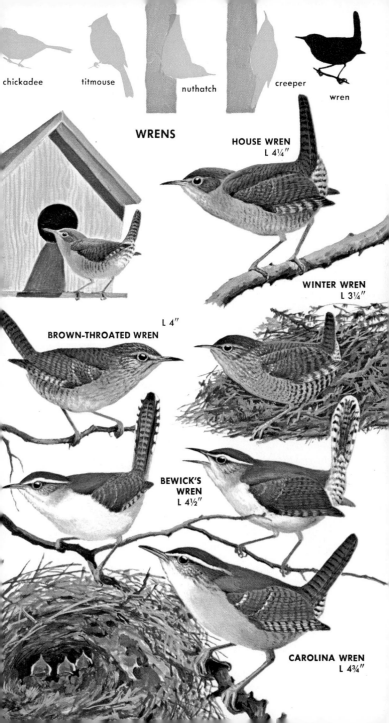

chickadee   titmouse   nuthatch   creeper   wren

WRENS

HOUSE WREN
L 4¼″

WINTER WREN
L 3¼″

L 4″

BROWN-THROATED WREN

BEWICK'S WREN
L 4½″

CAROLINA WREN
L 4¾″

224

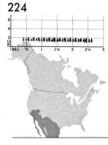

CACTUS WREN — *Campylorhýnchus brunneicapillus*

This common giant wren of the deserts is recognized by its broad white eye stripe and densely spotted breast. The tail is barred and white-tipped, usually not cocked upward. Flies low over the ground. Sage Thrasher (p. 226) is similar but has no white on its back. Generally found below 4,000' among thorny shrubs or large cacti. The song, one of the most familiar sounds of the desert, is an unmusical monotone of low-pitched notes.

ROCK WREN — *Salpinctes obsolétus*

Fairly common in rocky barrens. Best recognized by the light buffy tips on all but the central tail feathers, contrasting with the black subterminal band. Its buffy rump also contrasts with its gray back. No other wren, including the rather similar Bewick's (p. 222), has light streaking on the breast. Bobs as it walks. Song is a remarkable variety of trills, 8-20/min.

CANYON WREN — *Cathérpes mexicánus*

Fairly common in canyons. A clear white throat and breast contrasting with its chestnut-brown belly distinguish this bird at a distance from other cliff-dwelling canyon species. The Rock Wren, similar in size, is grayer and has a much lighter belly. The song is of loud clear descending whistles, slowing at the end.

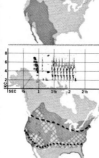

LONG-BILLED MARSH WREN — *Telmatódytes palústris*

Abundant in its limited habitat. Marsh wrens are quickly told from other small wrens by their streaked backs. This species also has a solid rusty cap and a distinct white line over the eye. It is seldom found far from cattails, rushes, sedges, or tall marsh grasses. Song is 1-3 musical rattles on different pitches, often preceded by a faint nighthawk-like buzz, 10-16/min.

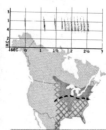

SHORT-BILLED MARSH WREN — *Cistóthorus platénsis*

Scarce and local in sedge meadows. Streaked crown and back, buffy underparts, short slim bill, cocked tail, and obscure buffy stripe over the eye identify this shy wren. It may even sing in hay fields during migration. An irregular migrant, it may arrive in some nesting areas as late as Aug. Song is soft, almost insect-like: about 3 introductory chips followed by an unmusical trill, 5-15/min.

WRENS

CACTUS
WREN
L 6½"

ROCK
WREN
L 4¾"

CANYON WREN
L 4½"

LONG-BILLED
MARSH WREN
L 4"

SHORT-BILLED
MARSH WREN
L 3¾"

226

MOCKINGBIRDS AND THRASHERS (*Family* Mimidae) are long-tailed, short-winged, slender-billed birds that sing loudly from conspicuous perches. Mockingbirds are known for their excellent imitations. Thrashers repeat phrases fewer times, mimic less. All prefer brushy habitats, wood margins, or residential areas. Eggs, 3-6.

MOCKINGBIRD
Mimus polyglóttos

Common and conspicuous throughout southern U.S. At a distance it is best told in flight; white wing patches show clearly, and wingbeats are slow enough to be counted (see shrikes, p. 242). At rest the slender bill and white on wings and tail will clinch identification. Flicks tail from side to side. An expert mimic; it repeats most phrases of songs many times. Sings both while perched and in flight, and more at night than do other mimids.

CATBIRD
Dumetélla carolinénsis

Common near dense cover. No other bird is plain dark gray with rusty undertail coverts. Note the distinct black cap. Catbird, named for its mewing call, often flicks its long tail. Song is of squeaky quality, with little or no repetition; it is a poor imitator.

BROWN THRASHER
Toxóstoma rúfum

Common. The only thrasher east of the Rockies and central Texas. It is heavily streaked below and rich rufous brown above. Most often confused with Wood Thrush (p. 232), which has shorter tail and dark eyes. Most phrases of the song are given twice rather than once (Catbird) or many times (Mockingbird), 25-42/min.

LONG-BILLED THRASHER
Toxóstoma longiróstre

Absence of rufous on head and back seperates this common resident of southern Texas from the Brown in the limited area of range overlap. Bill is longer and blacker. Song more like Catbird's than Brown Thrasher's.

SAGE THRASHER
Oreoscóptes montánus

A common short-tailed desert bird. No streaked thrush nests in the arid country where it occurs, but in winter compare it with other thrashers. Female Red-winged Blackbird, which has a similar call note, lacks tail spots, has dark eyes and a thick bill. Song, given from conspicuous perch or in flight, resembles Brown's, but is more melodious and lacks the pauses between phrases.

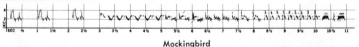

Mockingbird

hrasher thrush bluebird waxwing shrike

MOCKINGBIRD
L 9"

CATBIRD
L 7¾"

BROWN THRASHER
L 10"

im.

LONG-BILLED THRASHER
L 10"

SAGE THRASHER
L 7"

own Thrasher

UNSTREAKED THRASHERS require extreme caution in identification, especially in Ariz., where three or four species may occur together at water holes. These comparatively plain-breasted thrashers of the Southwest are similar in appearance and song. They feed mostly on the ground and nest in mesquite or cacti. Only Bendire's is migratory.

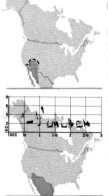

BENDIRE'S THRASHER *Toxóstoma béndirei*
The best field mark of this small thrasher is the short bill, which is nearly straight. Also note the indistinct breast streaks and the lemon-yellow eye. Often nests in cacti. Song is more varied than those of most thrashers, and phrases are not separated.

CURVE-BILLED THRASHER *Toxóstoma curviróstre*
Common in sparse desert brush. Told from Bendire's by the orange or red-orange eye of adult and by the tail, which is blacker than the back. The other thrashers in its range have plain breasts. Song is less varied than those of other thrashers, and phrases are not separated; call, a loud whistled *whit-wheet,* is more distinctive.

CALIFORNIA THRASHER *Toxóstoma redivívum*
Common in chaparral and other brushy habitats. Note the eye stripe and dark brown body, pale rusty below. Only the pale gray Le Conte's overlaps any part of this bird's U.S. range. The California flies less and runs more than other thrashers. When feeding on the ground, this species and the next two hold their tail more erect than the two above. Digs with curved beak rather than scratching with its feet. Song includes a great variety of phrases, many repeated; also is a good imitator.

LE CONTE'S THRASHER *Toxóstoma lecóntei*
Common in certain sagebrush and very open cactus deserts. The dark bill and black eye line contrasting with the pale gray body distinguish it from the darker California and Crissal Thrashers. Song is irregular; phrases not repeated as much as in other thrashers.

CRISSAL THRASHER *Toxóstoma dorsále*
Found in fertile valleys and densely vegetated canyons. The only other thrasher with rusty undertail coverts, the California, does not overlap Crissal's range. Crissal lacks the buffy eye stripe. Flies little. Call *pitchoorip.*

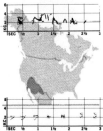

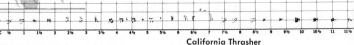

California Thrasher

UNSTREAKED THRASHERS

BENDIRE'S THRASHER
L 8¼"

CURVE-BILLED THRASHER
L 10"

CALIFORNIA THRASHER
L 10"

LE CONTE'S THRASHER
L 9¼"

CRISSAL THRASHER
L 10½"

THRUSHES, SOLITAIRES, AND BLUEBIRDS (*Family* Turdidae) are a varied family of fine singers. Young of all species have spotted breasts. All except bluebirds are often seen standing or running on the ground. They all eat worms, insects, and fruit. Typical thrushes migrate at night; Robins and bluebirds migrate in flocks by day. Bluebirds nest in cavities or bird boxes; other thrushes build nests in crotches of trees or shrubs. The 3-6 eggs are usually greenish-blue, plain, or lightly spotted.

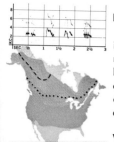

ROBIN
Túrdus migratórius

A common well-known bird often seen on lawns searching for insects and earthworms. In cold weather prefers moist woods or fruit-bearing trees. Adult is orange-breasted (head of female is paler than male's); breast of juvenal is spotted. Builds a nest of grass and mud in orchard trees or shrubs or on buildings. Song is a series of 6-10 whistled phrases of 3 or 4 notes, 5-20/min.

VARIED THRUSH
Ixóreus naévius

Common in moist coniferous woodlands of Pacific Northwest. Only similar species is the Robin, which it resembles in appearance, actions and habits. Note the orange wingbars and eye stripe and the black (male) or gray (female) breast band. Song is an un-Robin-like series of long musical notes on different pitches, each note loudest in the middle.

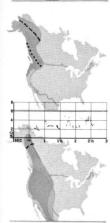

TOWNSEND'S SOLITAIRE
Myadéstes tównsendi

Uncommon; in coniferous forests in summer, woods or brush in winter. Like an erect, short-billed Mockingbird, but with a white eye ring, notched tail, and darker gray breast. Unlike typical thrushes, it flycatches from a conspicuous perch in the open and nests on the ground. At a distance it resembles a Robin. Song is a loud long warble. Call, a single piping note.

BLUETHROAT
Luscínia svécica

Summers in western Alaska; winters in Asia. Female and immature have a pale throat bordered with black as well as rusty base of tail. Tail is often jerked and spread. Song is a rather high-pitched gentle warbling.

WHEATEAR
Oenánthe oenánthe

Common from northern Alaska to Greenland; winters in the Old World. Note long wings, short tail, thin bill, white rump, black face mask, and flashy tail pattern. Female and winter male are brownish.

Robin

bluethroat

waxwing

shrike

starling

juv.

feeding

ROBIN
L 8½″

♂

♀

♂

VARIED THRUSH
L 8″

juv.

TOWNSEND'S SOLITAIRE
L 6¾″

WHEATEAR
L 5½″

♂

BLUETHROAT
L 4¾″

♂

summer

summer

● **SPOTTED-BREASTED THRUSHES** are typically slightly smaller than Robins. Their dark eyes, shorter tails, and spotted breasts distinguish them from thrashers. They prefer the forest understory; eat insects and berries. All are fine singers.

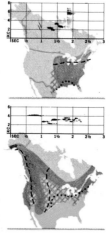

WOOD THRUSH　　　　　　　　　*Hylocichla mustelina*
The common nesting thrush in eastern deciduous forests and suburbs. Told from Brown Thrasher (p. 226) by round breast spots, dark eyes, and short tail; from other thrushes by the large breast spots and rusty head. Song is a series of loud flute-like phrases, each followed by a softer gutteral trill, 11-19/min.

HERMIT THRUSH　　　　　　　　　*Hylocichla guttáta*
Common and widespread in northern woodlands. Our only thrush with the habit of slowly raising its tail several times a minute. Note contrast of rusty tail and olive-brown back. Nearly all winter hylocichlids seen in U.S. are of this species. Song (seldom heard except on breeding ground) is a single high flute-like note followed by a rapid series of rising and falling notes; this pattern repeated in other pitches, 9-16/min.

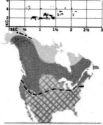

SWAINSON'S THRUSH　　　　　　　*Hylocichla ustuláta*
The best field marks for this common thrush are the buffy face and eye ring; compare carefully with the other thrushes on this page. Breeds like Gray-cheeked Thrush in evergreen forests. Song is a rolling series of rapid flute-like notes, rising up the scale, 8-14/min.

GRAY-CHEEKED THRUSH　　　　　*Hylocichla mínima*
Fairly common. Told from Swainson's by its gray face and absence of a distinct eye ring, from Veery by back color, and from Hermit by olive tail, which is the same color as the back. Song is like Veery's but softer, more nasal, and with a rising inflection at the end.

VEERY　　　　　　　　　　　　*Hylocichla fuscéscens*
Common. Typical plumage is entirely rusty above. Compare with Wood Thrush and Hermit Thrush. Spots on breast are less distinct and more restricted than in the other thrushes. Summers in deciduous forests; prefers wetter habitats than other thrushes. Nests on or very near the ground. The loud song is a rolling series of rapid flute-like notes, dropping down the scale, 8-14/min.

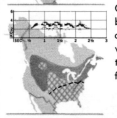

SPOTTED-BREASTED
THRUSHES

juv.

**WOOD
THRUSH
L 7"**

**HERMIT
THRUSH
L 6"**

**SWAINSON'S
THRUSH
L 6¼"**

**GRAY-
CHEEKED
THRUSH
L 6¼"**

dark race
im.

**VEERY
L 6"**

rusty race

234

● **BLUEBIRDS** are found in orchards, farmyards, roadsides, and open
woodlands, often in family groups or small flocks. When perched,
note the hunched shoulders; the bill often points slightly downward.
They sit on conspicuous perches, from which they drop to the ground
for insects. They also catch insects on the wing. In fall and winter
bluebirds add berries to their diet. Nests are in natural cavities or
bird boxes. Calls are given frequently in flight.

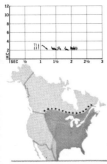

EASTERN BLUEBIRD   *Siália siális*

Only bluebird east of the Great Plains, fairly common along roadsides and in farmyards and abandoned
orchards. The male has a bright, entirely blue back
and rusty throat and breast. The much larger Blue Jay
is always crested and lacks the rusty breast. The Indigo
Bunting and Blue Grosbeak are all-blue below; the Lazuli
Bunting has wingbars. Recognize female and young as
bluebirds by the hunched posture, eye ring, and the
blue in wings and tail. Juvenal is spotted like a typical
thrush; compare with juvenal Western and Mountain.
Song and call are a melodious whistling, 30-40/min.

WESTERN BLUEBIRD   *Siália mexicána*

Fairly common. Adult male can be confused only
with the Eastern Bluebird. The blue throat and rusty
upper back are characteristic of the Western. The female
and juvenal Westerns are browner above than the Eastern Bluebird and have a grayer throat. Like other bluebirds, this species migrates by day, and generally is
found in small flocks outside the nesting season. The
usual song is a 3-fold or double whistle; a simple call
note is typical. A more varied song is heard at dawn.

MOUNTAIN BLUEBIRD   *Siália currucoídes*

Fairly common. The sky-blue plumage of the male is
diagnostic; neither the male nor the female has a rusty
breast. The female can be recognized by its gray breast,
and both sexes have a less hunched posture than the
Eastern and Western Bluebirds. The juvenal is told from
other bluebirds by its posture and by the paler blue of
wings and tail. More than other bluebirds, this species
hovers low over the ground hunting for insects. As its
name implies, it is typical of high elevations, being most
common above 5,000' and wandering in late summer
up to 12,000'. Generally silent except at dawn; song
is a soft warbling whistle.

asher thrush bluebird waxwing shrike starling

BLUEBIRDS

juv. ♀ ♂

**EASTERN
BLUEBIRD
L 5½″**

♂

♀

juv.

**WESTERN
BLUEBIRD
L 5½″**

hovering

♀

♂

**MOUNTAIN
BLUEBIRD
L 6″**

⬤ **GNATCATCHERS AND KINGLETS** (*Family* Sylviidae) comprise a large family of Old World warblers quite unrelated to New World warblers (p. 250). They are small, drab, and thin-billed; they are very active insectivorous birds. They have unspotted young, lay 4-8 spotted or speckled eggs.

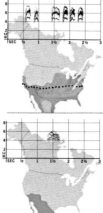

BLUE-GRAY GNATCATCHER — *Polióptila caerúlea*

A common treetop species of moist forests, recognized by its blue back, eye ring, fly-catching habit, and the sideways twitching of its long tail. The next species and the Painted Redstart of the Southwest are the only other small fly-catching birds with a long, dark, white-bordered tail. Its nest, coated with lichens, is easily found before leaves emerge. Its high nasal calls (65-85/min.) are more frequent than its soft vireo-like song.

BLACK-TAILED GNATCATCHER — *Polióptila melanúra*

Fairly common in desert scrub, washes, and ravines. Male is easily told in spring and summer by its black cap. Female, young, and winter male are best told by large amount of black on the underside of the tail.

GOLDEN-CROWNED KINGLET — *Régulus sátrapa*

Common; prefers conifers. Told from other tiny woodland birds by its brightly striped head. Female has a yellow crown. Song of 4 to 8 high notes, followed by a series of rapid, descending, chickadee-like notes, 4-8/min. Common call is 3-5 very high creeper-like notes.

RUBY-CROWNED KINGLET — *Régulus caléndula*

Common. Told from Golden-crown by eye ring, and from vireos or fall warblers by its smaller size, short tail, and kinglet habit of flicking of its wings. Ruby crown of the male may be concealed. Often hovers very briefly; prefers conifers. Gives a low-pitched, short, 2-note scolding call. Song is high and weak at the beginning and end, but has very loud ascending triplets in the middle.

ARCTIC WARBLER — *Phylloscópus boreális*

This drab Old World warbler breeds in western Alaska and winters in southern Asia. Resembles our wood warblers in size and actions and looks like an olive Tennessee. Note the prominent pale eye stripe and the single wingbar. Sexes are alike. Song is a short high trill.

chickadee

gnatcatcher

kinglet

vireo

warbler

side
s

Black-tailed   Blue-gray

**BLUE-GRAY
GNATCATCHER**
L 4″

♂

**BLACK-TAILED
GNATCATCHER**
L 4″

♂

**GOLDEN-
CROWNED
KINGLET**
L 3½″

♀

♂

♀

♂

**RUBY-
CROWNED
KINGLET**
L 3¾″

ARCTIC WARBLER
L 4¼″

PIPITS AND WAGTAILS (*Family* Motacillidae) are sparrow-sized birds with slender warbler-like bills; they have dark tails with white outer feathers. They feed on the ground, walk leisurely, and wag their tails continually. They do not hop. They lay 4-7 eggs in a nest on the ground. Pipits are streak-breasted, feed on insects.

WATER PIPIT
Ánthus spinolétta

Common in flocks during migration and in winter on muddy shores and plowed fields; nests on tundra and in alpine meadows. Characteristic white-edged tail bobs rapidly. Told from sparrows and longspurs by its slender bill, from Sprague's Pipit by the unstreaked back, dark legs, and voice. It rarely perches on trees or posts. Call, *pippit*, is frequently given in flight.

SPRAGUE'S PIPIT
Ánthus sprágueii

Unlike Water Pipit, this bird stays hidden in tall grass and is hard to see. When flushed, it flies a few hundred feet, then drops into heavy cover. Told from Water Pipit by the streaked back and flesh-colored legs. Nests on northern plains, where its weird hissing flight song is delivered high overhead. Its sharp distinctive call, generally a single syllable, is more squeaky than Water Pipit's. Red-throated Pipit (*A. cervínus,* L 5″) is casual in far western Alaska in summer, in California in winter. Told by rosy throat in summer. Winter birds resemble Sprague's, but streaking of breast, back and rump is bold and black, legs yellowish, tail shorter. Call is a hoarse *tseeh*.

WHITE WAGTAIL
Motacilla álba

Rare local breeder in coastal western Alaska and Greenland; winters in Asia and Africa. Adult is told by its black cap, bib, and central tail feathers, and its white face, wing patch, and outer tail feathers. Immature is known by the black necklace, white breast and belly. A black-backed race occurs in the Aleutians. Bobs head like a dove when walking. Call, *tschizzik*.

YELLOW WAGTAIL
Motacilla fláva

Locally common; breeds in arctic willow thickets and on tundra. Adult Yellow Wagtail is told from other arctic ground-walking birds by the long tail with white outer feathers, the white eye stripe, and the bright yellow underparts. Immature Yellow is buffy below. Both wagtails have an undulating flight. Call, *tsweep*.

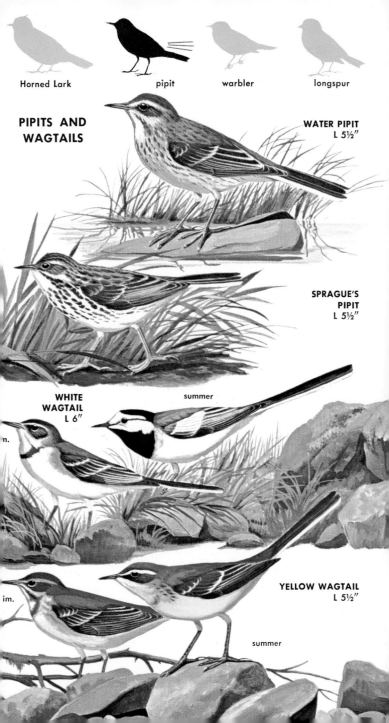

Horned Lark   pipit   warbler   longspur

PIPITS AND WAGTAILS

WATER PIPIT
L 5½"

SPRAGUE'S PIPIT
L 5½"

WHITE WAGTAIL
L 6"

n.

summer

im.

YELLOW WAGTAIL
L 5½"

summer

WAXWINGS (*Family* Bombycillidae), crested, gregarious, fruit-eating birds with black masks and yellow tips to their short tails, are named for the red wax-like spots on the wings of adult. They eat fruits and berries; also catch insects as flycatchers do. In flight their silhouettes and flock formations resemble those of Starlings. They lay 3-5 spotted eggs in a bulky shallow nest in late summer.

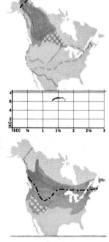

BOHEMIAN WAXWING
Bombycilla gárrulus

Abundant vagrant in large flocks except during the breeding season. Distribution is irregular, especially in eastern portion of winter range; may follow food supply. Recognized as a waxwing by the black mask, long crest, and yellow fringe to the tail. The cinnamon undertail coverts and distinctive yellow, black, and white wing markings identify it as the Bohemian. Females are similar to males. Young can be told by the tinge of cinnamon under the tail. Calls are similar to those of Cedar Waxwing, but recognizable with practice.

CEDAR WAXWING
Bombycilla cedrórum

Irregular in its wanderings, but at times abundant in compact flocks in berry-bearing trees and shrubs. Told from the grayer Bohemian Waxwing by the white undertail coverts, yellowish belly, and lack of conspicuous yellow and white markings on the wings. Sexes are similar. Young are grayer, with indistinct streaking below. Seldom seen alone except when nesting. Call is a very high thin monotone, generally with a slight quaver that distinguishes it from the Brown Creeper's.

SILKY FLYCATCHERS (*Family* Ptilogonatidae) are slim dark fly-catching birds with long pointed erect crests and long tails. Gregarious, they often travel in small flocks. Thickly speckled eggs (2-3) are laid in a shallow loose nest.

PHAINOPEPLA
Phainopépla nitens

Uncommon; in arid scrub, especially near streams. Recognized by its uniform dark color, tall crest, and long tail. In flight the male is best told by the white wing patch contrasting with the all-black body and tail. Female and immature are gray, with paler gray wing patches. Males generally outnumber females. Seen singly, making short flights from a conspicuous perch after insects, or in small flocks (15-20). Also eats small fruits and berries. Flight is slow and graceful. Call, a soft, short whistle.

thrasher   thrush   bluebird   waxwing   shrike

im.

BOHEMIAN WAXWING
L 6¼″

CEDAR WAXWING
L 5¾″

im.

PHAINOPEPLA
L 6¼″

♂

♀

♀

♂

● **SHRIKES** (*Family* Laniidae) are recognized by their heavy hooked beaks, black masks, large white wing patches contrasting with dark wings, and habit of pursuing insects, small birds, and rodents, which they impale on thorn trees or barbed wire. Shrikes perch alone, with tail held nearly horizontal, on treetops or telephone wires in open country. Their flight is low and undulating. Bulky nests with 4-6 eggs are in thorny shrubs or well hidden in small trees.

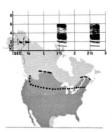

NORTHERN SHRIKE *Lánius excúbitor*

A rare Robin-sized bird that preys on small birds and mammals. Irregular winter visitor to northern states, where it is usually seen in brown immature plumage; immature Loggerheads are gray after Aug. Look for hooked bill, light base to lower mandible, faintly barred sides, and forward end of mask stopping at the bill. May hover over prey or pounce rapidly. Usually silent in winter, but has shrill cries and rattles.

LOGGERHEAD SHRIKE *Lánius ludoviciánus*

Uncommon. Often confused with Mockingbird, as it is gray above and white below, but note its blacker wing, facial mask, heavy hooked bill, and undulating flight with wingbeats too fast to count. Song is a slow chat-like series of calls and trills, often unmusical, 20/min.

● **STARLINGS** (*Family* Sturnidae), introduced and widespread in North America, are short-tailed, dark, and fat-bodied. Gregarious and aggressive, they are especially abundant at roosting sites. Diets are varied. Blue eggs (4-6) are laid in nest hole.

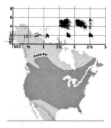

STARLING *Stúrnus vulgáris*

Told from true blackbirds (p. 280-282) by its short tail and, in flight, by its browner wings. The yellow bill is diagnostic in spring and summer; winter plumage is heavily speckled. Spends the night in large communal roosts from late summer until spring. Often an abundant pest in city parks, suburbs, and farms. Song is largely of squeaky notes, but it imitates many bird calls.

CRESTED MYNA *Acridótheres cristatéllus*

Introduced at Vancouver, B.C. Recognized by white wing patches contrasting with black wings and body and by its short crest. Habits and song are like Starling's, but Crested Myna is a much better imitator.

thrasher

thrush

bluebird

waxwing

shrike

im.

NORTHERN SHRIKE
L 8"

juv.

**LOGGERHEAD
SHRIKE**
L 7"

winter

summer

STARLING
L 6"

im. Starling

**CRESTED
MYNA**
L 9"

HONEYCREEPERS (*Family* Coerebidae) are nectar eaters with long, pointed, generally downcurved bills and short tails.

BAHAMA HONEYCREEPER — Coeréba bahaménsis

Casual in southeast Fla. Tame; probes blossoms in gardens. Told by bright yellow rump and breast band, striking face pattern, and white flash in wings and tail.

VIREOS (*Family* Vireonidae) are plain-colored sluggish birds that pick crawling insects from the foliage of shade and forest trees. Some vireos have spectacles (eye rings with a connecting band) and wing-bars; the others have eye stripes and no wingbars. Vireo bills are heavier than those of warblers and have a tiny hook at the end. They are persistent singers. Eggs, 3-5, are laid in nests suspended from crotches of thin branches.

BLACK-CAPPED VIREO — Vireo atricapilla

Locally common in cedar-oak thickets of central and west Texas. No other North American bird has white spectacles on a jet-black head. The female is told by the spectacles, the red eye, the buffy body, and the whitish wingbars. This tiny vireo is barely larger than a kinglet. Song is harsh but varied, suggestive of White-eyed Vireo's (p. 246).

GRAY VIREO — Vireo vicínior

Fairly common in pinyon-juniper and other arid scrub habitats. Drabbest of the wing-barred spectacled vireos; the single wingbar is faint. Easily confused with Bell's (p. 246), but the rump is gray, as is the back; the tail is much longer; and Gray inhabits drier areas. This is the only vireo that nervously twitches its tail as a gnatcatcher does. Song is slurred like Solitary's, but more rapid.

SOLITARY VIREO — Vireo solitárius

Common in mixed northern hardwood-coniferous forests. Its large size, prominent blue-gray or gray head, spectacles, and white throat are diagnostic. The gray-backed plumbeous form occurs in the Rockies. Its large white wingbars separate it from the Gray Vireo where ranges overlap, and the gray rump rules out Bell's and Black-capped Vireos. Rather sluggish and tame. Song consists of slow, slurred, Robin-like phrases, suggestive of Red-eyed Vireo's song (p. 248), but often with only 2 or 3 notes per phrase, 15-30/min.

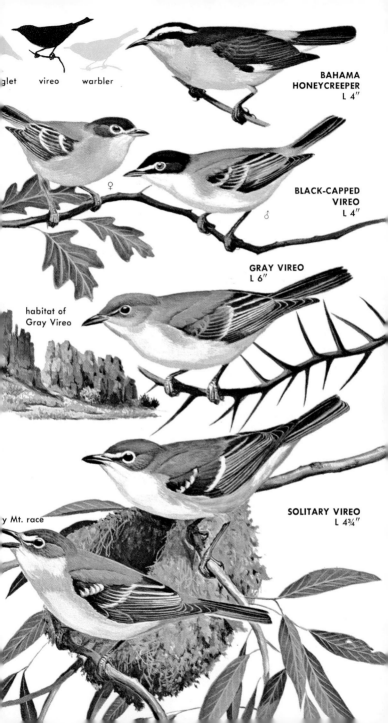

glet   vireo   warbler

BAHAMA HONEYCREEPER
L 4″

♀

BLACK-CAPPED VIREO
L 4″

♂

GRAY VIREO
L 6″

habitat of Gray Vireo

SOLITARY VIREO
L 4¾″

y Mt. race

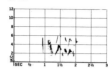

WHITE-EYED VIREO   *Vireo gríseus*

Common in dense moist deciduous thickets, wood margins, and hedgerows. The only vireo with a white iris in the eye (adult only). Its bright yellowish sides distinguish it from all wing-barred vireos except the Solitary and Black-capped, both of which show sharp contrast between head and throat. The dark-eyed immature resembles Bell's Vireo, but has more yellow on the flanks and the spectacles. *Empidonax* flycatchers (pp. 198-200) have dark eyes and light eye rings but no spectacles. The White-eyed Vireo is much easier to hear than see. Song is typically 5-7 loud notes slurred together, including an emphatic chip at the beginning and end, 6-12/min.

BELL'S VIREO   *Vireo béllii*

Common in moist thickets, wood margins, and mesquite. Western counterpart of White-eyed, but eye is always black. Note wingbars and light eye ring. Sexes are alike. Also similar to Gray Vireo (which has longer tail and obscure wingbar) and Hutton's (which has broad wingbars and dull gray throat and breast). Easily told from both by its rapid warbling song, which ends alternately with rising and falling inflection, 10-15/min.

HUTTON'S VIREO   *Vireo húttoni*

Common in evergreen oaks; also found in pines and firs. Told from other vireos by incomplete spectacles that do not join above the eye. Note the two distinct wingbars. Distinguished from Ruby-crowned Kinglet by its calls and its heavier bill, by having spectacles rather than an eye ring, and by its sluggish actions; also by its distinctive song, which is a monotonous repetition of a 2-note phrase accented on the higher note, 60-75/min.

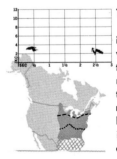

YELLOW-THROATED VIREO   *Vireo flávifrons*

Uncommon; in deciduous forests near water or in clearings; also in shade trees and mixed pine-deciduous woods. The only spectacled vireo with a distinct yellow throat and breast. Female and immature are similar to male. The heavy vireo bill and yellow spectacles distinguish it from the Pine Warbler, which it most closely resembles in plumage. Yellow-throated Vireo has much larger nesting territories than most vireos have. Song is hoarse, a repetition of 4-5 slurred phrases given again and again in about the same order, 19-35/min.

WING-BARRED VIREOS

im.

WHITE-EYED VIREO
L 6″

BELL'S VIREO
L 4¼″

HUTTON'S VIREO
L 4″

by-crowned Kinglet
for comparison

ne Warbler
r comparison

**YELLOW-
THROATED
VIREO**
L 5″

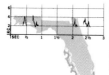

BLACK-WHISKERED VIREO   *Vireo altilóquuu*

Common and easily found in its limited U.S. range i
the Fla. Keys and south Fla. mainland, where it lives i
mangroves and hammocks from Tampa to Everglade
National Park. It is more easily recognized by its mo
notonous song than by its dark "whisker" marks. It
song resembles the Red-eyed Vireo's but with paire
phrases and less variable pitch, 20-32/min.

YELLOW-GREEN VIREO   *Vireo flavoviridi*

Rare in woods and shade trees along the lower Ri
Grande in southern Texas. Told from Red-eyed Viree
by its bright yellow sides and undertail coverts and les
distinct eye stripe. Immature Red-eyed has buffy undertai
coverts. Song closely resembles Red-eyed's.

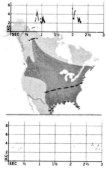

RED-EYED VIREO   *Vireo oliváceu.*

The most abundant bird in eastern deciduous forests
Red iris, prominent eye stripe, and blue-gray cap dis
tinguish this bird from all others except in the limitec
areas where the two preceding vireos occur. Immature
has a brown iris. Song is Robin-like, but phrases are
separated by brief pauses; the song typically continue
for many minutes without a long break, 35-70/min.

PHILADELPHIA VIREO   *Vireo philadélphicu*

Uncommon; in wood margins and deciduous scrub
This small elusive species is often mistaken for a Red-eyec
Vireo when heard and for a warbler when seen. Its yel
lowish breast and unmarked wings tell it from all othe
vireos. The vireo bill should separate it from all warblers
but it may be confused in fall with the Tennessee (p. 256)
which has a greener back, and the Orange-crowned (p
256), which has obscure head markings and yellow un
dertail coverts. Song is like Red-eyed's, but highe
pitched and slower.

WARBLING VIREO   *Vireo gilvu.*

This drab summer resident of tall deciduous shade
trees is more easily detected by its song than by sight
Look for the vireo bill and broad white eye stripe, whict
is not outlined in black. This vireo is so well concealed by
foliage that the male may sing from the nest. Song i
long and warbling, more like a hoarse Purple Finch's than
a vireo's, 6-11/min.

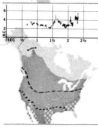

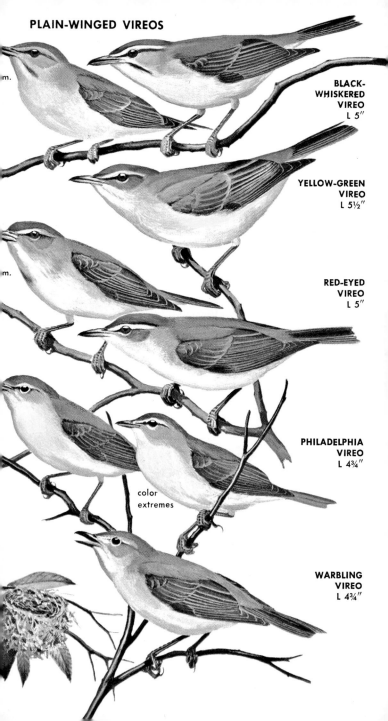

PLAIN-WINGED VIREOS

m.

BLACK-WHISKERED VIREO L 5"

YELLOW-GREEN VIREO L 5½"

m.

RED-EYED VIREO L 5"

PHILADELPHIA VIREO L 4¾"

color extremes

WARBLING VIREO L 4¾"

WOOD WARBLERS (*Family* Parulidae) are small, very active, brightly colored songsters with slender, straight, pointed bills. Males in spring and early summer (through July) are fairly easy to recognize if you can get a good look at them. Since males do the singing, the great majority of birds seen in spring and summer are males in their breeding plumage. Look first for wingbars and characteristic head markings. Note the song patterns, which are diagnostic for most species.

Fall birds and spring females are difficult at first. Most female plumage patterns bear some resemblance to those of spring males, but are duller. For comparisons of fall plumages see pp. 276-277.

Our warblers are divided into 15 genera. Those in the same genus have some similarity in habits as well as in plumage and structure, such as shape and size of bill. The genus *Seiurus* (Ovenbird and waterthrushes), for example, includes birds that teeter like the Spotted Sandpiper and walk on the ground in search of food. The genus *Oporornis* is composed of relatively sluggish warblers that feed on the ground. Members of the genus *Wilsonia* catch insects on the wing.

During the nesting season, warblers remain in or close to their preferred habitats. During migration they gather in mixed flocks, frequently in company with chickadees or titmice. Then nearly all species occur in wood margins, hedgerows, orchards, and wooded swamps, along streams, or even in desert oases. Warblers migrate mainly at

WOOD WARBLERS WITHOUT WINGBARS - SPRING MALES

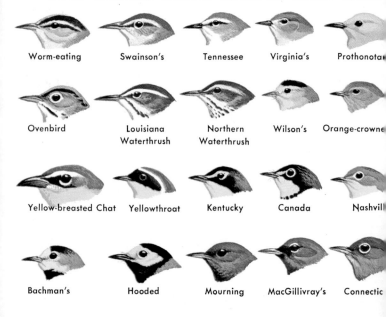

Worm-eating   Swainson's   Tennessee   Virginia's   Prothonotary

Ovenbird   Louisiana Waterthrush   Northern Waterthrush   Wilson's   Orange-crowned

Yellow-breasted Chat   Yellowthroat   Kentucky   Canada   Nashville

Bachman's   Hooded   Mourning   MacGillivray's   Connecticut

night, but watch for them flying within 500' of the treetops in early morning. Most winter in Mexico, Central America, or the West Indies.

The experienced observer can tell more than half the warblers just by their call notes. Learn the most distinctive chips first (such as those of Yellowthroat, Myrtle, Audubon's); then study the chips of the common birds in your area. Some will be impossible to recognize, but awareness of a chip that is different will aid you in fall by drawing attention to the less common species in a mixed flock.

Warblers are almost entirely insectivorous. Most warblers nest on or within 10' of the ground, but some, especially the Parula and some of the genus *Dendroica*, nest high in trees. Eggs, usually 4-5.

WOOD WARBLERS WITH WINGBARS - SPRING MALES

| Cerulean | Myrtle | Chestnut-sided | Blackpoll | Brewster's |

| Parula | Audubon's | Yellow-throated | Grace's | Blackburnian |

| Blue-winged | Yellow | Kirtland's | Olive | Bay-breasted |

| Palm | Pine | Prairie | Magnolia | Cape May |

| Black-throated Blue | Black-throated Gray | Black-and-white | Golden-winged | American Redstart |

| Black-throated Green | Townsend's | Golden-cheeked | Hermit | Red-faced |

⬤ **WOOD WARBLERS** do not warble, but nearly all species have gay
distinctive songs. Many species have 2 or more characteristic song
patterns: frequently a longer song with a distinctive ending and a
shorter one (heard more in late summer) that is harder to recognize.
In general the more distinctive one is illustrated in Sonograms.

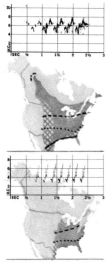

BLACK-AND-WHITE WARBLER   *Mniotilta vária*

Common in deciduous woods. This, the Blackpoll and
the western Black-throated Gray (p. 264) are the only
warblers that are black and white. Neither of the others
has the white streak through the crown, nor do they
share the Black-and-white's habit of feeding primarily
along the trunks and larger branches. In this behavior it
is more like a nuthatch (p. 220), though its posture is
different. The crown is striped in all plumages, but female
and immature lack the black cheeks. Nests on the ground.
Song is a high thin whistle, 4/min.

PROTHONOTARY WARBLER   *Protonotária cítrea*

Common in wooded swamps and along streams.
Golden head and plain blue-gray wings distinguish this
brilliant bird in all plumages. Note also the long dark
bill and white in and under the tail. Seldom seen far from
water. Nests in tree cavity low over water. Song is loud
and clear, of slurred ascending notes, 6-8/min.

SWAINSON'S WARBLER   *Limnóthlypis swainsoni*

Uncommon; in wooded swamps and canebreaks; rare
and very local in rhododendron thickets in mountains. The
plain brown back and wings, solid rusty cap, and plain
underparts are diagnostic. Compare with Worm-eating
and female Black-throated Blue (p. 264); other brown-
backed warblers are heavily streaked below. Note
Swainson's large bill. Sexes and immature are similar.
Inactive and hard to see. Song of about 5 clear slurred
notes is suggestive of Louisiana Waterthrush's, 5-8/min.

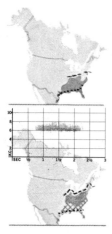

WORM-EATING WARBLER   *Helmitheros vermivorus*

Uncommon; inconspicuous on deciduous slopes. Prominently streaked head, plain brown back and wings,
and plain buffy underparts separate Worm-eating in all
plumages from other warblers. Except for its slender
bill, it resembles a sparrow. Often walks along limbs.
Nests on ground. Song is much like Chipping Sparrow's,
but is higher and generally more rapid, 4-6/min.

flycatcher

kinglet

vireo

warbler

sparrow

BLACK-AND-WHITE WARBLER
L 4½"

♂

Blackpoll for comparison

♀

PROTHONOTARY WARBLER
L 4¾"

♀

♂

SWAINSON'S WARBLER
L 5"

WORM-EATING WARBLER
L 4½"

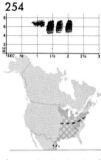

GOLDEN-WINGED WARBLER   *Vermívora chrysóptera*

Uncommon; in gray birch and other young deciduous growth and in abandoned pastures. Male looks like a chickadee, but has a yellow crown and yellow wing patch. Females and immatures always have enough of the male's pattern to identify them. No other warbler has the combination of black or gray throat and yellow wingbars. Song, which is given from a conspicuous perch, is buzzy: typically 1 note followed by 4 on a lower pitch, 6-10/min.

BLUE-WINGED WARBLER   *Vermívora pínus*

Uncommon; in old pastures overgrown with scattered saplings more than 10′ tall. The narrow black eye line and white wingbars are diagnostic. Most of the other bright yellow warblers with unstreaked breasts have no wingbars. Female and immature Yellow Warbler (p. 260), which are common in migration at the same time as the Blue-wing, have much less contrast on the wing and have yellow tail spots. First note of the buzzy song is like Golden-winged's; its other high note is of more vibrant quality.

HYBRIDS occur locally where ranges of the above two species overlap. Several different plumages occur. The typical hybrids are known as Brewster's and Lawrence's. Brewster's, which is more frequently seen, is mostly white below with yellow (or occasionally white) wingbars. Lawrence's, with a black throat and yellow underparts, is extremely rare. Female Golden-wing can be mistaken for Brewster's, male Hooded for Lawrence's. Brewster's may have a pure white breast. Songs of the hybrids may be the same as either parent's or may be a combination of the two songs.

BACHMAN'S WARBLER   *Vermívora báchmanii*

Rarest woodland warbler, very local in moist deciduous woodlands. The yellow forehead and face separate adult male's black crown from the black throat; its eye ring is yellow. There is no white in the tail. In the other plumages yellow or yellowish forehead, gray crown, and white undertail coverts will rule out similar species. Hooded Warbler, which frequents the same habitat, has entirely different song and call notes. Bachman's sings from 20-40′ up in the forest understory, giving distinct notes in a monotone, but with the quality of the alternate song of the Golden-winged Warbler.

EASTERN VERMIVORAS

♀

♂

**GOLDEN-WINGED
WARBLER**
L 4¼″

♀

**BLUE-WINGED
WARBLER**
L 4¼″

♂

BREWSTER'S WARBLER
hybrid   L 4¼″

LAWRENCE'S WARBLER
hybrid L 4¼″

im.

♀

♂

**BACHMAN'S
WARBLER**
L 4¼″

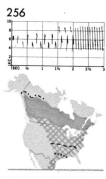

TENNESSEE WARBLER   *Vermívora peregrína*

Common in aspen and spruce woods. The only warbler except Lucy's with completely white underparts in spring. Its slender bill and bright greenish back separate it from sparrows. Similar to vireos (p. 248), but is slimmer and has a very slender bill. Female is washed with olive-green on the crown and yellowish on underparts. In fall the bright greenish back, white undertail coverts, and indistinct wingbar and eye stripe are diagnostic. Stays high in trees in spring. Song, of loud unevenly spaced chips, more rapid at the end, 6-9 songs/min.

ORANGE-CROWNED WARBLER   *Vermívora celáta*

A nondescript warbler common in West; rare in East except along the Gulf Coast in winter. Frequently forages in low trees and brush. The crown patch seldom is visible. Note the absence of white in all plumages. The very faint streaking on the sides of the breast helps distinguish this bird, especially in fall, when it is very similar to Tennessee (which has white or whitish undertail coverts). Most immatures approach the immature Tennessee in color; the one pictured here is the gray extreme. Song is a weak chippy-like trill.

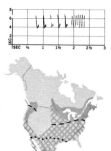

NASHVILLE WARBLER   *Vermívora ruficapílla*

Common in open second-growth deciduous woods and spruce bogs. Only North American warbler with the combination of bluish-gray head, white eye ring, bright yellow throat, and no wingbars. In fall it may be confused with dull Connecticut, Mourning, and MacGillivray's Warblers (p. 272), but these never have the bright yellow chin and throat. Reddish cap of the male is often concealed. The song is in two parts: the first half suggests the Black-and-white's, but notes are separate; the rest (sometimes omitted) is a lower, slow trill, 4-6/min.

OLIVE WARBLER   *Peucédramus taeniátus*

The buffy brown head and black eye stripe of the male are diagnostic. Note also the broad white wingbars and dark wings and tail. The female is the only western warbler with broad wingbars and an unstreaked yellowish breast; note also the yellow triangle around the dusky eye patch. Uncommon; nests high in sugar-pine and fir forests above 8,000'. The song is short; it consists of 2 to 5 pairs of loud, low-pitched slurred notes.

im.

summer

♂

**TENNESSEE
WARBLER**
L 4¼″

**ORANGE-CROWNED
WARBLER**
L 4¼″

gray race

NASHVILLE WARBLER
L 4″

**OLIVE
WARBLER**
L 4½″

♀

♂

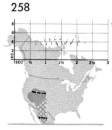

VIRGINIA'S WARBLER — *Vermivora virginiae*

The unmarked gray back and wings distinguish this species and the two below from all except the gray-plumaged Orange-crowned Warbler (p. 256), which has an eye stripe rather than a white eye ring. Virginia's is told from Lucy's and the large Colima by its greenish-yellow rump and undertail coverts. Common in dense scrub at 6,000-9,000'. Song suggests Yellow Warbler's.

COLIMA WARBLER — *Vermivora crissális*

Rare and local in young deciduous oaks and maples at Boot Spring (6,500'), in the Chisos Mts. of western Tex., and in adjacent Mexico. Very similar to Virginia's, but is larger, more robust, and heavier billed. The spring male can be told from Virginia's by the breast, which is mostly gray in Colima. Female and immature Colimas have more orange-yellow rump and undertail coverts, not greenish-yellow, as in Virginia's. Song suggests Chipping Sparrow's, but is much more musical and ends with 1 or 2 separate, sliahtly lower notes.

LUCY'S WARBLER — *Vermivora lúciae*

Common in mesquite, generally nesting in cavities. Similar to the two species above, but can be told in all plumages by the white undertail coverts. The only warbler with a chestnut rump; immature has at least a trace of this color. Song is a series of musical chips (like Colima's) followed by 4-8 slower, slurred notes.

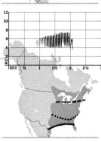

PARULA WARBLER — *Párula americána*

Common at all heights in mature deciduous and coniferous woods, especially river swamps in the Southeast. The only eastern warbler with yellow throat and blue back. Note also the yellow patch on the back, small size, narrow eye ring, and broad white wingbars. Builds its nest of Spanish moss when available. Song is a rising buzzy trill, dropping abruptly at the end; 6-7/min.

OLIVE-BACKED WARBLER — *Párula pitiayúm*

This southern counterpart of the Parula Warbler is an uncommon summer resident in the lower Rio Grande Valley. Resembles Parula in plumage, song, and habits. Male is told by its distinct black mask and very faint rusty breast band. Wingbars of female are smaller than Parula's, and the eye ring is lacking.

im.

VIRGINIA'S WARBLER
L 4¼"

im.

COLIMA WARBLER
L 4¾"

LUCY'S WARBLER
L 4¼"

im.

Lucy's
nest
in
tree
cavity

PARULA WARBLER
L 3¾"

nest

juv.

OLIVE-BACKED WARBLER
L 3¾"

● **GENUS DENDROICA**, a large group (pp. 260-268), includes primaril‹ arboreal warblers with wingbars and tail spots.

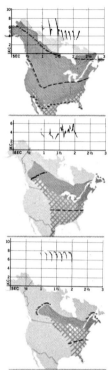

YELLOW WARBLER　　　　　　　*Dendroica petéchi‹*

Common in willow thickets, orchards, and suburba‹ shrubbery. The only yellow-breasted warbler with yellov tail spots; no white on plumage. Note the rusty streaks o‹ the male. Female and young are told from the simila‹ Hooded and Wilson's by the yellow tail spots. Song ha‹ about 7 clear sweet notes, second half slightly faster typically with the final note slurred upward, 4-10/min

MAGNOLIA WARBLER　　　　　　*Dendroica magnóli‹*

Common in moist hemlock and spruce forests. The onl‹ yellow-throated bird with a broad white tail band. Th‹ other dendroicas have spots on fewer tail feathers. Not‹ the bright yellow rump and conspicuous wingbars. Im‹ matures have a distinctive narrow gray breast band. Son‹ is the quality of Yellow Warbler's, but is softer and lim‹ ited to about 5 notes, 5-8/min.

CAPE MAY WARBLER　　　　　　*Dendroica tigrin‹*

Uncommon. Nests in spruce and fir. Yellow rump, ches‹ nut cheeks, and large white wing patch of the male ar‹ diagnostic. The female has a yellow patch back of th‹ ear and a yellow rump. In fall note the finely streake‹ breast, white belly and undertail coverts, olive-gree‹ rump, and small yellowish ear patch (usually visible)‹ Song is a series of very high thin separate slurred notes 8-12/min.

MYRTLE WARBLER　　　　　　*Dendroica coronát‹*

Abundant, especially along the coast during migra‹ tion and in winter. Nests in spruce-fir forests. The onl‹ white-throated, yellow-rumped warbler. Yellow or dul‹ orange side patches are always present. Eats bayberrie‹ and poison ivy berries in cold weather. Song resemble‹ Audubon's; 7-11/min.

AUDUBON'S WARBLER　　　　　*Dendroica aúdubon‹*

This western counterpart of the Myrtle differs chiefl‹ in having a yellow throat (very dull in some females), ‹ little more white in the tail, and, in the male, more white on the wing. Some fall birds are not safely separable Hybridizes with Myrtle Warbler. Song, a soft warble

YELLOW
WARBLER
L 4″

♀ ♂

MAGNOLIA
WARBLER
L 4¼″

im. ♀ ♂

CAPE MAY
WARBLER
L 4¼″

im. ♀ ♀ ♂

MYRTLE
WARBLER
L 4¾″

♀ ♂

im. ♀

AUDUBON'S
WARBLER
L 4¾″

♀ ♂

im. ♂

● **GOLDEN-HEADED WARBLERS** Males of these four are easily recognized by the head patterns and back color. Breeding ranges are separate except in Wash. Females and especially the immatures in fall pose identification problems in the Southwest during migration.

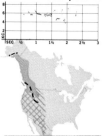

TOWNSEND'S WARBLER — Dendroíca tównsendí

Common in coniferous forests. The dark cheek patch outlined in yellow should tell it in all plumages from all other warblers except female Blackburnian (p. 266), which is strictly eastern. The fall Black-throated Green and Golden-cheeked Warblers have only a suggestion of the dark cheek patch; their throats are white or pale yellow, not bright yellow. Song is slightly wheezy, often with 1 or 2 high clear notes at end.

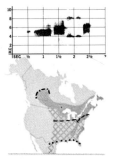

BLACK-THROATED GREEN WARBLER — Dendroíca vírens

Common, nesting high in northern conifers, oaks, and cypresses. The golden cheek is the most distinctive feature; no other eastern warbler has cheeks of this hue. Also note the black throat, white wingbars. Female is similar but duller, with the throat mottled darkly. Some fall birds lack black on the throat, but all have the bold gold triangle on the face. Immature has a yellowish-white throat. Typical song is slow; third and fourth notes are a clear whistle; others are wheezy, 5/min. Second song has 4 similar notes, then 1 lower, 1 higher, all wheezy.

GOLDEN-CHEEKED WARBLER — Dendroíca chrysopária

Uncommon and local; in virgin stands of Mountain Cedar, 25-40' high, on the Edwards Plateau, Texas. Only North American warbler with golden cheeks outlined in black (male). The similar Black-throated Green has olive-green crown and back. In fall, in the narrow zone of overlap with Black-throated Green and Townsend's, note that the males' face patterns are faintly present in all immatures. Song is similar to Black-throated Green's, but lower pitched, all notes wheezy.

HERMIT WARBLER — Dendroíca occidentális

The unique male has an unmarked golden head and a small black bib. Female and immature have the entire face yellow, which distinguishes them from Townsend's; they are told from female and young Black-throated Green by their gray back. Common in tall conifers. Song is like Yellow Warbler's, but is higher.

winter ♂

**TOWNSEND'S
WARBLER**
L 4¼"

♀

♂

im. ♀

**BLACK-
THROATED
GREEN WARBLER**
L 4¼"

im. ♀

♀

♂

im. ♀

**GOLDEN-
CHEEKED
WARBLER**
L 4¼"

♀

♂

**HERMIT
WARBLER**
L 4¼"

im. ♀

♀

♂

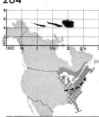

BLACK-THROATED BLUE WARBLER

Dendroica caeruléscens

Common in evergreens (or deciduous undergrowth in the Appalachians). Male is unique at all seasons with its black cheeks and throat and its blue-gray back; immature male is almost identical to adult. Wing patch of the female is frequently small, but is usually present. Note female's eye stripe, lack of streaking, and junco-like chip. Song is slow, slurred, wheezy, and ascending.

BLACK-THROATED GRAY WARBLER

Dendroica nigréscens

Common in dry western deciduous or coniferous scrub. The combination of dark cheek patches and very faintly streaked back distinguishes it in all plumages from the Black-and-white and Blackpoll Warblers. The tiny yellow spot in front of the eye is hard to see, but diagnostic. Song is of slightly wheezy notes; pattern suggests Audubon's.

CERULEAN WARBLER   *Dendroica cerúlea*

Locally common in deciduous woods in river bottoms and near streams. This is our only blue-backed, white-throated warbler. Note the thin black throat band of adult male. Female and young have a dull bluish-gray crown; this, together with a greenish tinge on the back and light buffy underparts, aids in identification. Song is typically of 6-8 buzzy notes, the middle ones rapid.

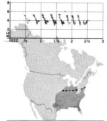

YELLOW-THROATED WARBLER   *Dendroica domínica*

Common, high in pines or sycamores. The yellow throat, white belly, and black and white head are diagnostic. Black streaks border the breast. Song is loud and clear, 4-6/min. Sutton's Warbler *(Dendroica potómac)*, probably a Parula-Yellow-throated hybrid, resembles latter but has a yellow back patch. Very rare; in eastern W. Va. Song like Parula's, given twice.

GRACE'S WARBLER   *Dendroica gráciae*

Locally common in pine-oak forests above 7,000'. The only western warbler with a yellow eye stripe and a yellow throat contrasting with the white lower breast and belly. Adults and immatures are similar. Compare with head pattern of Yellow-throated, Townsend's (p. 262), and Blackburnian (p. 266). Song, a series of musical chips on the same pitch, slightly faster at the end.

THROATED WARBLERS

♀

♂

**BLACK-THROATED
BLUE WARBLER**
L 4½″

im. ♀

♀

♂

**BLACK-THROATED
GRAY WARBLER**
L 4″

♂

**CERULEAN
WARBLER**
L 4″

im.

♂

**YELLOW-
THROATED
WARBLER**
L 4½″

♂

**GRACE'S
WARBLER**
L 4¼″

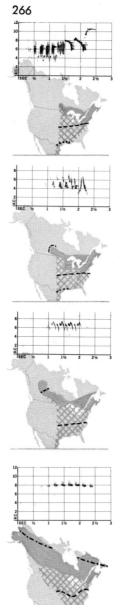

BLACKBURNIAN WARBLER — *Dendroica fúsce*

A treetop warbler common in spruce-fir forests (in oaks in the Appalachians). The bright orange throat and head markings of the male are distinctive. Female and young have similar but paler markings; the only other eastern warblers with this face pattern are the Black-throated Green (p. 262) and Yellow-throated (p. 264). In West compare with female and immature Townsend's (p. 262). Song is very high and thin, often with an exceedingly high-pitched ending, 4-6/min.

CHESTNUT-SIDED WARBLER — *Dendroica pensylvánica*

Common in deciduous brush. The yellowish crown and distinct chestnut side markings identify both male and female in spring. The only other warbler with chestnut sides is the Bay-breasted. Immatures are usually without chestnut marks, but can be told by their bright unstreaked green back, white underparts, and narrow eye ring. Song is very similar to Yellow Warbler's, but typically the next to last note is accented and the final note is slurred downward, 5-8/min. Another song lacks this ending.

BAY-BREASTED WARBLER — *Dendroica castáne*

Fairly common in northern coniferous forests. Chestnut sides, throat, and crown and buffy patch back of head are diagnostic of the spring male. The female is much duller. Fall birds often lack all traces of chestnut and are very similar to fall Blackpolls; the Bay-breasted is more buffy below, especially on the undertail coverts, and has black, not buffy yellow, legs and feet. Song is a very high weak one, like the Cape May's, but notes are more often run together rather than distinct.

BLACKPOLL WARBLER — *Dendroica striáte*

Abundant in coniferous forests. Spring male has distinct black crown, white cheeks, and white throat, which distinguish it from the Black-and-white (p. 252) and Black-throated Gray (p. 264). Streaked back, buff yellow feet and legs, white undertail coverts, and prominent white wingbars on the olive wings are good field marks of the female and all fall birds. This is an abundant migrant in the Atlantic states, often seen on low branches. Song is high, thin, and distinctive; either fast or slow, but of separate notes in a monotone, often loud in the middle, soft at both ends, 4-7/min.

im. ♀

♀

♂

BLACKBURNIAN WARBLER L 4¼"

im. ♀

♀

♂

CHESTNUT-SIDED WARBLER L 4¼"

♂

♀

BAY-BREASTED WARBLER L 4¾"

Bay-sted

♂

BLACKPOLL WARBLER

kpoll

♀

L 4½"

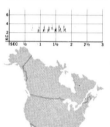

PINE WARBLER   *Dendroica pinu*

Common in mature pines; during migration also i orchards and other deciduous trees. This large plair backed warbler is highly variable in the amount c yellow on the underparts. The female and immature ar hard to recognize when not in pines. The male resemble the Yellow-throated Vireo (p. 246), but that vireo ha prominent "spectacles." The Pine can be told in a plumages by the combination of large white wingbar: unstreaked back, white belly, faint eye stripe, an white tail spots. Immature Blackpoll and Bay-breaste are similar, but are streaked on the back. Song is musical trill, slower than Chipping Sparrow's, 4-7/mir

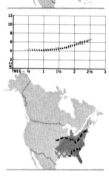

KIRTLAND'S WARBLER   *Dendroica kirtland*

Rare and local, occurring only in large tracts of jac pines, about 6-18' tall. Known to nest only in north central Mich. Believed to winter in the Bahamas; almo: never seen in migration. No other eastern tail-waggin warbler has a gray back. Note the distinct black streak on the gray back and along the yellow sides; also th black lores and white eye ring. Females are similar b: duller. Compare with Magnolia Warbler (p. 260). Nes: on the ground. Very tame. Song is low, loud, 6-9/mi:

PRAIRIE WARBLER   *Dendroica discolc*

Not found on prairies, but common in deciduous sar lings (in heavily logged or burned areas), in young stanc of pine (10'-30' tall), wood margins, and mangroves. Th is the only tail-wagging warbler with an olive back. Th chestnut streaks on the back of the male are some times concealed. Note the eye and cheek marking yellow and black in adult, gray and whitish in the im mature. Streaking of the underparts is restricted to th sides. Song, which may be slow or fast, consists of buzz notes ascending in a chromatic scale, 4-7/min.

PALM WARBLER   *Dendroica palmáru*

Fairly common, nesting on the ground in bogs; in wir ter found at field edges. Bright yellow undertail covert bright olive rump, and tail-wagging habit identify th ground-feeding warbler. The rusty cap should be looke for in spring. Color of breast and belly varies geograpl ically and seasonally from yellow to gray. Song is rapid, slightly buzzy, junco-like trill.

PINE WARBLER
L 4¾″

♀
♂

im. ♀

KIRTLAND'S WARBLER
L 4¾″

♂

♂

im. ♀

♀

PRAIRIE WARBLER
L 4″

im. ♀

yellow race

PALM WARBLER
L 4½″

♂

western race

♂

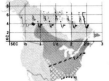
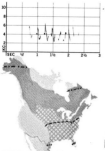

OVENBIRD
Seiúrus aurocapíllus

Common in deciduous woods. Plain olive upperparts, the heavily streaked breast, and black stripes on the crown separate this common ground-walking species from all other warblers. Waterthrushes have a light eye stripe rather than an eye ring. Builds domed nest on ground. Sings from an exposed perch in the understory, a loud and clear *tea-cher* repeated about 10 times, louder and louder, 3-4/min. Flight song is given at dusk.

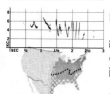

NORTHERN WATERTHRUSH
Seiúrus noveboracénsis

Common in northern bogs. Waterthrushes walk with bobbing motions like Spotted Sandpipers. Note the horizontal posture. Told from Ovenbird by head pattern. Northern is separated from Louisiana by its streaked throat and smaller bill. Northern's eye stripe ranges from cream to yellow. Feeds on ground near water. Song is loud and ringing, 3-8/min.

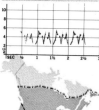

LOUISIANA WATERTHRUSH
Seiúrus motacilla

Uncommon; along rivers and in swamps. Females and immatures are similar to male (see Northern). Song, about 3 slow, high, slurred notes followed by a rapid jumble in descending pitch, 4-12/min.

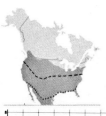

YELLOWTHROAT
Geóthlypis tríchas

Abundant in moist grassy or shrubby areas. Black mask distinguishes the male. Female's chin, throat, and breast are more yellow than its belly, which is dull white. Other similar species have an eye line extending both forward and backward from the eye. Seen near or on the ground. Song, *wichity* or *wichy,* is repeated several times; 4-6/min. Ground-chat (*Chamaéthlypis poliocéphala,* L 5"), a casual visitor to extreme south Texas, is intermediate in size and color between Yellowthroat and Chat. Underparts are all yellow, bill is chat-like. Male has gray head and black lores.

YELLOW-BREASTED CHAT
Ictéria vírens

Fairly common in deciduous thickets. By far the largest warbler. All plumages have white spectacles, plain olive-green upperparts, and a bright yellow breast. Note also the heavy bill. Song is an amazing alternation of caws, whistles, grunts, and rattles, frequently given in flight and even at night; 12-28/min.

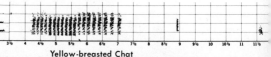

Yellow-breasted Chat

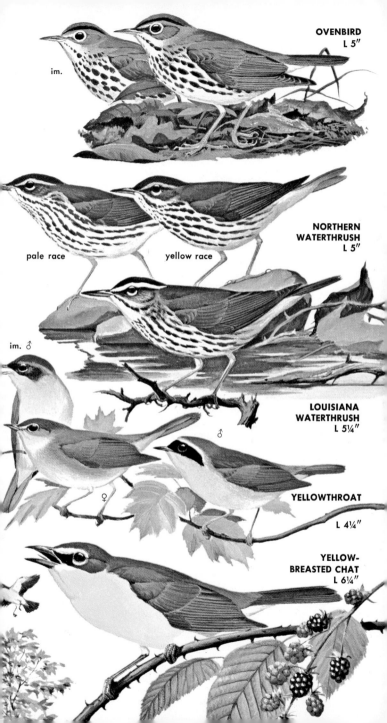

OVENBIRD
L 5″

im.

**NORTHERN
WATERTHRUSH**
L 5″

pale race

yellow race

im. ♂

**LOUISIANA
WATERTHRUSH**
L 5¼″

♂

♀

YELLOWTHROAT

L 4¼″

**YELLOW-
BREASTED CHAT**
L 6¼″

● **OPORORNIS WARBLERS** are sluggish heavy warblers with rather short tails. They stay close to the ground except when singing. All are generally hard to see except the Kentucky, which often sings from an exposed understory perch.

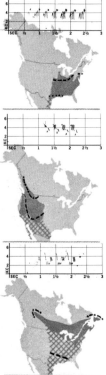

KENTUCKY WARBLER *Oporórnis formósus*

Common; nests on the ground in moist deciduous woods with ample ground vegetation. The black mustache and yellow eye ring are diagnostic, but the black is largely concealed in immature. The male Yellowthroat (p. 270) has a black mask but its belly is white. Song, a loud *churree* repeated 7-10 times, is often mistaken for Carolina Wren's; 4-5/min.

MACGILLIVRAY'S WARBLER *Oporórnis tólmie*

Fairly common in dense thickets. The gray hood and broken eye ring are diagnostic except in fall, when it is impossible to separate this species from the immature and female Mourning Warbler in the limited area where both occur. The larger heavier Connecticut Warbler has a conspicuous complete eye ring in all plumages, and in spring the Mourning Warbler has no eye ring at all. Song is similar to Mourning's, 8-10/min.

MOURNING WARBLER *Oporórnis philadélphia*

Uncommon; in heavy underbrush. This eastern equivalent of MacGillivray's Warbler has the same gray hood and black throat (male), but lacks the eye ring in spring. A broken eye ring in fall confuses the female and immature with the larger duller-colored Connecticut Warbler in the East and with MacGillivray's in the West. Song is short and soft, typically a 5-note warble, 5-8/min.

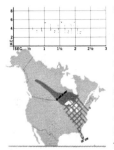

CONNECTICUT WARBLER *Oporórnis ágilis*

Uncommon and local; in moist woodlands with dense understory. The gray hood and conspicuous white eye ring are the best field marks in spring. The yellow undertail coverts of this species are even longer than on the two above. Nashville (p. 256) has a yellow throat and short undertail coverts. In fall the immature Connecticut has a buffy eye ring and a more olive hood. The loud single chip resembles the softer double chip of Magnolia. Song is very loud, clear, and jerky; suggests Yellowthroat's but is accented on last syllable, 5-7/min.

KENTUCKY WARBLER
L 4½″

im. ♀
♀
♂

MACGILLIVRAY'S WARBLER
L 4½″

im. ♀
♂
♀

MOURNING WARBLER
L 4½″

♂
im. ♀
♀

CONNECTICUT WARBLER
L 5″

im. ♀
♂
♀

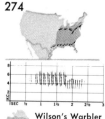

Wilson's Warbler

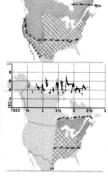

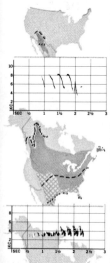

HOODED WARBLER — Wilsónia citrína

Common in moist deciduous woods with abundant undergrowth. Male is recognized by the yellow face and black hood; female by the yellow face pattern and white tail spots, which it displays as it often spreads its tail. Wilson's Warbler lacks tail spots. Nests close to ground. The loud musical chip is distinctive. Song is loud, clear, usually with an accented, slurred ending, 5-9/min.

WILSON'S WARBLER — Wilsónia pusílla

Fairly common in thickets, especially of willows. The male is recognized by the glossy black cap, the female by the plain bright yellow underparts, lack of tail spots, and yellow forehead. Song is of 15-20 musical chips, dropping slightly in pitch toward the end, 5-10/min.

CANADA WARBLER — Wilsónia canadénsis

Common in northern forest underbrush. Black necklace, usually present at least faintly, is the best field mark; if this is lacking in fall, note yellow spectacles and plain gray back, wings, and tail (with greenish cast). Song is rapid and varied, starting with a low chip, 6-8/min.

RED-FACED WARBLER — Cardellína rúbrifrons

Locally common in summer in pine and spruce forests above 6,500' in southeast Ariz. and southwest N. Mex. Unmistakable; immature and female are like male. Jerks tail sideways. Song like Yellow Warbler's, but thinner.

AMERICAN REDSTART — Setóphaga ruticílla

Common in deciduous forest understory, especially near water. An extremely active fly-catching warbler with prominent salmon or yellow patches in its long fanned tail; no other warbler has this wing and tail pattern. Song is a series of similar high notes, with or without a characteristic lower terminal note, 6-13/min.

PAINTED REDSTART — Setóphaga pícta

Common at 5,000-8,000' in oak canyons. Adults and immatures are alike and unmistakable, with red breast, black head and throat, and large white patches on the wings and tail. Catches flying insects as American Redstart does. Song suggests that of Audubon's (p. 260), but is more varied in pitch, 5-7/min.

HOODED WARBLER L 4½"

WILSON'S WARBLER L 4¼"

♂

♀

RED-FACED WARBLER L 4½"

♂

♀

CANADA WARBLER L 4¾"

♂

AMERICAN REDSTART L 4½"

1st yr. ♂

♀

merican edstart

PAINTED REDSTART L 4½"

FALL WARBLERS Immature warblers in dull plumages generally outnumber adults in fall. Most adults are less brilliantly colored than in spring, but adult males (except the Blackpoll and Bay-breasted Warblers) retain distinctive patterns. Immatures, especially females, require careful study.

OLIVE OR YELLOW IMMATURES WITHOUT WINGBARS ...

Seen near grour
no tail spe

Connecticut

♂ Mourning ♀

MacGillivray's

Seen near grour
no tail sp

Canada

Kentucky

♂ Yellowthroat

♀ Yellowthroat

Seen high or lo

tail spots

tail spots

Prothonotary

Hooded

Wilson's

Bl.-thr. Blue

Very slender b
no tail sp

Virginia's

Nashville

Orange-crowned

Tennessee

Below are immature females (and a few immature males) of all warblers except: (1) those restricted to the Southwest, (2) those on pages 252 and 270 that look much like the adults, and (3) American Redstart and the bluish-backed Parula and Cerulean. Note the faint wingbars of the Palm (p. 268) and Tennessee (p. 256).

... WITH WINGBARS AND TAIL SPOTS

...ked   ♂   ♀   Bay-breasted   Blackpoll   Blackburnian

...aked   Pine   Chestnut-sided   Bl.-thr. Gray   Townsend's   Bl.-thr. Green

Yellow   Myrtle   Audubon's   Magnolia   Cape May

...ers   Kirtland's   Prairie   Palm (yellow race)   Palm (western race)

WEAVER FINCHES (*Family* Ploceidae) are a large Old World family represented in North America by two introduced species. Both resemble our native sparrows, but have shorter legs and thicker beaks. They are non-migratory. They nest in bird boxes or on buildings or make bulky, woven grass nests in trees; lay 4-7 eggs.

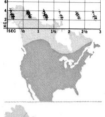

HOUSE SPARROW
Pásser domésticus

Abundant on farms and in cities and suburbs. The male is recognized by his black bib and bill and white cheeks. The female often is confused with other sparrows or female buntings; the unstreaked dingy breast, the bold buffy eye line, and the streaked back are the best field marks. Often seen in flocks. Song is a long series of monotonous musical chirps, 30-120/min.

EUROPEAN TREE SPARROW
Pásser montánus

Locally common around St. Louis, Mo., and nearby Ill. Told in all plumages by bright chestnut crown, black ear and throat patches. Calls like House Sparrow's.

BLACKBIRDS AND ORIOLES (*Family* Icteridae) are medium to large, heavy-billed birds, mainly iridescent black or black with yellow or orange. Some walk on the ground; others are arboreal. The upper ridge of the bill parts the feathers of the forehead. Eggs, 3-6.

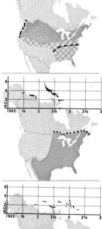

BOBOLINK
Dolichónyx oryzívorus

Locally common in hayfields and in fall migration in large flocks near marshes. Spring male is only North American land bird dark below, light above. Female and fall male resemble large sparrows, but have buffy crown stripes, buffy breast, and narrow pointed tail feathers. Song is long, loud, and bubbling, 5-15/min.

EASTERN MEADOWLARK
Sturnélla mágna

Common in fields and on fences. Adults and immatures known by black V on bright yellow breast, and white outer tail feathers. Gregarious. In flight it alternately flaps and sails. Song, a clear slurred whistle, 5-11/min.

WESTERN MEADOWLARK
Sturnélla neglécta

Common, and similar to Eastern Meadowlark in plumage, habits, and habitat, but yellow of throat extends farther onto cheek. Where both occur together in winter flocks, Western can be told by its paler back and tail. Song is loud and flute-like, 4-8/min.

Song Sparrow

House Sparrow

Starling

oriole

grackle

♂

HOUSE SPARROW
L 5¼"

♂

♂

EUROPEAN TREE SPARROW
L 5"

im.

fall ♂

♀

summer

BOBOLINK
L 6"

♂

hers

WESTERN MEADOW-LARK
L 8½"

E.

EASTERN MEADOW-LARK
L 8½"

YELLOW-HEADED BLACKBIRD
Xanthocéphalus xanthocéphalu

Locally common to abundant in cattail and tule marshes. No other North American bird has yellow head and black body. White wing patch is lacking in female and first-year males. The brownish females are easily overlooked in large flocks of blackbirds. Look for the unstreaked yellowish throat. Song of low rasping notes ends in a long descending buzz, 3-5/min. Call is a distinctive low hoarse croak.

RED-WINGED BLACKBIRD
Agelaius phoeniceu

Abundant in marshes and fields. The red-shouldered male can be confused only with the western Tricolored Blackbird. Females and immature males resemble large sparrows, but are longer billed and more heavily streaked, often with a tinge of red on shoulder or throat. Feed, fly, and roost in huge flocks. Song, a squeaky *kong-ka-ree*, 4-9/min.

TRICOLORED BLACKBIRD
Agelaius tricolo

Common in flocks in cattails or tules. Male is told from Red-winged by the darker red of the shoulders and the white border; female by the solid dark belly and lower back (obscuring the streaking). Song, quite different from Red-winged's, is harsh and unmusical.

RUSTY BLACKBIRD
Eúphagus carolinu

Fairly common in wooded swamps; rarely seen in fields with other blackbirds. Size and shape of Red-winged, but has a slightly longer tail. Adult is told from cowbird, Red-winged, and female Brewer's by its light eyes. Brown eye of young Rusty is yellowish by Oct. Rusty lacks iridescence. Its bill is more slender at base than in other blackbirds. Song is high, squeaky.

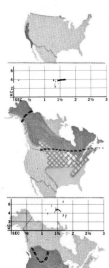

BREWER'S BLACKBIRD
Eúphagus cyanocéphalu

Common around farms, fields, and roadsides, especially in West. Spring male can be told in good light by light eye, purplish sheen on head, and greenish tint on body. Note similarity to both cowbirds (p. 282) and to Common Grackle. Female is told from female Rusty by the dark brown eye and in winter by the absence of rusty wash. Starling (p. 242) is much shorter tailed. Song is a soft hoarse whistle. *Chuck* note resembles Rusty's.

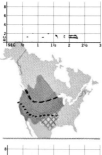

BLACKBIRDS

YELLOW-HEADED BLACKBIRD L 8½″

Yellow-headed

ed-winged ♀

Red-winged ♀

RED-WINGED BLACKBIRD L 7¼″

♀

♂

Rusty

♀

♂

TRICOLORED BLACKBIRD L 7½″

♂

fall

RUSTY BLACKBIRD L 8″

♂

♂

BREWER'S BLACKBIRD L 8″

BOAT-TAILED GRACKLE
Cássidix mexicánus

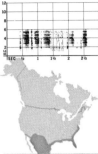

Common on shores and in coastal marshes, along inland lakes and streams (Fla.), and in towns, mesquite, and arid farmlands (Southwest). Male, much larger than female (12″), is about length of Fish Crow (p. 212). Its very long slender V-shaped tail widens at the end. A distant flock can be recognized by the contrast in size and color between males and females. The male has unbarred steel-blue iridescence on back; may have dark eyes in Florida and yellow elsewhere. Female is paler and browner than female Common Grackle. The two species seldom flock together. Song, unlike Common Grackle's, is a distinctive mixture of ascending squeaky calls and gutteral gurgles.

COMMON GRACKLE
Quíscalus quíscula

Abundant on farmland; nests in evergreens if present. Has a long keel-shaped tail, broader at the end. Flocks with cowbirds, Red-wings, and Starlings. The plumage is variable; head iridescence may be green, blue, or violet. Inland and northern males have unbarred bronzy backs; southeastern ones have iridescent bars. Female is smaller; its long keel-shaped tail separates it from other blackbirds. Young have brown eyes until Oct. Song is a loud ascending squeak.

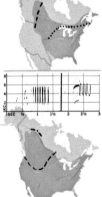

BROWN-HEADED COWBIRD
Molóthrus áter

Common on farmland, often feeding in mixed flocks with Red-wings, Brewer's, or Common Grackles. Note its heavier bill, slighter build, and uptilted tail when it walks. The plain mouse-gray female lays its speckled egg in the nests of other species, especially of warblers, vireos, and sparrows. Young resemble female but have faint breast streaks; they beg noisily for food from their foster parents. Song is a thin whistle, 4-7/min.

BRONZED COWBIRD
Tangávius aéneus

Locally common on farms, where it flocks with other blackbirds. Larger and much longer billed than Brown-headed Cowbird, it is more like Brewer's, but told from it by red eye and shorter bill. In poor light both sexes appear uniformly dark (female not much paler, as in Brown-headed and Brewer's). Both sexes have an inflatable ruff on the hind neck. Song is similar to Brown-headed's, but the notes are shorter and wheezier.

GRACKLES AND COWBIRDS

♂

BOAT-TAILED GRACKLE
L 16"

♀

♂

ronzed race

♀

COMMON GRACKLE
L 10-12"

♂

purple race

wn-headed removing egg

♂

BROWN-HEADED COWBIRD
L 6½"

♀

♀

♂

BRONZED COWBIRD
L 7"

● **ORIOLES** are colorful arboreal icterids, quite different in habits, appearance, habitat preference, and nest structure from their ground-feeding relatives. All North American orioles have the same basic pattern. Adult males and most first-year males are strikingly marked with brilliant breasts, bellies, and rump patches that contrast with black wings, black throats or heads, and in many species black rounded tails. Most females are similar to one another and pose a real problem in the Southwest, where several species occur. All have conspicuous wingbars and very sharply pointed beaks. Female tanagers (inset) have heavier, lighter-colored beaks and notched tails. Orioles migrate primarily by night, but loose bands of 5-10 may sometimes be seen just above the treetops in the early morning.

ORCHARD ORIOLE   *Ícterus spúrius*

Locally common in unsprayed orchards, wood margins, and shade trees. Adult male is our only brick-red oriole and (except in southern Fla.) the only oriole east of the Mississippi River with a solid black tail. First-year male has a well-defined black bib. Female is the only eastern oriole with greenish-yellow rather than orange-yellow breast. Migrates south early (July-Aug.). Song is a medley of melodious whistles and flute-like notes, quite different from the short phrases of the Baltimore, 4-8/min.

BLACK-HEADED ORIOLE   *Ícterus graduacáuda*

Uncommon; in dense woods and thickets. The only North American oriole with combination of black head and yellow (male) or olive-green (female and young) back. All our other adult male orioles have black upper back. Young of both sexes acquire the black head in Aug., but black wings and tail do not appear until the second fall. In spite of its large size, it often goes undetected because of its retiring nature, preference for heavy cover, and infrequent singing. Song is a soft low whistle.

SCOTT'S ORIOLE   *Ícterus parisórum*

Common in joshua trees, yuccas, pinyons, and junipers of Southwest. No other adult male oriole in its range is black and yellow. Note the redstart tail pattern. Black throat of first-year male is poorly defined in contrast to similar Orchard's and Hooded's (p. 286). Female closely resembles these two species, but can be identified by its straight heavy bill and prominently streaked back. Scott's Oriole is 1″ longer than Orchard. Song is suggestive of Western Meadowlark's.

Robin   oriole   tanager   grosbeak

YELLOW ORIOLES

♀   ♂

**ORCHARD ORIOLE
L 6"**

1st year
♂

**BLACK-HEADED
ORIOLE
L 8"**

♂

♂

**SCOTT'S
ORIOLE
L 7"**

...ger for
...arison   1st year ♂

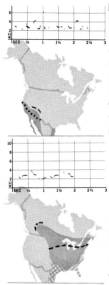

HOODED ORIOLE
Ícterus cucullátus

Common in palm trees where present, otherwise in cottonwoods and other tall trees with shrubby undergrowth, often in residential areas. Golden crown and solid black tail separate the adult male from all but the much larger Lichtenstein's. The bill is more decurved than in other N. A. orioles. Compare first-year male with Scott's and Orchard (p. 284). Female is greener than female and young Baltimore and has a more rounded tail. Song is soft and warbling, interrupted by harsh metallic trills.

BALTIMORE ORIOLE
Ícterus gálbula

Common in tall elms and other shade trees, where its deep pendant nest is a familiar sight. Except near Miami, Fla., this is the only orange oriole east of Mississippi River in spring and summer. Hybridizes with Bullock's; compare head pattern, wingbar, and tail pattern. Adult male Orchard and adult Spotted-breasted have solid black tails. Female is told from Bullock's, which occasionally winters in Southeast, by orange-yellow belly; Orchard has greenish-yellow plumage. Song is clear flute-like whistles, either singly or in a varied series of 4-15.

BULLOCK'S ORIOLE
Ícterus búllockii

Locally common in shade trees from Great Plains west. Black eye stripe, large white wingbar, and tail pattern separate adult male from the Baltimore; other orange orioles have orange crowns. Female resembles Baltimore and Hooded females, but belly is pale gray and back is an unstreaked pale gray. Bullock's tail is much less rounded than Hooded's. Song is similar to Baltimore's but less varied and more repetitious.

LICHTENSTEIN'S ORIOLE
Ícterus guláris

Very rare resident near Brownsville, Texas. Adult is told from the male Hooded by larger size, heavier bill, and broad yellow upper wing patch. Females and young males (after their Aug. molt) are duller, with dark grayish-brown wings and yellowish-olive back. Song is 1 or more separate whistles interrupted by harsh notes.

SPOTTED-BREASTED ORIOLE
Ícterus pectorális

Introduced in eastern Dade Co., Fla. Native to Central America. Female is duller than male, but both are recognized by the black spots on the sides of the breast and the large amount of white on the wing. Song is loud, varied, and more continuous than those of most orioles.

ORANGE ORIOLES

♀

♂

1st year ♂

**HOODED
ORIOLE**
L 7"

1st year ♂

♂

**BALTIMORE
ORIOLE**
L 6½"

♀ ♂

**BULLOCK'S
ORIOLE**
L 7"

♂

**LICHTENSTEIN'S
ORIOLE**
L 8½"

**SPOTTED-BREASTED
ORIOLE**
L 7½"

● **TANAGERS** (*Family* Thraupidae) are brilliant thrush-sized forest bird whose "swollen" beaks are thicker than the slender pointed beaks o orioles and longer than the conical ones of grosbeaks. Males often sing from the topmost branch. Eggs, 3-5.

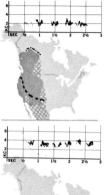

WESTERN TANAGER — *Piránga ludoviciáno*

Fairly common in Douglas fir, spruce, pine, and aspen forests. Note the male's red head or face, yellow body and black wings and tail. Head is yellow-green in fall but wings and tail remain black. Female and young are recognized by their wingbars, pale tanager beak, and notched tail. Song is Robin-like, but hoarse with a pause after each phrase. Call, *pit-ik* or *pit-er-ik*.

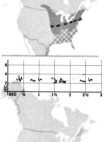

SCARLET TANAGER — *Piránga oliváceo*

Common in deciduous and pine-oak woods. No othe North American bird has red body with black wings and tail. First-year males occasionally are orange instead o red. In July-Aug. greenish feathers gradually replace the red ones, but the black wings are retained. Females are told from female Summer by yellow-green plumage and smaller darker bills. Song of 6 or 7 hoarse continuou Robin-like phrases. Call is a low toneless *keep-back*.

SUMMER TANAGER — *Piránga rúbro*

Common in southern oak-pine woods; in the Southwes in willows and cottonwoods along streams at low eleva tions. Adult male remains red all winter. Young male resembles female. Female is orange-yellow in contras to yellow-green of Scarlet, and has longer yellowish bill Song is Robin-like, not hoarse, as in other tanagers, 3-5, min. Call is a low, rapid, descending *chicky-tucky-tuck*

HEPATIC TANAGER — *Piránga flávo*

Uncommon; in pines and oaks of mountain canyons a 5,000-7,500'. The dark bill and dark cheek distinguish the brick-red male from the Summer Tanager. Female and young are told from Western Tanager and oriole by lack of white wingbars; from Summer Tanager by the dark bill, dark cheek patch, and call, *chuck*, repeated several times. Song is like Scarlet's, but slightly lower

BLUE-GRAY TANAGER — *Thraúpis virens*

Introduced in Miami, Fla., from tropical America. Has silver shoulders, blue wings and tail. Sexes similar.

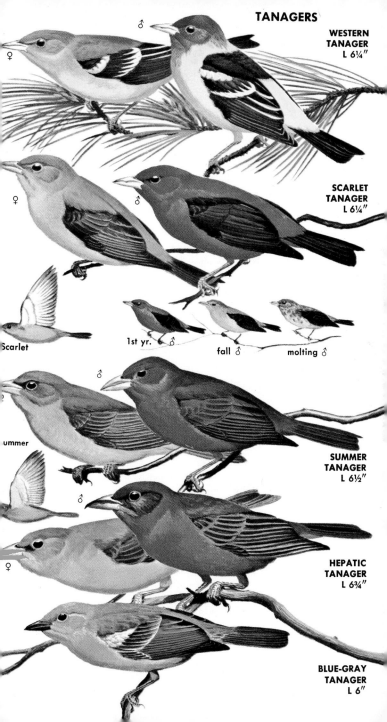

TANAGERS

♀ ♂

WESTERN TANAGER
L 6¼″

♀ ♂

SCARLET TANAGER
L 6¼″

Scarlet

1st yr. ♂   fall ♂   molting ♂

♂

ummer

SUMMER TANAGER
L 6½″

♂

♀

HEPATIC TANAGER
L 6¾″

BLUE-GRAY TANAGER
L 6″

● **GROSBEAKS, FINCHES, SPARROWS, AND BUNTINGS** (*Family Fringillidae*) comprise the largest family of North American birds. The best field mark is the short heavy conical beak, which is well adapted for cracking seeds. Only weaver finches, Bobolinks, and cowbirds have similar beaks. In the grosbeaks, finches, buntings, longspurs, Dickcissel, seedeater, and some of the towhees the males are much brighter than the females and young. In a few of these species (Indigo Bunting, American Goldfinch, Lark Bunting, longspurs) the winter male resembles the female. In the other towhees and the sparrows the sexes are similar at all seasons. Fringillids occupy all land habitats; crossbills and Pine Grosbeaks prefer evergreens; other grosbeaks, deciduous trees. Male buntings, goldfinches and Blue Grosbeaks often perch on wires. Towhees scratch among fallen leaves. In winter the smaller finches prefer weed seeds. Finches and northern grosbeaks often call or sing during their undulating flight. Fringillids occur in flocks during migration and winter. They nest in trees, shrubs, weeds, or on the ground; eggs, 3-6. Northern species are highly migratory or erratic wanderers.

Feeding shelf in winter

CARDINAL   *Richmondéna cardinális*

Common in hedgerows, wood margins, and suburbs. Our only crested bird with a conical beak except in the Southwest, where it is replaced by the Pyrrhuloxia. Bright red male with black throat is unmistakable. Both male and yellow-brown female have pointed crests and thick red (or dusky in immature) beaks. Song is a repetition of loud slurred whistles, 5-10/min.

PYRRHULOXIA   *Pyrrhulóxia sinuáta*

Fairly common in Southwest. Nests to 3,500'. The male is gray above except for its red crest. The female is told by its stubby yellow beak with an abruptly curved upper mandible and its gray back and tail. Usually feeds on the ground and remains near cover. Song and calls often are indistinguishable from Cardinal's.

Pine woods

Wire near hedgerow

Oak woods

Shrubs in Southeast

Weed patch

Brush

♀　♂

CARDINAL
L 7¾"

♀　♂

PYRRHULOXIA
L 7½"

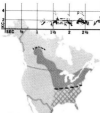

ROSE-BREASTED GROSBEAK   *Pheúcticus ludoviciánus*

Common in northern deciduous woods, suburbs and old orchards. Rose bib of adult male is diagnostic. In flight note the rose wing linings and white wing patch. Female resembles Purple Finch (p. 296), but is much larger, with proportionately heavier beak and broad white or buffy midline through the crown; orange-yellow wing linings are conspicuous in flight. No other grosbeak except female Black-headed has streaked breast or sides. Song is a long continuous Robin-like whistle. Call, a single loud sharp *peek,* is easily recognized.

BLACK-HEADED GROSBEAK

Pheúcticus melanocéphalus

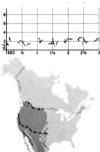

Common in open woodlands, especially deciduous. Male is easily recognized by its orange underparts, black head, and white wing patches. Female is best told from female Rose-breasted by extremely fine streaking on sides, unstreaked breast, and bright lemon-yellow wing linings. Many females have a yellow wash on the belly in spring. Towhees (p. 304) lack head streaks. Song and call are similar to those of the Rose-breasted, with which the Black-headed hybridizes.

EVENING GROSBEAK   *Hesperiphóna vespertína*

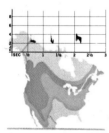

Locally abundant in conifers. Irregular (sometimes common) in southern part of its winter range. Partial to sunflower seeds at feeding stations. Male is told by its large size, huge beak, yellow body, and large white wing patches. Female has yellow on nape and sides. Bill varies from chalky white in winter to pale green in spring. Usually flies in loose flocks; note the undulating flight and the short tail. The most frequent call (at right in Sonagram) is a loud House Sparrow-like chirp.

BLUE GROSBEAK   *Guiráca caerúlea*

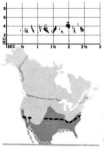

Fairly common, especially in hedgerows. Our only other blue bird with a conical beak is the little Indigo Bunting. Both are commonly seen on roadside wires. Note the much heavier beak, broad rusty wingbars and, in the male, the deeper, almost violet blue of Blue Grosbeak. In poor light either sex could be mistaken for Brown-headed Cowbird (p. 282) if wingbars are not noticed. Seen singly or in family groups; watch for occasional tail-flicking. Song is long, rich, and warbling, more like Purple Finch's than Indigo Bunting's, 4-7/min.

GROSBEAKS

♂

♀

♂

**ROSE-BREASTED
GROSBEAK
L 7¼"**

Rose-
breasted

♂

♀

♂

♀

lack-headed

♂

**BLACK-HEADED
GROSBEAK
L 7¼"**

Evening

♂

♀

♀

**EVENING
GROSBEAK
L 7¼"**

♂

♂

Indigo Bunting
for comparison

♀

**BLUE
GROSBEAK
L 6¼"**

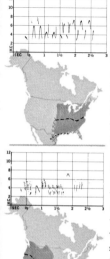

INDIGO BUNTING
Passerína cyánea

Common in hedgerows and wood margins; perches on wires during nesting season. Male resembles Blue Grosbeak (p. 292), but is much smaller, more brilliant, almost iridescent blue, and darker on the crown, with a sparrow-like beak and no wingbars. The plain brown female and immature have a tinge of blue on the tail or the shoulder. The unstreaked back separates them from all sparrows. Note the very fine blurred streaking on sides. Young have faint wingbars. Seen in flocks during migration. The song, especially conspicuous at midday, is long and varied, with most phrases paired, 5-9/min.

LAZULI BUNTING
Passerína amoéna

The common western counterpart of Indigo Bunting, which it resembles in its habits. Found in scattered deciduous or scrub growth, especially near water. The pattern of the male suggests a bluebird (p. 234) except for the wingbars, but the short conical beak and sparrow-sized body are diagnostic. Female and young are told from all sparrows by the plain, unstreaked, brown back; from Indigo Buntings by the broad whitish wingbars. Song, faster than Indigo's, has a few scratchy notes.

VARIED BUNTING
Passerína versícolor

Uncommon and local along the Mexican border in thickets, generally near water. Male looks uniformly dark in poor light, but its purple body, bluish rump, and the bright red head spot leave no doubt when it is well seen. Female and young are similar to Indigo Bunting, but are grayer above and have no trace of faint streaking on the sides. Because of variation in Indigo's plumages, the female Varied is not safely separable in the field outside its normal range. Song resembles Indigo's.

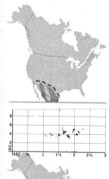

PAINTED BUNTING
Passerína círis

Locally common in thickets, but is hard to see except when the colorful male sings from an exposed perch. No other bird has red underparts and a blue head. The red breast and rump may suggest a Purple Finch (p. 296), but note the difference in color. Female Painted is a brilliant yellow-green, quite unlike the color of any other North American bird except escaped cagebirds. Note its yellowish belly, sparrow-like beak, narrow eye ring, and lack of wingbars. Song is a rather soft warble.

TROPICAL BUNTINGS

juv.

♀

summer ♂

INDIGO BUNTING
L 4½"

molting ♂

♀

♂

LAZULI BUNTING
L 4½"

♂

VARIED BUNTING
L 4½"

♂

PAINTED BUNTING
L 4½"

♀

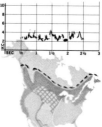

PURPLE FINCH · · · · · · · · · · *Carpódacus purpúreus*

Common in open woodlands and suburbs, often at feeding stations. The wine-colored male is more uniformly colored than other red finches. West of the Great Plains, compare with the brighter-crowned Cassin's. The heavily streaked female and immature resemble a sparrow except for the heavier beak, deeper tail notch, and undulating flight. Female is told from female House Finch by the broad white line back of eye and the larger beak. The sharp musical chip of the Purple, often given in flight is distinctive. Song is a long, loud, rich warbling.

CASSIN'S FINCH · · · · · · · · · · *Carpódacus cássinii*

Fairly common in western conifers. Where its range overlaps Purple or House Finch, Cassin's is often recognized by its call note or song before plumage differences can be studied. Best mark of male Cassin's is the brilliant crown, contrasting with browner hind neck. Female has narrower streaks below than Purple Finch and stronger head markings than House Finch. The wing tips of Cassin's extend nearly to the tip of the tail. Song is more varied than Purple's.

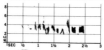

HOUSE FINCH · · · · · · · · · · *Carpódacus mexicánus*

Abundant in bottomlands, canyons, suburbs, and ranches in the West; uncommon but increasing and spreading in East, especially at feeders. Nests to 7,000'. Red of male is much more restricted than in Cassin's or Purple, and sides are streaked with brown. Female is plain-headed, without an eye stripe or dark mustache, and with a smaller bill than Purple or Cassin's. Tail is less notched than in other finches. Call suggests House Sparrow's. The warbling song has a few harsh notes.

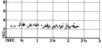

PINE GROSBEAK · · · · · · · · · · *Pinícola enucleátor*

These tame birds are locally common in northern forests of spruce and fir. Male is like a large Purple Finch, but has white wingbars contrasting with its dark wings. The White-winged Crossbill (p. 302) is much smaller and has a shorter tail. The female in poor light looks plain gray except for its wingbars; the olive on the head and rump are characteristic. In flight Pine Grosbeak is told from Evening Grosbeak by its long tail. Feeds on seeds and fruits. Song like low Purple Finch's. Call is 3 high weak whistles suggesting that of Greater Yellowlegs.

RED FINCHES

PURPLE FINCH L 5½"

♂
♀

CASSIN'S FINCH L 6"

♀
♂

HOUSE FINCH L 5¼"

♀
♂

PINE GROSBEAK L 7¾"

♂

1st year ♂

ROSY FINCHES nest in western Arctic and above timberline in western U.S. and Canada. These tame birds spend much time on the ground, gleaning seeds and insects from snowbanks. Rosy wings and rumps of males show both at rest and in flight. Pink of female is visible at close range. No other reddish finches have unmarked dark breasts. Calls are low and hoarse, or high sharp chips.

GRAY-CROWNED ROSY FINCH   *Leucosticte tephrocótis*
Locally common. Nests above 7,000' (in Wash.) and winters in lowlands. Told from the Black Rosy Finch by the brown back and breast and from the Brown-capped by the well-marked gray headband. Some female Gray-crowns with little gray over the eye closely resemble the Brown-capped, but have a browner body.

BLACK ROSY FINCH   *Leucosticte atráta*
Uncommon. The dark blackish-brown breast and back distinguish this bird from other rosy finches.

BROWN-CAPPED ROSY FINCH   *Leucosticte austrális*
Locally common. Breeds above timberline in central and northern Rockies; most easily found on Mt. Evans, Colo. Winters in nearby lowlands. All plumages lack the gray headband, as do some female Gray-crowns.

REDPOLLS wander south irregularly in winter, sometimes in huge flocks. They feed on weed seeds in snow-covered fields; also eat alder and birch catkins. They are sparrow-like but have a black chin spot, red crown, deeply notched tail, and undulating flight.

HOARY REDPOLL   *Acánthis hórnemanni*
Uncommon in Far North; rare in border states and provinces. Occurs with flocks of Common Redpolls, whose geographic color variations make identification of a Hoary risky except under ideal conditions. Examine each redpoll flock for pale-backed birds, then look for the unstreaked rump, which is the Hoary's only reliable field mark. Calls are like Common Redpoll's.

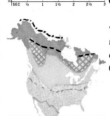

COMMON REDPOLL   *Acánthis flámmea*
Irregularly common in snow-covered weedy fields, where it feeds much like goldfinches. The black chin and red cap are diagnostic. Common call, a hoarse *chit-chit-chit*, given frequently in flight, suggests a White-winged Crossbill's but is more rapid.

finch

ger   grosbeak   bunting sparrow longspur

gray-headed race

**GRAY-CROWNED
ROSY FINCH**
L 6¼"

♂

♀

♂

**BLACK
ROSY
FINCH**
L 6"

♂

♀

**BROWN-CAPPED
ROSY FINCH**
L 6¼"

♀

♂

**HOARY
REDPOLL**
L 5"

♀

♂

♀

♂

juv.

**COMMON
REDPOLL**
L 5"

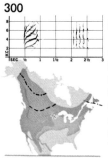

PINE SISKIN
Spinus pinu

Irregularly common in large flocks, especially i conifers. Amount of yellow at the base of the tail an in the wings varies greatly. Note the heavily streake underparts, deeply notched tail, and slender sharp bil Siskins, smaller and slimmer than female Purple Finche (p. 296), are more finely streaked below, and lack th dark patch at the side of the throat. In form and action they resemble goldfinches, with which they often flock Tame. Wheezy voice is diagnostic.

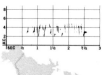

AMERICAN GOLDFINCH
Spinus tristi

Common in flocks in weedy fields, bushes, and roac sides and in seed-bearing trees. Fond of thistles, sur flowers, and dandelions. Our only other bright-yellov bird with black cap and wings is the much larger Eve ning Grosbeak (p. 292). Female and young can be tol by the unstreaked back and breast, stubby finch bil wingbars, notched tail, whitish rump, and roller-coaste flight. Male in winter and immature resemble female Song is long, high, and sweet. Call, *per-chik-o-ree*, i diagnostic of this species. Both are given in flight.

LESSER GOLDFINCH
Spinus psáltri

Common in flocks in same or drier habitats than Amer ican Goldfinch. Breeds to 7,500′. Both a black-backe and a green-backed form occur. Males of both races are easily told from American by the dark rump and, ir flight, by the large white wing patch. Females are tol by lack of contrast between back and rump. Calls mor scratchy than American's.

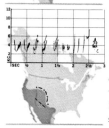

LAWRENCE'S GOLDFINCH
Spinus láwrence

Locally common, but erratic. They flock at times wit other goldfinches but prefer drier habitats. The flesh colored bill of the male contrasts with its black face anc throat at all seasons. Head and back of female are grayer than those of other goldfinches, and the wingbar are yellower. The song is lower pitched than othe goldfinches', with distinctive harsh notes.

EUROPEAN GOLDFINCH
Carduélis carduélis

Introduced and rare; not well established anywhere in North America. Face pattern of adult is distinctive, as is wing pattern of immature. Song suggests American's.

SISKINS AND GOLDFINCHES

PINE SISKIN
L 4¼"

♀

flight pattern

summer ♂

**AMERICAN
GOLDFINCH**
L 4¼"

im.

winter ♂

♀

green-backed
♂

**LESSER
GOLDFINCH**
L 3¾"

black-
backed ♂

summer ♂

♀

juv.

winter
♂

**LAWRENCE'S
GOLDFINCH**
L 4¼"

juv.

**EUROPEAN
GOLDFINCH**
L 4½"

CROSSBILLS are irregular vagrants partial to conifers, in which they may nest at any season. They are especially fond of salt and are very tame. Only when they are close can one notice the crossed bill. Like other northern finches they call frequently in flight.

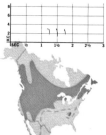

RED CROSSBILL
Lóxia curviróstra

Unpredictable but common at times in pine woods. The brick-red plumage of the adult male is distinctive; immature is more orange-red. All plumages lack wingbars on their blackish wings. The female, heavier billed and distinctly larger than a goldfinch, has a yellow rump like some subadult Purple Finches' but lacks the heavily streaked breast. They cling to pine cones, from which they noisily extract seeds with their peculiar bills. Call, *kip-kip-kip,* is frequently given in flight.

WHITE-WINGED CROSSBILL
Lóxia leucóptera

Less common and more irregular than Red Crossbill. Prefers spruces, pines, and larches. Distinctive pinkish color and broad white wingbars identify the adult male. Similar wingbars are the best mark of the female and young male. Note also the bright rump and fine streaking on flanks. In flight, has a 3- or 4-note call suggesting a redpoll. Song is long and canary-like, 5-10/min.

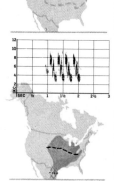

DICKCISSEL
Spiza americána

Abundant in grain fields and weed patches, but variable from year to year. The black-bibbed male sings from a conspicuous perch; the sparrow-like female is seldom noticed. The chestnut wing patch, narrow streak at side of throat, and trace of yellow separate winter Dickcissel from House Sparrow (p. 278). Migrates in enormous flocks. Stray birds reach the Atlantic Coast or winter with sparrows at feeders. Song is 1 or 2 *dick's* followed by a gutteral trill; in flight a low *br-r-r-r-rt.*

WHITE-COLLARED SEEDEATER
Sporóphila torqueóla

Resident, locally common in flocks in weed patches in Rio Grande Delta. This tiny Mexican finch is much smaller than the sparrows with which it flocks. The stubby bill is the best field mark. Seedeaters are slimmer bodied, longer tailed, and much buffier than goldfinches and lack the notched tail. Most birds seen are females or immatures. The loud song has 4 or 5 upward slurred notes followed by fewer notes on a lower pitch.

tanager grosbeak crossbill bunting sparrow longspur

im. ♂ ♀ ♂

RED CROSSBILL
L 5½″

im. ♂ ♀

WHITE-WINGED CROSSBILL
L 5¾″

im. ♂ ♀ ♂

ouse Sparrow
r comparison
♀

DICKCISSEL
L 5¾″

♀ ♂

sub-adult ♂

WHITE-COLLARED SEEDEATER
L 3¾″

TOWHEES, large ground-feeding sparrows with long rounded tails, are often seen scratching for insects and seeds in shrubbery or brush. They hop and kick with both feet together; usually fly close to the ground, pumping their tail. Young are finely streaked below.

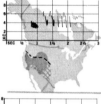

GREEN-TAILED TOWHEE

Chlorúra chlorúra

Fairly common in underbrush or chaparral. They nest up to 9,000'; are found to 11,000' in fall. The clear white chin and greenish tinge of the upperparts separate it from all other towhees. Call is a soft mew.

RUFOUS-SIDED TOWHEE

Pípilo erythrophthálmus

Common in brush, heavy undergrowth, wood margins, and hedgerows. Note the rufous sides, white belly, and long rounded tail with its large white spots. Female differs from the male only in the replacement of black by brown. In the West, the back is spotted with white. Juvenal loses its streaking in early fall. The iris of the adult is red in most of North America but may be white or orange in the Southeast; iris of immature is brown. Call is a slurred *chewink*. Song, *drink-your-tea*, 7-12/ min., the last note trilled, varies geographically.

BROWN TOWHEE

Pipilo fúscus

Common near dense shrubbery in residential areas, and in chaparral and stream borders with shrubby growth. Male and female are alike, colored much like thrashers (p. 226) but distinguished by the conical beak and smaller size. Juvenal is streaked and sparrow-like. Where range overlaps Green-tailed's, note the plain brown back and tail. Female Blue Grosbeak and cowbirds have shorter notched tails. Call is a musical finchlike *peenk*. Song of loud chips and then often a trill.

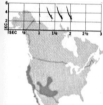

ABERT'S TOWHEE

Pípilo áberti

A common towhee in brushlands of the arid Southwest. More secretive than the Brown Towhee, from which it is told by its black face and buff underparts. Song is similar to Brown's, with the final trill more gutteral.

OLIVE SPARROW

Arremónops rufivirgáta

Locally common in southern Texas in brushy areas. The unstreaked body, olive upperparts, and rounded tail make this bird look more like a Green-tailed Towhee than a sparrow. Note median stripe through crown and lack of a white chin patch. Song is a series of musical chips.

TOWHEES

juv.

GREEN-TAILED TOWHEE L 6¼"

western race

eastern race

♀

juv. ♀

RUFOUS-SIDED TOWHEE L 7¼"

♂ eastern race

white-eyed race

♂

Rocky Mt. race

BROWN TOWHEE L 7¼"

juv.

wn Towhee cific race

ABERT'S TOWHEE L 7¾"

OLIVE SPARROW L 5¾"

● **SPARROWS** are small brown-bodied birds with streaked backs and short conical beaks. Their food, mostly seeds except during the nesting season, is obtained on or near the ground. When not nesting, most are seen in flocks. Each species has its own habitat preferences; these may be diagnostic. Head and breast patterns are most helpful for identification; note also the length and shape of the tail. In most species females are very similar to males. Heads of adult males of most species are shown on this spread. The juncos and longspurs are represented by one head each; the very local Cape Sable Sparrow is omitted, as are the striking Lark Bunting, the Snow Bunting, the towhees and the Olive Sparrow. Immatures of some species are much duller, especially those species with black or rufous on the head. Songs and chips of sparrows are often more easily distinguished than are their plumages. See pages 308-324 for further details.

STREAKED BREASTS

| Vesper | Song | Lincoln's | Savannah |

| Le Conte's | Sharp-tailed | Henslow's | Baird's |

| Purple Finch for comparison | Seaside | Fox | Sage |

UNSTREAKED BREASTS

 Slate-colored Junco

 Black-chinned

 Black-throated

 Lapland Longspur

 White-crowned

 White-throated

 Golden-crowned

 Harris'

 Tree

 Field

 Chipping

 Swamp

Brewer's

Clay-colored

Grasshopper

 Rufous-crowned

 Lark

 Rufous-winged

 Cassin's

Bachman's

308

SAVANNAH SPARROW   *Passérculus sandwichénsis*

Common in large fields with short or sparse grass or weeds. The heavily streaked breast without a central spot and the short notched tail are characteristic. The yellow lores, when present, are also a good field mark. Extremes of geographic variation are illustrated. Savannah runs and hops, rarely walks. When flushed, it flies for a short distance and usually returns to the ground. The song consists of 2-6 faint musical chips followed by 1 or 2 thin trills, 4-8/min.

IPSWICH SPARROW   *Passérculus prínceps*

Rare. Nests only on Sable Island, N.S.; winters in coastal dunes from Mass. to Ga. Larger and paler than eastern races of Savannah, but both dark and medium races of Savannah winter in the range of Ipswich. Note the difference in size as well as color. Walks or runs, rarely hops. Calls and songs are like Savannah's.

GRASSHOPPER SPARROW   *Ammódramus savannárum*

Common in hayfields and weedy fallow fields. The unstreaked buffy breast is characteristic of adult. At close range note the yellow at bend of the wing, the yellow lores, and the unique back color. The tail is very short and narrow. Sings from a tall weed or utility line. When flushed, the Grasshopper flies a short distance, then descends suddenly to the ground and disappears. The relatively large flat-topped head is thrown far back when singing. The song is grasshopper-like: 2 or 3 *ticks,* then an insect-like trill, 4-8/min.

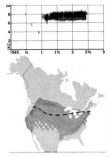

BAIRD'S SPARROW   *Ammódramus bairdii*

Uncommon. The broad orange-brown median stripe through the crown separates this bird from the solid-capped Sharp-tail, the white-striped Le Conte's, and the faintly striped Savannah. Note also the finely streaked breast band. Song is 3 short ticks followed by a musical trill. 5-9/min.

HENSLOW'S SPARROW   *Passerhérbulus hénslowii*

Rare and local in broomsedge fields. No other sparrow has an olive head that contrasts strongly with a brown back. This large-headed short-tailed bird sings its insignificant song from such a low perch that often it is not visible. Song is ventriloqual, an unmusical *ssllick.*

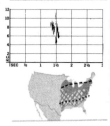

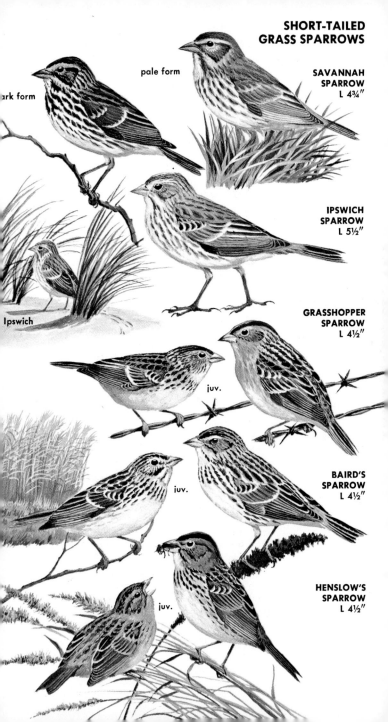

SHORT-TAILED GRASS SPARROWS

pale form

dark form

SAVANNAH
SPARROW
L 4¾"

Ipswich

IPSWICH
SPARROW
L 5½"

GRASSHOPPER
SPARROW
L 4½"

juv.

BAIRD'S
SPARROW
L 4½"

juv.

HENSLOW'S
SPARROW
L 4½"

juv.

LE CONTE'S SPARROW *Passerhérbulus caudacútus*

Common in tall marsh grass in summer, rare in dry fields in winter. Broad purplish collar, bright orange eye stripe, and white stripe through crown distinguish this sparrow from all others. No other sparrow except Sharptail and immature Swamp has the combination of a clear buffy breast and finely streaked sides. Most easily recognized by its insect-like song, *tickity-tshshshsh-tick.*

SHARP-TAILED SPARROW *Ammospiza caudacúta*

Common in short grass salt marshes and fresh marshes. The broad orange triangle on the face is diagnostic. Note the unstreaked crown. Sharp-tails spend most of their time on the wet ground. If flushed they fly weakly for a short distance, then drop back into the marsh. In flight, they appear smaller and browner than the Seaside Sparrows, with which they often associate. Song is a high faint trill preceded by almost inaudible chips.

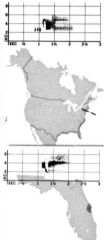

SEASIDE SPARROW *Ammospiza marítima*

Common in short grass tidal marshes with scattered shrubs. Seaside Sparrow is recognized by its dark gray head and body, very long bill, and the yellow line before the eye. Its tail is short and narrow for the size of the bird. Like the Sharp-tailed, when flushed it flies short distances and drops back in the marsh. It eats fewer seeds and more insects and crustaceans than other sparrows. Call is a low *chuck;* song is like a distant Redwinged Blackbird's.

DUSKY SEASIDE SPARROW *Ammospiza nigréscens*

Uncommon; resident locally in salt marshes of eastern Orange and northern Brevard Cos. (Merritt Island area), Fla. This blackest of the seasides is the only one in its range. Recognized by the heavy black streakings on its breast and back. Habits and song like Seaside's.

CAPE SABLE SPARROW *Ammospiza mirábilis*

Rare and very local resident; known only in brackish marshes of southwest Fla. (Ochopee marshes to Shark River basin). Destruction of marshes by hurricanes threatens its existence. It is the only seaside sparrow in southwest Fla. Note the greenish tinge on back and the more distinct streaking below, contrasting with the white background color. Song is similar to other seasides'.

MARSH SPARROWS

juv.

LE CONTE'S
SPARROW
L 4¼"

d race

northeastern race

eastern
race

SHARP-TAILED
SPARROW
L 5"

Sharp-tailed
Sparrow im.

juv.

SEASIDE
SPARROW
L 5½"

DUSKY SEASIDE
SPARROW
L 5½"

CAPE SABLE
SPARROW
L 5½"

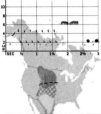

LARK BUNTING — *Calamospíza melanócorys*

Common on or near the ground in short grass prairie, irregular near margins of its range. Spring and summer male can be confused only with Bobolink (p. 278). Heads of female and winter male resemble female Purple Finch's. Note the broad white wingbars, rounded tail, white tips to tail feathers, and crisp streaking of the underparts. Gregarious. Song, often given in flight, is long and varied, with trills and repeated single notes.

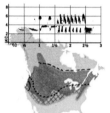

VESPER SPARROW — *Pooécetes gramíneus*

Fairly common in meadows, pastures, and hay and grain fields. Told from all other brown sparrows by white outer feathers of its notched tail. Note the narrow eye ring and chestnut shoulder. Lark Sparrow has white around the tip of its rounded tail. Pipits have white outer tail feathers but warbler-like bills, and are more often seen in dense flocks. Song suggests Song Sparrow's but is recognized by 2 longer, slurred, introductory notes.

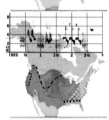

LARK SPARROW — *Chondéstes grámmacus*

Fairly common in West (local east of Mississippi River) in dry fields near brush or trees. Told by the rounded white-tipped tail, black breast spot, and chestnut head markings. Immature lacks breast spot but has white tail margin and dull face pattern. Song is melodious notes and trills, interrupted by unmusical buzzes, 4-10/min.

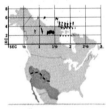

BLACK-THROATED SPARROW — *Amphispíza bilineáta*

Common desert bird of cactus, sage, and mesquite. Gray with white underparts; other black-bibbed sparrows have streaked backs. Immature is told by the finely streaked breast, face pattern, dark rounded tail with white on outer feather, and lack of wingbars. Song is high, sweet, and trilled, much like Bewick's Wren's.

SAGE SPARROW — *Amphispíza bélli*

Fairly common in sagebrush and chaparral. This large, dark-headed sparrow is recognized by its single breast spot and its habit of flicking its dark tail. Look for the white spot below the ear. The narrow white margin on the outer tail feather may be lacking. The streak-breasted immature suggests a Lark Sparrow but has a dark head, a plain crown, and much less white on its tail. Wary. Song of 4-7 high thin notes, third note highest.

WHITE-TAILED SPARROWS

♀

LARK BUNTING L 6″

♂

VESPER SPARROW L 5½″

Lark Sparrow juv.

LARK SPARROW L 5¾″

juv.

BLACK-THROATED SPARROW L 4½″

♂

♂

SAGE SPARROW L 5″

juv.

● **JUNCOS** are common to abundant, rather tame sparrows with light pink bills, gray or black hoods, white outer tail feathers, and, in the West, rusty backs or pinkish sides. Often in large flocks, they hop on the ground and pick up small seeds but seldom scratch with their feet. Streaked juvenals on breeding ground resemble sparrows except for tail and voice. Song (except Mexican's) is a simple slow trill, more musical than Chipping Sparrow's, 5-12/min.

WHITE-WINGED JUNCO *Júnco aiken*

Common in its restricted range in yellow pine forests in the Black Hills; no record east of Great Plains. This large junco is told by the two white wingbars, the broad pale margins on its secondaries, and the excessive white on the tail (at least 3 feathers on each side are completely white). Has typical junco song.

SLATE-COLORED JUNCO *Júnco hyemális*

Abundant in brushy clearings and borders of coniferous forests in summer and in weedy fields, brush, and wood margins in winter. Head, back, and breast are uniformly slate-gray. Immatures, especially in or from far Northwest, have varying amounts of pink on the sides; these birds may be confused with Oregon Juncos.

OREGON JUNCO *Júnco oregánus*

Abundant in western conifers, and in winter in suburbs, farmyards, and fields. Plumage and size vary geographically. Some races have a black breast and head, contrasting sharply with the rusty back. Others have a pale gray head and breast with no head-back contrast, and a broad pink stripe down the sides.

GRAY-HEADED JUNCO *Júnco cániceps*

Common in coniferous forests. Told by gray head and pale gray breast and sides, contrasting with rusty upper back. Lores are dark gray or black. Told from Mexican Junco by its dark eye. A Rocky Mountain race has a light bill and a Southwest race a dark upper mandible.

MEXICAN JUNCO *Júnco phaeonótus*

Locally common in coniferous and pine-oak forests above 5,000'. Bright yellow eye is the best field mark. The entire underparts are whitish; the lores are black. Generally walks instead of hopping. Tame. Song is varied for a junco; call is like Chipping Sparrow's.

tanager   grosbeak   crossbill   bunting   sparrow   longspur

JUNCOS

♂

Slate-colored

im.

♀

WHITE-WINGED JUNCO
L 6″

♂

SLATE-COLORED JUNCO
L 5¼″

juv.

♂

OREGON JUNCO
L 5¼″

sided

southern race

GRAY-HEADED JUNCO
L 5½″

MEXICAN JUNCO
L 5½″

northern race

RUFOUS-WINGED SPARROW   *Aimóphila carpális*
Rare and local in tall grass amid thorny desert shrubs. Looks like a large dusky Field Sparrow with a gray stripe through the crown. Unlike Field and Chipping, it has a black whisker mark and a rounded tail. Small rusty shoulder patch can be seen (except in juvenal) at close range. Song, towhee-like, about 2 notes, and a trill.

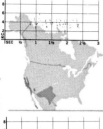

RUFOUS-CROWNED SPARROW   *Aimóphila rúficeps*
Locally common on steep slopes with scattered bushes. A handsome sparrow with an unstreaked crown, unlike its somber-hued relatives. Told by the deep rufous crown, black whisker mark, lack of wingbars, obscure back streakings, dusky breast, and rounded tail. Other rusty-capped sparrows are on pp. 318-322. Song is a jumble of short rapid notes.

CASSIN'S SPARROW   *Aimóphila cássinii*
Fairly common on dry plains with short grass and scattered low brush. Recognized by its plain breast, finely streaked crown, gray-brown back, and dark gray tail. Grasshopper Sparrow (p. 308) is smaller and shorter tailed and has a prominently streaked crown in all plumages. Brewer's is smaller and slimmer, with notched tail and wingbars. Unlike similar species, Cassin's Sparrow often gives its song in flight, a high musical trill preceded and followed by 1 or 2 short notes.

BOTTERI'S SPARROW   *Aimóphila bótterii*
Rare and local summer resident in the tall grass of brushy coastal prairies of Texas and in portions of southeast Ariz. deserts. Similar to Cassin's, it occurs with it in Ariz. Note at close range the rusty tinge of the wings and tail, the pale buffy breast and sides, and the heavier black streaking on the back. The song, always given from a perch, is 2 to 4 notes followed by a trill.

BACHMAN'S SPARROW   *Aimóphila aestivális*
Uncommon and local; in abandoned fields with scattered shrubs, pines, or oaks, usually in dense ground cover. Told from Field Sparrow (p. 318), which often occurs with it, by the yellow bend of the wing, dark upper mandible, purplish back, darker crown, and dark tail. Song is beautiful and varied, 4-10/min.

AIMOPHILA SPARROWS

juv.

RUFOUS-WINGED SPARROW
L 5¼"

RUFOUS-CROWNED SPARROW
L 5"¼

ins race

juv.

♂

CASSIN'S SPARROW
L 5½"

juv.

BOTTERI'S SPARROW
L 5½"

juv.

BACHMAN'S SPARROW
L 5½"

TREE SPARROW
Spizélla arbóre

Common in willow thickets, weedy fields, and hedg rows. This brightest and largest of the rusty-capped spa rows is seen in large flocks in winter. It is the only or with a large central breast spot. Note also the 2-tone b and dark legs. Immature is like adult. Song has the po tern of Fox Sparrow's, but is higher, thinner, and softe A musical 2-note twitter is diagnostic in winter.

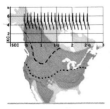

CHIPPING SPARROW
Spizélla passerín

Common on lawns or sparse grass under scattere trees. In winter it flocks with other sparrows in hedgerov and weedy fields. Black bill and very white eye strip separate spring adults from other rusty-capped sparrow Immatures and winter adults, with lighter bills and du streaked crowns, are told by the contrast between th gray rump and brown back. Song is of rapid chips.

CLAY-COLORED SPARROW
Spizélla pállia

Locally common in open brushland. Brown cheek patc and light median streak through crown are distinctive. rump color is not seen it may be mistaken in fall for Chip ping Sparrow. Song is a distinctive series of 2-5 ide tical, slow, low-pitched buzzes, 5-10/min.

BREWER'S SPARROW
Spizélla bréwe

Common; in sage and desert scrub. The crown, pa brown and finely streaked with black, lacks a medic line. Note also the small size, slim build and clear breas Song is a varied series of rapid trills.

FIELD SPARROW
Spizélla pusíl

Common; in abandoned fields with tall grass or sco tered saplings. Told by its pink bill and legs, unstreake crown, and lack of dark eye line. Song is a series slurred whistles in increasing tempo, 4-6/min.

BLACK-CHINNED SPARROW
Spizélla atrogulár

Uncommon; in chaparral and sage. Pink bill contras ing with gray head and breast make it appear junc like, but Black-chinned is easily told by the streaked bac and absence of white on the tail. Song suggests Fiel Sparrow's, but is higher pitched and more rapid.

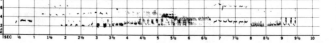

Brew
Spar

SPIZELLA SPARROWS

TREE SPARROW
L 5¼"

CHIPPING SPARROW
L 4¾"

im.

CLAY-COLORED SPARROW
L 4½"

im.

BREWER'S SPARROW
L 4½"

juv.

FIELD SPARROW
L 5"

BLACK-CHINNED SPARROW
L 5¼"

♂

320

HARRIS' SPARROW
Zonotrichia quérula

Fairly common. Breeds at timberline; in winter it prefers hedgerows, wood margins, and brush. Our largest sparrow; recognized by the combination of the pink bill, black or blotched bib, black crown, and streaked sides. No other pink-billed sparrow has streaked sides. The sexes are alike. Song consists of 2-4 identical high whistles; repeated on a different pitch.

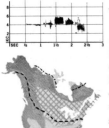

WHITE-CROWNED SPARROW
Zonotrichia leucóphrys

Abundant in West, in thickets, hedgerows, or wood margins adjacent to fields or open areas. Recognized by its pink or yellowish bill, erect posture, gray throat and breast, and prominently streaked crown. Adult and immature are told from White-throated by posture, bill color, and lores. Geographic races show minor differences in head pattern and bill color. The White-crowned shuns the woodland thickets so favored by the White-throated. Song is of clear whistles and buzzy trills; it varies geographically.

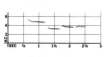

GOLDEN-CROWNED SPARROW
Zonotrichia atricapilla

Fairly common, breeding at higher elevations near timberline and at openings in stunted spruce forests. Often seen in winter with the White-crowned Sparrow, which it most closely resembles. Golden-crowned is best told by the crown pattern and dusky bill. The immature could be mistaken for immature White-throated except for its plain throat, larger size, and lack of a buffy median stripe. Its song consists of 3-5 whistled notes, with or without a softer final trill.

WHITE-THROATED SPARROW
Zonotrichia albicóllis

Abundant in dense undergrowth and brush; seldom found far from dense cover. The well-defined white throat is the best field mark. The yellow lores are diagnostic, but are inconspicuous in immatures and some fall adults. The dark bill and short-necked posture separate it from the White-crowned in all plumages. The similar immature Swamp Sparrow has a white throat and dingy breast, but is smaller and has rufous wings and a rounded tail. White-throated usually feeds on the ground. Song is a clear high whistle, *Old Sam Peabody Peabody Peabody.*

CROWNED SPARROWS

**HARRIS'
SPARROW
L 7"**

im.

**WHITE-CROWNED
SPARROW
L 5¾"**

Gambel's
face

im.

second
winter

fall ♂

**GOLDEN-CROWNED
SPARROW
L 6¼"**

**WHITE-THROATED
SPARROW
L 5¾"**

♀

spring. ♂

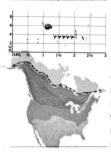

FOX SPARROW — *Passerélla ilíaca*

Common in dense coniferous thickets and deciduous brush. It is recognized by its heavily streaked underparts and in the East (where it is the largest sparrow) by its bright orange-brown rump and tail. Like the Song Sparrow, it has a central breast spot. It feeds by scratching, towhee-fashion, with both feet. Western Fox Sparrows are a deep chocolate or dark gray-brown, almost devoid of head and back markings. They may be confused with Hermit Thrush (p. 232) and with large northwestern races of the Song Sparrow, except for the yellow lower mandible and slightly notched tail. Song is loud and clear, starting with characteristic slurred notes.

LINCOLN'S SPARROW — *Melospíza líncolnii*

Fairly common in thickets along bogs and streams; uncommon in East. In migration and winter it prefers brush piles and wood margins. Note the fine neat streakings on the buffy breast band and the semblance of a tiny eye ring. Its gray face and longer rounded tail separate Lincoln's from the grass and marsh sparrows. Secretive. Seldom sings in winter or migration. Note the juncolike chip. Song suggests House Wren's, 3-6/min.

SWAMP SPARROW — *Melospíza georgiána*

Common in bogs and marshes but not heavily wooded swamps; in migration it is also seen in weedy fields. Adult is told by its red cap, gray eye stripe and gray face, white throat, and solid dark bill. Immature is grayer breasted than Lincoln's and lacks the clear-cut breast streakings. Also note the rusty wings in all plumages. Feeds on or near the ground. Song is a slow trill of similar slurred liquid notes, suggestive of a Chipping Sparrow's song but much more musical and slower, 4-6/min.

SONG SPARROW — *Melospíza melódia*

Abundant in East, locally in West in moist areas with bushes, hedgerows, and wood margins. Told by the heavily streaked breast with a central spot, by the lack of yellow or buffy color, and by the long slightly rounded tail which it "pumps" in flight. Geographic races vary from rusty to gray and light to dark. Short-tailed juvenal, which lacks central breast spot, can be mistaken for Savannah. Song is lively and varied, of many short notes and a trill near the end, 4-6/min.

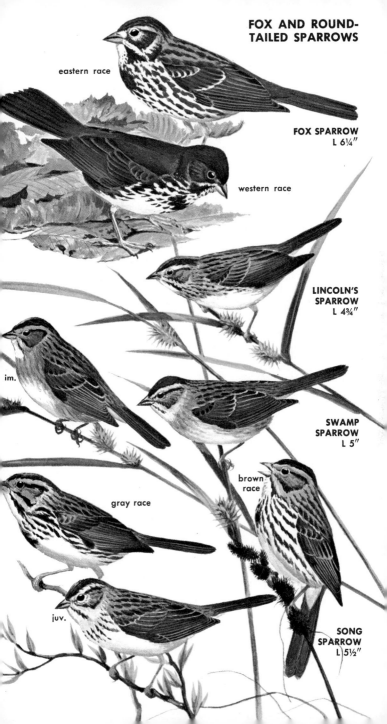

FOX AND ROUND-TAILED SPARROWS

eastern race

FOX SPARROW
L 6¼"

western race

LINCOLN'S SPARROW
L 4¾"

im.

SWAMP SPARROW
L 5"

brown race

gray race

juv.

SONG SPARROW
L 5½"

LONGSPURS AND SNOW BUNTINGS are gregarious sparrow-like ground birds of open fields, tundra, and dunes. Adult male plumage seldom is seen outside the nesting ground. Watch for distinctive patterns on the rather short tails.

Mc COWN'S LONGSPUR   *Rhynchóphanes mccównii*

Less common than Chestnut-collared on arid plains. The tail is mostly white, with only narrow median and terminal bands. The only longspur with rusty bend of wing (often concealed). Note the gray hind neck. Flight song is a long twittering warble; call, a dry rattle.

CHESTNUT-COLLARED LONGSPUR   *Calcárius ornátus*

Common in fallow plains and prairies. Told in all plumages by the dark triangle on the white tail and by lack of a well-defined ear patch. Song is like a faint Western Meadowlark's, 3-8/min. Call is finch-like, 2 syllables; does not give the typical longspur rattle.

LAPLAND LONGSPUR   *Calcárius lappónicus*

Abundant in Arctic and locally in interior; uncommon in East. Flocks with Horned Larks, Snow Buntings, or other longspurs. Winter male is told by chestnut hind neck and gray throat blotch. Tail with white outer feathers is like pipit's (p. 238) or Vesper Sparrow's (p. 312). A dry rattle is given in flight.

SMITH'S LONGSPUR   *Calcárius píctus*

Uncommon and local; winters on short grass plains and airports. Told from other longspurs by the broad white wingbar of male and by the buffy coloration and flesh-colored legs. Common flight call is a rapid clicking.

SNOW BUNTING   *Plectróphenax nivális*

Common in tundra; local on beaches, dunes, and in short grass; often seen with Horned Larks or longspurs. Most readily identified in flight by large white wing patches; no other flocking songbird in its range has these. Flight call is a short descending whistle.

McKAY'S BUNTING   *Plectróphenax hyperbóreus*

Common breeder on Bering Sea islands. Winters in coastal western Alaska. Female is told by pure white head and male by white head and back. Song is like American Goldfinch's.

McCOWN'S LONGSPUR
L 5¼"

summer ♂

♀

**CHESTNUT-COLLARED
LONGSPUR**
L 5"

summer

♀   ♂

summer

**LAPLAND
LONGSPUR**
L 5¾"

winter ♂

summer

♂

♀

**SMITH'S
LONGSPUR**
5¾"

♀

winter ♂

er ♀

**SNOW
BUNTING**
L 6"

winter ♂

winter ♀

er

Bunting

summer ♂

cKay's Bunting

**McKAY'S
BUNTING**
L 6¼"

BIBLIOGRAPHY

American Ornithologists' Union. *Check-List of North American Birds*, 5th ed. Balitmore, Md.; American Ornithologists' Union, 1957

Austin, Oliver L., Jr. *Birds of the World*. N.Y.; Golden Press, 1961

Bent, Arthur Cleveland. *Life Histories of North American Birds*, 20 vols. Wash., D.C.; U.S. Nat. Mus., 1919-1967

Blake, Emmet Reid. *Birds of Mexico*. Chicago; Univ. of Chicago Press, 1953

Broun, Maurice. *Hawks Aloft*. N.Y.; Dodd, Mead, 1949

Bull, John. *Birds of the New York Area*. N.Y.; Harper and Row, 1964

Fisher, James and Roger Tory Peterson. *The World of Birds*. Garden City, N.Y.; Doubleday, 1964

Forbush, Edward Howe. *Birds of Massachusetts and Other New England States*, 3 vols. Boston; Commonwealth of Mass., 1925, 1927, 1929

Gabrielson, Ira N. and Frederick C. Lincoln. *Birds of Alaska*. Wash., D.C.; Wildlife Mgmt. Inst., 1959

Godfrey, W. Earl. *The Birds of Canada.* Ottawa; Nat'l Museum of Canada, 1966

Grinnell, Joseph and Alden H. Miller. *The Distribution of the Birds of California*. Berkeley; Cooper Ornithological Club, 1944

Griscom, Ludlow and Alexander Sprunt, Jr. *The Warblers of North America*. N.Y.; Devin-Adain, 1957

Hickey, Joseph J. *A Guide to Bird Watching*. N.Y.; Oxford Univ. Press, 1943, Doubleday, 1963

Imhof, Thomas A. *Alabama Birds*. University, Ala.; Univer. of Alabama Press, 1953

Jewett, Stanley G. and others. *Birds of Washington State*. Seattle; Univ. of Wash. Press, 1953

Kortright, Francis H. *The Ducks, Geese and Swans of North America*. Wash., D.C.; Wildlife Mgmt. Inst., 1953

Lowery, George H., Jr. *Louisiana Birds*. Baton Rouge; Louisiana State Univ. Press, 1955

Palmer, Ralph S. (Ed.). *Handbook of North American Birds*. Vol. 1, *Loons Through Flamingos*. New Haven; Yale Univ. Press, 1962

Peterson, Roger Tory. *A Field Guide to the Birds, 1947; A Field Guide to the Birds of Texas and Adjacent States, 1963; A Field Guide to Western Birds, 1961;* all, Boston; Houghton Mifflin

Peterson, Roger Tory. *The Birds*. N.Y.; Time, 1963

Peterson, Roger Tory, Guy Montfort and P. A. D. Hollom. *A Field Guide to the Birds of Britain and Europe*. Boston; Houghton Mifflin, 1966

Pettingill, Olin Sewall, Jr. *A Guide to Bird-Finding East of the Mississippi, 1951; A Guide to Bird-Finding West of the Mississippi, 1953;* both N.Y.; Oxford Univ. Press. Editor. *The Bird Watcher's America*. N.Y.; McGraw-Hill, 1965

Phillips, Allan R. and others. *Birds of Arizona*. Tucson; Univ. of Arizona Press, 1964

Pough, Richard H. *Audubon Land Bird Guide, 1949; Audubon Water Bird Guide, 1951; Audubon Western Bird Guide, 1957;* all, Garden City, N.Y.; Doubleday oberts, Thomas S. *Birds of Minnesota*, 2 vols. Minneapolis; Univ. of Minneapolis; Univ. of Minnesota Press, 1932, 1936

alomonsen, Finn. *The Birds of Greenland*. Copenhagen; Ejnar Munksgaard, 1950

aunders, Aretas A. *A Guide to Bird Songs*. N.Y.; Doubleday, 1959

nyder, L. L. *Arctic Birds of Canada*. Toronto; Univ. of Toronto Press, 1957

prunt, Alexander, Jr. *Florida Bird Life*. N.Y.; Coward-McCann, 1954

prunt, Alexander, Jr. *North American Birds of Prey*. N.Y.; Harper and Bros., 1955

ufts, Robie W. *Birds of Nova Scotia*. Halifax; Nova Scotia Museum, 1962

Van Tyne, Josselyn and Andrew J. Berger. *Fundamentals of Ornithology*. N.Y.; John Wiley and Sons, 1959

Welty, Carl. *The Life of Birds*. Philadelphia; Saunders, 1962

Wetmore, Alexander and others. *Song and Garden Birds of North America; Water, Prey and Game Birds of North America*. Wash. D.C.; Nat. Geographic Society, 1964-65

PERIODICALS OF PRINCIPAL ORNITHOLOGICAL SOCIETIES

Audubon Magazine, Audubon Field Notes, National Audubon Society, 1130 Fifth Ave., New York, N.Y. 10028
These publications are of interest to the general reader; others listed below are mainly research and professional literature.

Auk, American Ornithologists' Union (Dr. L. Richard Mewaldt, Sec., Dept. Biol. Sciences, San Jose State College, San Jose, Calif.)

Condor, Cooper Ornithological Society, Museum of Vertebrate Zoology, Berkeley, Calif.

Wilson Bulletin, Wilson Ornithological Society (Dr. Pershing B. Hofslund, Sec., Dept. of Biol., Univ. of Minnesota, Duluth, Minn.)

RECORDINGS

Cornell Univ. Laboratory of Ornithology has produced some 23 records, most released by Houghton Mifflin Co., Boston. These include *Birds of Florida, Birds in the North Woods, Bird Songs in Your Garden, A Field Guide to Eastern Bird Songs, A Field Guide to Western Bird Songs,* and *Songbirds of America.*

Federation of Ontario Naturalists, 187 Highbourne Road, Toronto, Ontario, with the Canadian Broadcasting Corporation, has produced the "Sounds of Nature" series, including *Birds of The Forest, A Day in Algonquin Park, A Day at Flores Moradas, Finches, Songs of Spring, Warblers of Eastern North America,* and others.

National Network of American Bird Songs reproduces the Stillwell Collection, records distributed by Ficker Records, Old Greenwich, Conn. These include *Birds From the Great Plains to the Atlantic,* 2 vols., and *Birds From the Great Plains to the Pacific.*

Sveriges Radio, Stockholm, Sweden, has a series, *Radions Fagel Skivor,* which includes many of our northern species.

INDEX

Individual species names, both common and scientific, are indicated with the text page only (even page) when the illustration is on the facing (odd) page, as it is for most birds. When there is more than one entry, the principal entry is indicated in bold face type. For orders, families, and other groups inclusive page numbers are given.

Common and scientific names of species are those of the A. O. U. CHECKLIST, 5th ed. Names formerly used on a wide scale for common birds are usually given in parentheses after the accepted common name. Those requiring separate listings are indicated by "see" references.

The boxes at the left of the common name can be used for checking the birds you have identified.

332

335

337

MEASURING SCALE (IN 10THS OF AN INCH)

340